Praise for *Savage Arena:*

"Joe will long be remembered for *Savage Arena*—the compelling story of men climbing the hardest routes up this world's highest mountains...running the razor's edge with death, the greatest triumph to return alive. We will all miss him."
—Rob Taylor, author of *The Breach*

"A tremendously evocative book about climbers and climbing."
—Laurence Leamer, author of *Ascent: The Spiritual and Physical Quest of Willi Onsoeld*

"There is a quality of total sincerity in Joe Tasker's writing ...which must carry conviction in the minds of every reader, whether or not they are mountaineers."
—Lord John Hunt, leader of the original 1953 Everest expedition in which Sir Edmund Hillary and Sherpa Tenzing reached the summit for the first time

"Few books about mountain climbing have so well captured the pain, travail and anguish that are a part of the sport."
—*Publishers Weekly*

"*Savage Arena* is a sensitive and comprehensive view of the rare breed of men who can't sit still, but must always climb.... It should be standard reading for anyone interested in the outdoors, even if they are only curious about what makes climbers tick."
—*Chattanooga Times*

"[It rings] with such authority that no reader can fail but be moved by the honesty with which each confronts the issues that climbing raises: life and death, trust and fear."
—*Outside* magazine

"If any writer has expressed the essence of winter climbing in the Himalayas, it is Joe Tasker. In *Savage Arena*, his life's work stands before us. It is both instruction and literature."
—Reinhold Messner, world-famous climber and author

SAVAGE ARENA

SAVAGE ARENA

Joe Tasker

St. Martin's Press

NEW YORK

Library of Congress Catalog Card Number: 82-6093

ISBN 0-312-69985-9

Contents

	Publisher's Note	*page* 11
1	Or Men Will Come For You	13
2	It is Forbidden to Walk on the Track: The Eiger	20
3	It Could be Worse: Dunagiri	40
4	Figures on a Screen: Changabang	91
5	'Let's Draw Matchsticks': K2	127
6	In the Treasure House of the Great Snow: Kangchenjunga	159
7	Apocalypse: K2	214
	Postscript	259
	Chronology	261
	Index	265

Illustrations

PLATES

1. The North Face of the Eiger   *between pages* 32 *and* 33
2a. Dick at the first bivouac on the Eiger
 b. Dick on the Hinterstoisser Traverse
3a. Dick coming past the Swallow's Nest
 b. Dick traversing along the top of the Second Ice Field
4a. The van on the way to Dunagiri
 b. Dunagiri seen from Changabang
5a. Dick approaching the couloir   80 *and* 81
 b. Joe approaching the shoulder
6a. Joe on the shoulder, site of the third bivouac
 b. Dick on the snow band at the bottom of the rock barrier
7a. Dick approaching the summit of Dunagiri
 b. Dick joining the ropes together after his fall
 c. Dick's frostbitten hands
8a. Dick at Base Camp after his return
 b. Vera and the American girl guarding Joe's baggage
9a. Changabang   112 *and* 113
 b. Pete on the walk-in to Changabang
10. Joe coming up the edge of the ice field
11a. Pete on steep granite in the lower part of the wall
 b. Joe at Camp 2 at 20,000 feet
12a. Pete just three feet below the summit of Changabang
 b. Joe abseiling down to the ramp below the summit slopes
13a. K2   144 *and* 145
 b. Nick Estcourt in the bank at Islamabad
14a. Hiring porters at Skardu
 b. Porters crossing the Punmah river
 c. Quamajan, our Hunza high-altitude porter
15a. The porters with Doug and Joe at the glacier camp
 b. The porters in the middle of the Savoia glacier
16a. Nick and Tony Riley on the way up to Camp 1
 b. Joe in the snow-buried tent at Camp 2

17a. Pete leading above Camp 2   *facing page* 160
   b. Doug re-crossing the avalanche slope
   c. The memorial plaque to Nick
18a. The team for Kangchenjunga   161
   b. The village on the ridge at 8,000 feet, with
      Kangchenjunga beyond
19a. Pete being carried in a basket by a porter   192
   b. Dawa, the lovely girl from Ghunza
   c. The north side of Kangchenjunga
20a. Georges on the wall up to the North Col   193
   b. Doug coming through the ice-fall to Camp 2
   c. Camp 2 at 19,000 feet
21a. Pete leaving the snow cave at 26,000 feet   224
   b. Doug on the summit of Kangchenjunga
22a. K2 as seen from Concordia   225
   b. Gohar bringing us cups of tea
23a. Doug prusikking up the ropes   240
   b. Pete on the lower part of the Abruzzi Ridge
   c. Joe on the radio to Base during the retreat
24a. Pete and Dick at the fourth camping place of
      the second attempt   241
   b. Coming up from the fourth camp

MAPS

1. The Eiger and surrounding area   *page* 21
2. General location of mountains in the Karakaram
   and Himalayas   42
3. The approach and area surrounding Dunagiri and
   Changabang   51
4. The ascent and separate descent routes of Dunagiri   56
5. The route up Changabang   99
6. The location and walk-in route to K2   137
7. The attempted lines of ascent in 1978 and 1980 on K2   147
8. The location of Kangchenjunga   174

DIAGRAMS

1. The line of ascent on the Eiger   *page* 31
2. The ascent of Dunagiri   61
3. The ascent of Changabang   103

4. The route up the West Ridge of K2   151
5. The ascent of the North Ridge of Kangchenjunga   178
6. The line up the Abruzzi Ridge of K2 in 1980   232

All the photographs, unless otherwise credited in the captions, were taken by Joe Tasker. The maps and diagrams were drawn from the author's roughs by Neil Hyslop.

Publisher's Note

Joe Tasker delivered the typescript of this book on the eve of his departure
with the British Everest Expedition 1982. The aim of the expedition was
to tackle the unclimbed North-East Face by the East-North-East Ridge of
Mount Everest. On 17 May Joe and his close friend and long-time climbing
companion, Peter Boardman, were last seen at a height of over 27,000 feet,
making a push for the summit.

In mourning the death of two such young and gifted men, we hope that
the publication of *Savage Arena* will act as a fitting memorial to Joe Tasker
– climber, writer and photographer.

ONE

Or Men Will Come For You

The mountains of the Alps formed a difficult school in which to learn but, for whatever unfathomable reason, I found it hard to avoid going back time and again. And although I tried to find partners who would allow themselves a little luxury and who were similarly bemused by their own involvement with climbing mountains as I was by mine, each time I found myself teaming up with one person more often than with any other, a person whose single-mindedness and asceticism were the opposite of my own nature.

It is easy to understand the attraction of rock-climbing, which is an exercise of physical skill, gymnastic ability and intense concentration to scale increasingly smoother walls of rock, larger overhangs and fiercesome cracks. The physical and mental effort is in itself rewarding, but the greater pleasure is attempting to climb a rock face, which seems hardly possible, and succeeding against all odds with those skills being tested to the limit.

At some point there is a transition from an interest in solving the problems of climbing a rock face, and the idyllic days in the sun which one always hopes for, to an interest in solving the problem of climbing bigger mountains, and the acceptance of a more gruelling way of life. The bigger mountains take more physical effort, more total commitment, and escape from them is not easy if the weather should take a turn for the worse.

The mountains of the Alps have a stark beauty, but this alone is not enough to elicit the extreme exertion which is needed to climb there. It is possible to go up in some places on a mountain railway or in a cable car which will open up vast panoramas for the price of a ticket, and if it were only the view that was sought, no one would ever climb. For a climber there is more, though it may be little understood. The mountains are a testing ground where he is confronted by challenges which not only demand all his skill in meeting them but make him face up to his own motivation, perseverance and resilience when danger, hardship and fatigue all conspire to turn him back from his chosen objective.

Given the chance, few can explain the compulsive fascination which draws them back year after year to this difficult school and makes them want to look further and higher, to push themselves all the harder.

I was no exception but found in a companion from university days, Dick Renshaw, someone who accepted without question the hardship entailed and who seemed motivated by a blind drive to climb and climb, without stopping to wonder about the purpose of it all.

Unlike me, he could switch his mind off to the tedium and effort which are inevitable in the mountains and, though opposites, we climbed together and learned together: how to negotiate crevasses, deep snow, loose rock and altitude; how to cope with hunger, fear and exhaustion. We climbed on small peaks carrying too much and taking too long; we graduated to climbing the Matterhorn and the Eiger, to classic routes from the past and to bold new routes. We began to prefer the shadowy north faces of the mountains, thinking we should climb these precipices of ice-coated rocks while we were young and save the more pleasant walls of sun-warmed granite and limestone for later years.

We accumulated a shared store of experiences; the midnight starts from alpine huts, hurrying to reach safety while the rocks were frozen into immobility; the many sleepless, anxious hours of waiting for and wanting to escape the moment of departure into the dark night, and those dreadful and unavoidable moments when we left the safe eyrie of the hut and climbed away, ill-tempered from nerves, picking a way on crampon points by dim torchlight into a dark no man's land.

It is necessary to start in the middle of the night or very early hours of the morning to reach a chosen climb because often the route to its start is menaced by other parts of the mountain from which ice or rocks may fall, or avalanches come sweeping down. In the night, when the temperature drops below zero, the blocks of ice and loose rocks are frozen into place, and snow slopes become firm, and passage through these hazards is safest, but there is a surreal quality about the midnight fumblings and preparations to leave at an hour when most people are sound asleep.

Again and again Dick and I were companions in the night across glaciers, over crevasses and under avalanche zones to reach the mountain of our choice. On one occasion we huddled together, afraid, under blocks of ice as pitiful shelter against an unexpected avalanche which we heard roaring down out of the darkness; on another we clung together for warmth as we stood all night on a wall of ice waiting for a storm to abate and dawn to arrive.

We saw many sunrises and saw mountains turning pink at sunset; we shared the satisfaction of overcoming difficulties, of succeeding on climbs we had hardly dared dream of, and in our minds we stopped looking for those climbs which we knew we could do and started looking for those which were more difficult.

Arguments and misunderstandings became fewer, we recognised the strains imposed by the harsh discipline of the mountains; there was less and less need for talk between us, our aims and evaluations were the same.

We felt at home in the mountains, but we still had much to learn. When three British climbers disappeared in a blizzard on Mont Blanc we, in the valley below, did not know what we should do to institute a search or where to turn to summon help. When the search had taken place and all possibility that the three climbers should still be alive was ruled out, we asked a mountain guide who had helped organise the search what we should do in any similar event in the future to get things under way more quickly. He had smiled, flattered by such a request from two whom he saw as apprentices looking to a master for advice, but his reply was unhelpful. 'Look for an old hand like myself,' he had said, 'one who has been around a long time, and ask him.' I took him to be saying that if you lived long enough in the mountains you accumulated the necessary experience to deal with most things, but that was not of much use for the present, and we were made aware that there is no tidy answer to accidents.

The mountains filled our dreams and permeated our subconsciousness. We were so conditioned by the sounds experienced during a climb that we found ourselves ducking for shelter if a plane droned overhead, thinking that it was the sound of an avalanche starting. On one climb, sleeping on a ledge under the shelter of a prow of rock, I believed that I could hear the purr of a paraffin stove heating some tea, but woke to find that the sound was the hum of stones falling from above.

There were odd coincidences which we could not explain, such as the time in 1972 when Dick dreamt one night, as we slept in a hut, that he was falling from the side of a mountain and that I was not holding the rope to which he was attached. He woke me with his shouts, telling me to catch him. Two days later he did fall – on the North Face of the Dent d'Hérens in Switzerland – eighty feet down a wall of ice and landed head first in a bank of snow above a 2,000-foot drop, and at the time, thinking him safe, I was not holding the rope.

There were faint superstitions too. We went in wintertime to Wengen, a mountain village near Interlaken. Wengen is close to the famous ski resort of Mürren, high up above the cliffs of the Lauterbrunnen valley. The valley is encircled by steep-sided mountains, the most impressive of which are the Eiger, Mönch and Jungfrau, forming a solid rampart with the ridges which link them together into the Lauterbrunnen wall. We were intending to climb the North Face of the Gspaltenhorn, one of the biggest walls in the Alps, hidden away up a secluded side valley. The old lady who ran the hostel where we stayed heard of our plans and warned us, 'You should come here to ski in winter, not to climb. It is too dangerous. If you go to climb the Gspaltenhorn you will not do it and come back, or men will come for you and you will be dead.' We did not do it.

Across the valley from Wengen the sombre wall of the North Face of the Eiger seemed to hold an air of brooding menace. We had climbed it in the summer of 1973, taking two nights and two days. We knew how hard, intricate and long the route was up the North Face and I could not conceive

of climbing it in winter. We knew that only two or three parties had done
so and that each time it had taken almost a week on that forbidding wall
before they had reached the top. As we watched, we would see, even at the
distance we were, avalanches sweeping constantly down the face, and I
shuddered at the long nights, the cold and the storms which would have
to be endured to climb it in winter. I looked with respect on that mountain
and with awe for the parties who had dared to climb it in winter, but for
myself felt that such an ascent was outside my ambitions. I had no wish to
take on such difficulty and danger for the many days that an ascent would
entail. Our knowledge of the mountain made us no less daunted; if anything
we had more to be afraid of, since we knew how much harder the North
Face would be in the deep snow and hard ice of winter.

We parted after that winter and went our separate ways, odd-jobbing,
climbing and mixing with new friends. But we were as hand to glove and
the next winter we met and, probing with words for a hint of the other's
thoughts, we sounded each other out:

'Yes, a winter route in the Alps.'

'What were you thinking of?'

'I wondered about the Eiger.'

'Yes, I've come round to thinking of that too.'

'It will be hard. Need a lot of preparation.'

So we worked as temporary teachers to raise the money, having to impose
a discipline, which I did not feel myself, onto the rebellious youth of Moss
Side in Manchester. We accumulated the equipment needed and made
some of the clothing such as climbing salopettes and specialised pieces of
gear such as over-boots ourselves when we could not obtain the right item
for our purpose in the shops. We made calculations on how many days it
would take us, how much food and fuel we would need, how much weight
we could carry. We told no one of our plans except Ellis Brigham, a climbing
shop owner, who lent a fatherly ear to the young aspirants who came to him
for advice. He made us a gift of one-piece suits of fleecy pile material as
an under-garment into which we inserted zips, all the way round to the small
of the back, so that we would be able to relieve ourselves without
undressing.

Neither of us felt at home in the classroom and were relieved to leave in
the February of 1975 for Switzerland, driving there in my old Ford Anglia.

Dick and I had been climbing together in the Alps for four years by this
time, but journeying now towards the greatest test we had yet faced I knew
him little more than at the start. He still had the same quiet, relentless
dedication to climbing that he had when I first met him. When the rest of
us were lying in our sleeping bags on a summer's morning in the Lake
District, Dick would be outside the tent cooking breakfast, making more
tea and waiting, eager to be off climbing, without a word of complaint, for

us to stir ourselves. I never knew what drove him; he seemed unaffected by discomfort, undaunted by the folly of what we were doing. When we stood, clinging to each other all night through snow-storm and avalanche on the north face of the Dent Blanche, passing the long, chill night with idle chatter, all he could think to say was, 'What climb do you fancy doing next?'

I felt he looked askance at my self-indulgence if I bought a glass of beer, as if I was recklessly squandering valuable resources, but never a word passed.

In smoking, as in all things, he was completely controlled. He would take along one cigarette for each bivouac, so friends could estimate how long we thought a climb might take us by the number of cigarettes Dick took. Three cigarettes meant a serious route.

Physically, Dick was the opposite to me, 'Little Richard' we used to call him, but he was broad in the chest. He looked more suited to weight-lifting or body-building than climbing.

It always puzzled me whether he did not feel cold and discomfort as much as me or whether he just put up with it more stoically. Tall and thin as I was, I always felt the cold and could not sleep if I was not comfortable. I passed many nights shuffling myself about on uneven ledges trying to find the optimum position while Dick snored gently, sleeping where he had first settled down. I suspected that, as with everything else, he had long since disciplined himself not to pay attention to physical discomfort and had he done so would have regarded it as a weakness, a flaw in the overall plan he had for himself. It was as if he was training his body for something, toning it into shape, with no place in the design for feelings such as comfort. There was something of a religious asceticism in him. I could recognise it but I had chosen a different path.

Dick was a creature of nature, he had seen no need as yet to learn to drive. I even felt self-conscious that I actually possessed a car.

The Eiger, or more accurately, its North Face had permeated my first years of climbing. In the seminary where I spent seven years training to be a Catholic priest, two mealtimes of the day were made more formal by the reading out of a book. Originally the books read out were probably intended to be of a spiritually edifying nature but by the time I was there the criteria seemed to be simply that the book should be 'good'. Any books were, of course, carefully vetted before being read out.

In 1965 I was in the fourth year when a book called *The Climb up to Hell* by Jack Olsen was chosen for the supper-time reading. The book described how the North Face of the Eiger, a mountain which I had hardly heard of, was the most difficult and dangerous of all the mountain faces in the Alps. The mountain, in the Bernese Oberland of Switzerland, is part of the

northern bulwark of the Alps and is thus particularly subject to violent
changes in weather. Air movement and air pressures are sharply altered
when the air comes up against this first obstacle of the main Alpine mass.
Sudden and prolonged storms can occur, and the concave wall of the Eiger
can seem to be holding its own furious storm when the meadows below are
clear. The wall is so big and the route up it so intricate, long and difficult
that several tragic accidents took place as climbers attempted to be the first
to solve the problems of climbing that face. So many accidents occurred that
the Swiss government at one stage banned all attempts on the North Face;
but still men came. In 1938 an Austro/German party of four succeeded in
being the first to reach the top via the North Face, but the accidents did
not lessen and the Eiger became notorious for the dramas enacted in full
view, when the clouds permitted, of the binoculars and telescopes on the
verandah of the hotel at Kleine Scheidegg, only an hour from the foot of
the wall and reachable by rock and pinion railway from Grindelwald or
Lauterbrunnen.

The Climb up to Hell recounted the struggles and tragedies of the attempts
to climb the Eiger's North Face, culminating in the disappearance in 1957
of two German climbers and the death of an Italian, stranded high on the
face. He died within shouting distance of the rescue party who were trying
to reach him, when the snow-storm had closed in on him for the last time.
The book is full with the drama of the attempts on the mountain and for
the only time I ever knew the whole dining hall of three hundred people
subsided into absolute quiet. Not a knife rattled, not a cup clattered as
another tragedy was described, that of a party of four in 1937, making one
of the earliest attempts on the face. Toni Kurz, sole survivor of the four
young Germans, was trying to reach the guides who had come to rescue him.
One of his arms was frozen and he was very weak, but after two days of
rescue efforts he was at last sliding down a rope to the waiting guides. Then
a knot in the rope jammed in the karabiner attaching the rope to his waist
and he had no strength left to free himself. Only an arm's length away from
the waiting rescuers he keeled over and died. None of us students understood the terminology of climbing, none of us knew what abseiling was, nor
what karabiners were, but every one of us was enthralled by the account
of this moving tragedy.

During the days when that book was being read out, days when we looked
forward as never before to supper time for the next rivetting chapter, I was
unexpectedly asked by one of the teaching priests in the college if I would
like to try a bit of climbing myself. Although I had never remotely
considered the possibility of climbing before I was asked, it suddenly
seemed the most enthralling prospect. Rather than being deterred by the
dangers as described in *The Climb up to Hell*, the book provided an
inspiration for my own first steps and those of another friend on the small

sandstone walls of the quarry from which the college had been built. The quarry, though only twenty feet high with two walls only thirty feet across, was the focal point of my days. My every thought was taken up by the sport, though for months at a time our activities were confined to that tiny quarry. It was as if a wondrous new world had been opened up to me. I read avidly every book on the subject that I could get hold of. I borrowed Heinrich Harrer's book, *The White Spider*, which documented all the attempts and successes to date on the Eiger's North Face and devoured it by torchlight at night. I read it at every spare moment and for long after 'lights out', until my eyes grew weary and the words seemed to dance on the page.

Shortly after I first started climbing, early in 1966, the siege was on to make the first winter ascent of a direct line on the North Face. In order to climb as directly as possible to the summit, avoiding the zig-zags entailed by following natural fault lines as on the 1938 route, the climbers would leave themselves exposed to the rockfall in many sections. Two teams had had the same idea of attempting such a line in winter when, though conditions would be more rigorous, the rocks would be frozen in place day and night.

The siege lasted a month. They used the tactics developed on Himalayan expeditions of climbing a certain distance, fixing rope on that section, then descending to a well-established camp at the bottom of the face or a snow hole on the face itself. Once most of the wall had the rope fixed up it they would make a bid to reach the summit.

As a young climber I swallowed greedily the regular news reports and television bulletins. I was awestruck by the bleak lives of the climbers in their snow holes or battling upwards in blizzards. The death in an accident on the wall of John Harlin, the driving force behind one of the teams, came as a great shock. He was an American who had settled in Switzerland, and though at first his team were in competition with the team of Germans whom he found to have the same designs, he died in trying to assist them. Both teams were pinned down on the mountain by storms and he was carrying up to the Germans some much-needed supplies when a damaged rope snapped and he fell to his death.

In 1966 I had no thoughts of going to the Eiger, even though I called myself a climber, any more than when flying in an aeroplane I think of going to the moon. I considered such climbers to be of a different order of people and though I was fascinated by every aspect of the sport I was content to climb rock and my aspirations only stretched as far as acquiring sufficient skill to do some winter climbing in Scotland.

TWO

It is Forbidden to Walk on the Track

THE EIGER

I

Ten years later I was on my way to climb the Eiger a second time. Our ascent in summer had been a traditional one. Though we had known more about that mountain by reputation and accounts than any other, we still had to go and climb it, and having climbed it we were coming back because it was the longest and most complex route we could think of and, if we dared admit it to ourselves, the most difficult. We wanted something substantial, something we could get our teeth into. We did not want to overcome a mountain with ease, we needed to struggle, needed to be at the edge of what was possible for us, needed an outcome that was uncertain. Sometimes I wondered if the climbing had become an addiction, if the pleasure of this drug had gone and only the compulsion to take it in ever stronger doses remained.

The brakes on the Anglia were terrible. We called in to see André in Switzerland, an engineering contractor for whom Dick and I had both worked instead of returning to Britain after the summer's climbing in 1973. His foreman gave us a hand to mend the brakes and a tongue-lashing for driving such a suicidal machine. We did not have to tell them our plans, the name of the group of mountains was enough – the Bernese Oberland. Their concern was matched by their pride. I borrowed a crash helmet from Danielle, André's cousin; my own had somehow been left behind.

In the Lauterbrunnen valley we found lodgings in the Naturfreundhaus, a hotel run by a kindly Frau Gertsch. She was surprised and pleased to find she had climbers staying rather than the periodic groups of skiers. We had the place to ourselves – long communal platforms of foam mattresses to stretch out on for beds, but none of the summer crowds to share them with.

When we returned from a five-day outing making an ascent of the North Face of the Breithorn, Frau Gertsch took us as sons. She assigned the second dining-room completely to us for sorting out and drying our gear.

The North Face of the Breithorn was a preparatory climb for us, something on which we could try ourselves out and get the feel of climbing in winter. There was deep snow all the way to the foot of the mountain and it took eight hours of agonising toil before the climbing started. Then for three days we steadily made our way up gullies of snow, turning to ice, and of loose rock held in place by ice. As a climb it was interesting, well within our capabilities. We did not want an epic, did not want to stretch ourselves so much that we would lose the drive for our real purpose. Winter climbing is solitary; we had the mountains to ourselves. A lone plane one day was the only sign of life we saw the whole time we were away in that frozen wilderness.

We had a few days' rest after that, rest from climbing, not rest from activity. Dick went off on a nature trek on cross-country skis, shunning the contrived sport of skiing on a piste with cable cars, chair lifts and tows. He had worked in the resort of Montana one winter as a dish-washer. During the afternoon break he would hoist his skis onto his shoulder and walk up the piste rather than indulge in taking the *téléphérique*. In this way he became very fit but did not improve his skiing much as it took him all his time to walk up for a single run down. I did not find Dick much company. I took the train up to Kleine Scheidegg, the station at the foot of the Eiger, and skied below the dark wall of limestone, ice and snow, trying to absorb

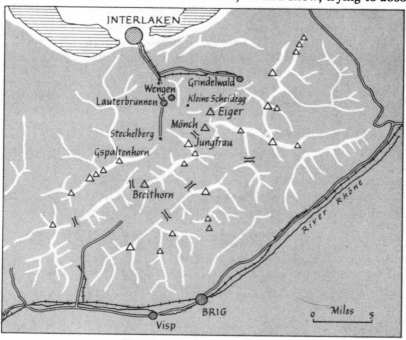

1. The Eiger and surrounding area.

some impression from it, trying to attune myself to it, trying to penetrate its inscrutable aspect. At sunset I slid away, down to the cosy warmth of the Naturfreundhaus. It was time for us to make ready and go.

Twenty rock pitons, thirty-two aluminium karabiners, eleven ice pitons, ice axes, ice hammers, crash helmets, we laid all the gear and food and clothing out on the tables in the dining-room. There was a lot of weight, but it was a huge wall and if we had to retreat we would need many pitons to drive into rock or ice to safeguard our descent. There was much snow low down, I had noticed, but the ice fields in the middle of the face seemed to be nothing but dark, hard ice. We expected our progress to be slow and we were consequently taking food for a week.

On 14 February, early in the morning, we joined the skiers who were boarding the train to Scheidegg to make best use of the morning snow. There were curious glances at our untidy appearance amidst the sleekly clad throng. There were hostile glances at the ice axes protruding from our bulging rucksacks; we did not fit into the normal pattern.

It was strange to think that the railway track continued up inside the mountain we were intending to climb. In order to reach the Jungfraujoch, a vantage point on a ridge between two valleys, a tunnel has been carved through two mountains. The ventilation holes from the tunnel open onto the lower part of the North Face of the Eiger and have sometimes been used to avoid descending the last few hundred feet by parties retreating in bad weather. I had not been able to locate through binoculars any sign of the entrance to these air shafts, and assumed that they were concealed deep beneath the snow. The idea of a train trundling up inside the mountains we would be living on for days was bizarre but it did not detract from the seriousness of the mountain, since the air vents are located low down where there are few difficulties.

When the train disgorged its load, the skiers busied themselves clipping on skis and Dick and I trudged off away from the crowds, into the shadow cast by the wall. There were hundreds of people around us but I felt quite alone. Our tracks led away from the ski pistes in a rising contour until, after an hour of wading through deep snow, we reached steepening ice, the start of the climbing. The crevasses along the foot of the face were covered by the winter snows.

Always I feel nagging doubts and uncertainties before a climb, always I wonder what I am doing launching out, away from more immediate pleasures and certain comforts. Now, faced with the long, unpredictable voyage ahead, up this wall, the feeling was stronger than ever, reinforced by the stray shouts of the tiny skiers in the distance. Dick, as ever, seemed unaffected by any such self-questioning and I wondered to what extent I rode on the wave of this determination.

The sky was clear, the air chill, but there was no wind. I felt I was lingering over the ritual of strapping crampons to boots, of uncoiling ropes and tying on, one of us to each end. We needed the points of the crampons to dig in to the steep ice in front of us, but there was much snow too. We sandwiched a layer of polythene between the crampon framework and the sole of each boot so that the snow would not stick, forming a heavy, unstable ball beneath each foot. Then Dick was off, no reasons for delay left, sack on his back, karabiners and pitons jangling from his seat harness, ice axe and hammer driven alternately into smooth ice and himself moving with increasing certainty upwards on the front points of his crampons.

In summer the lower part of the North Face is not difficult, the first 1,500 feet can be climbed in a few hours, up terraces littered with loose rocks, avoiding steep walls by taking a zig-zag course along ledges. Now we were confronted by a largely featureless area of snow, broken only by infrequent outcrops of rock. Had the snow been firm, had it supported our weight, it would have made our task much easier, but we sank into it, knee deep, thigh deep, and beneath there was sometimes steep rock, sometimes ice. We could not see or feel the ledges up which we had zig-zagged in summer, it was as if we were runners on a race track we knew but with a ball and chain on each foot.

Our ropes were 150 feet long. We had two, and each of us attached one end of both ropes with a karabiner to the harness round our waists. Like this, whichever of us was leading a pitch could climb for the full length of the ropes, clipping them one at a time, with karabiners, onto pitons or nylon loops on rock spikes, to safeguard movement upwards. With two lengths of rope there is more safety, but using the two alternately also prevents the friction of the ropes, as they run through karabiners, placed unavoidably in a zig-zag manner, from becoming too great. In retreat, too, having two ropes of 150 feet enables long sections to be descended with ease, provided a sound anchor point is found. A rope longer than 150 feet becomes unmanageable, or the friction through the snap-links usually becomes too great after a certain distance.

By mid-afternoon, taking it in turns, we had run out the rope only nine times. Not much more than 1,000 feet, given that some of the rope was taken up with the knots tying the rope to our waists and to the pitons or other anchor points used to fasten one of us to the side of the mountain whilst the other was leading. There is 10,000 feet of climbing on this wall – 6,000 feet – more than a mile – in height. The route follows the lines of weakness, avoiding overhanging sections where possible, thus almost doubling the distance to be covered. Nearly two miles upwards on hands and knees. In one day we had barely done one-tenth, and the major difficulties were still to come. It was dark by 4.30 p.m. so we had to have chosen our bivouac site for the night before then. There were no natural ledges, all was concealed by the blanket of snow. Dick traversed to the left, towards a feature called the Shattered Pillar, but there was nowhere there to rest. We set to digging out a ledge in the snow and ice beneath a small wall of rock. It felt safer to have a solid wall beside us and some pitons driven into the rock to secure ourselves to during the night.

Night overcame us before we were settled down, facing each other, warm in sleeping bags and down jackets, insulated from the cold ledge of snow by a light foam mat each. We had a plastic bag containing the food for each day, six of these bags in all, and a litre of petrol for the stove. We were disappointed at ourselves and at the mountain, alarmed at all that lay ahead, but for the moment we had the consolation of food and sleep. Little whispers of icy wind troubled my face as I settled down, so I pulled the sleeping bag tight over my head, leaving only a small hole through which to breathe.

My sleep was disturbed by the wind penetrating even that small hole and blowing snow onto my face. I turned and pulled the hood closer round my face but still the snow stung me. I thought, through the mental inertia of only half-wakefulness, that the wind must have grown very strong. I tried to regain sleep, having exerted myself to the minimum to escape the plaguing winds. I could not bear the thought of making a radical effort to solve the problem, such as getting into our bivouac tent. But Dick woke me with his shout: 'Joe, it's snowing, let's put the tent up.'

I roused myself, fought clear of the constrictions of the hoods of the sleeping bag and by torchlight saw the thickly falling, swirling flakes coating everything on the ledge. We had intended to use the bivouac tent as little as possible because it was not much more than a nylon envelope and the condensation from breathing and cooking would cause our sleeping bags and down jackets to get damp and, in a couple of nights, useless. On a still, clear night we could sleep outside, with our sleeping bags tucked into our rucksacks as protection against the windblown snow, but we needed the tent in snowfall such as this. It was of course Dick, unhampered by any sense of lethargy or inertia, who had made the move which was most sensible, chill as it was at first to leave the warmth of the sleeping bag.

We gathered up food, stove and gear before they should disappear in the snow and struggled one by one into the tent, shuffling about to find a tolerable position. The tent was designed for two people lying side by side, but our ledge was long and narrow. We strained against opposite ends, both of us trying to lie full length without one of us sliding off the edge of the ledge. There were no poles in this tent. We attached the two corners at the top to the pitons driven into the rock and the loose fabric of the tent sagged down onto us with the weight of the falling snow. We each had a rope tied to our waists and fastened to the pitons too, just in case a heavy slide of snow from above should knock us off the ledge. A fitful sleep returned.

I think I was glad next morning when it was still snowing and the mountain was covered in cloud. I did not feel rested at all after the disturbed night and though it would not be good in the long run to consume a day's rations if we should run short of food higher up, I did welcome the prospect of a day's rest, waiting for the weather to improve. It was too wild outside the tent to contemplate moving and we passed the day, pressed close against each other, with little conversation, dozing and nibbling at morsels of food.

It was airless inside the tent. We had to choose between ventilation and the chill wind streaming in with flurries of snow, or stale air and near suffocation, but we were snug.

The grey day of silent mist and hissing snow-slides passed into night. Tiny avalanches of snow had slid between the tent and the wall so that the tent fabric inside bulged between Dick and me. It only happened at dark so we did not want to move. We settled down to sleep with even less space than the night before, and growing doubts about the point of staying on the mountain in this spell of bad weather.

I woke to the sound of rushing snow, a senseless, brutal pounding down onto the tent, onto my head, between the tent and the wall, prising the tent irresistibly from the mountain. Dick was awake too and we struggled together in darkness, breathless, pressing as hard as we could against the side of the tent nearest the wall, trying to halt the slow advance away from it, trying to make the falling snow slide over us before the tent was wrenched from the pitons holding it in place and we should tumble down the mountain.

It only lasted seconds, not a word had passed between us; when the snow stopped pouring down we were encased in snow, but able to work ourselves free. Snow had entered the tent and our cosy cocoon was contaminated by an alien whiteness which penetrated every gap in clothing and sleeping bags. But we were alive.

Dick wormed his way outside to dig clear the snow from between the tent and rock before the taut nylon should tear. I found my head torch but before I could join him another remorseless battering started up. The light from my head torch danced to the rhythm of the falling snow as I was struck again and again. This time I could see by the shaking light the dark blue tent shrinking before my helpless eyes as I was crushed and I thought of Dick outside, catching the full force of the avalanche and wondered if he was gone. It stopped. I was held fast as if in concrete. I started to move.

'Joe, are you all right?' It was Dick still there. 'I couldn't see the tent at all when that stopped – I thought you were a goner.'

'I thought the same about you.'

We shifted enough snow for us to breathe and move. 'What can we do?'

It was snowing steadily, thick heavy flakes, more avalanches were certain to come. We had survived two small ones but we could not hope to last the night in this spot.

'The rock bulges out just over here. If we can dig a hollow out beneath it we should at least be out of the way if any more do come.'

We dug by the light of our torches into the bank of snow with a little protective roof of rock jutting out above us. It was not at all comfortable or convenient but we thought that if it would help us survive the next few hours until dawn it would suffice.

Some of our gear we could not find in the snow which covered the ledge we had vacated, but most things we recovered and packed crudely into our sacks. We thrust the sacks into the snow in the protected hollow and crouched on top of them. The tent we draped over ourselves and sat for the rest of the night, weary, stamping our feet to keep the blood flowing in them, shivering and waiting. More avalanches slid past. They came frequently so they had not accumulated the devastating force which some avalanches possess. We were just protected by the roof above us. We contrived to make a warm drink. I held the stove on my knee and Dick held the pan on the stove, melting some of the snow gathered from round our feet.

Cold cramps shook my body but the heat from the stove helped in spite of the clammy condensation.

'How long do you think it will take us to get down?' I asked Dick.

'Down? What if the weather clears up?'

We were thoroughly damp and weary. Sometimes I used to think we were on the same wavelength and at other times I realised we were poles apart.

'We've got to go down, we're soaking, we've lost half the food and we've hardly started the climb.'

'I suppose you're right.'

The admission was wrung from him with such reluctance that I felt as if I was chickening out, but I could not see how we could possibly continue without dying of exposure.

It was still snowing at daybreak and even Dick could not offer a good case for staying on the mountain longer.

'We'll have a hard enough time getting down as it is,' I said, to reaffirm and justify my point of view.

Dick went first down the two ropes held in the snap-link attached to a piton. He disappeared, snow coating his dark clothes, and camouflaging him in the mist. He was only 150 feet away but I could see nothing, and I waited for his shouts to tell me he had hammered in another piton, he was attached and it was safe for me to slide down the ropes and join him. As I arrived, Dick was already busy preparing the next abseil. The doubled rope passed through the karabiner above, I pulled one end of the rope, the other end disappeared up the slope to pass through the karabiner and back down to us. At each anchor point we had to abandon the piton and karabiner, but this was the most rapid way to descend. We did not want to waste time in case we were caught in the open by another avalanche.

Dick set off again. This time the piton was only half embedded in a crack. It was a thin blade of a piton, only 3 inches long. The 1½ inches protruding from the crack flexed and bent as Dick's weight came on it. I took his weight on the rope in my hands, relieving the strain on the piton as he carefully edged downwards. It was a long time before he shouted up to me to come and I nervously put my weight on the rope, watching the piton bend before my eyes, trusting that Dick had found a really good anchor point this time and that he would have tied the other ends of the ropes to it. If the piton above me did come out I thought I might have some chance if at least the bottom ends of the rope were securely attached.

When I came alongside him I saw nothing.

'Where's the anchor?'

He looked sheepish. 'I couldn't find anywhere, it's hopeless with all this snow.' Anger was pointless since I had arrived safely.

Nine times we had to rig up the ropes and abseil down. Nine times my heart was in my mouth until the last leap, clear of the vertical step of ice at the bottom of the wall, and we hurried, as best we could, away from any avalanche zone, before stopping to catch our breaths and pack away harness and ropes.

It was a little warmer down out of the wind and I felt overdressed. We made for the black line of the railway track cutting through the white hillside. We were floundering thigh deep, sometimes waist deep in the snow, and the railway line, kept open for the trains bringing the skiers, was the only clear track. We could relax mentally, there was no danger, just tedium and effort as we sank helplessly into the snow at every step.

At last we staggered clear, out of the wilds, back to civilisation and communication with the real world.

We walked tiredly up the track towards a small hut near a siding. A round, florid rail guard appeared from the hut. He spoke in German.

'Where have you come from? The Wall?'

'Yes.'

'How many days?'

'Two or three.'

He looked wonderingly at us.

'It is forbidden to walk on the track.'

'Where do you want us to walk?'

He gestured at the snow we had just left.

'Which is the nearest station, Alpiglen or Scheidegg?'

'It is forbidden to walk on the railway.'

We set off downhill, along the line, away from him. We reached the

station at Alpiglen and climbed onto the platform. The station master came
rushing out.

'Can we buy tickets for Lauterbrunnen please?'

'It is forbidden to walk on the railway line.'

He would not sell us tickets. We boarded the train when it came and paid
a fine for not having tickets when we got on.

II

Frau Gertsch fussed over us, beaming her pride. Mountaineering is in the
blood of the Swiss. There was a meter on the shower, half a franc for ten
minutes. I put six coins in and stood letting the hot jets of water stroke away
the discomforts, the memories, the anxieties of the last few days. The huge
sleeping platforms were wonderful to stretch out on full length and sleep
on in complete security.

We skied and waited. I could not relax in this period. It was as if a very
difficult exam was hanging over us, one whose starting date we did not
know. I did not look forward with excitement to getting back on the
mountain, the experience would be too cold, too painful to be enjoyed, but
neither could I walk away from the objective we had set ourselves. We did
not have to do it. All those skiers were quite happy to ski below the
mountain, they did not feel the need to go up and spend days and days trying
to climb it. I could not answer to myself why I should want to.

After a day's rest I went up to ski again at Scheidegg and was surprised
to see that much of the snow had come off the face. Instead of the white
wall we had last seen, the rock stood out bare and the dark expanses of the
ice fields were just ice. It shook me a little. We had expected to wait a week
for the snow to clear or consolidate so that there was less risk of avalanche,
but the cold of winter caused the snow to stay light and mobile instead of
fusing together as in the warmer temperatures of summer. It had all slid
off immediately or been blown off by the winds. Now we would have to
face up to going back on the mountain immediately.

When I got back I persuaded Dick that we should postpone departure
for a day. The forecast was not too certain but inwardly I was not prepared
for so sudden a return. I needed time to adjust to it, time to be quiet, to
savour normal life, without the distraction of conversation and activity
before committing myself to the wild forces of the mountain.

We journeyed up again on the train on 25 February, managing to find a seat
this time so I was able to stare dumbly out at the passing woods, heavy with
snow, the chalets sending up blue tendrils of smoke from roofs which almost
merged with the snowy hillside. It was beautiful but it meant nothing. I was
a prisoner, stunned by a sentence just received, on my way back to serve
out my time, and my senses only observed, they did not appreciate.

We needed some more pitons to replace the ones lost on our retreat. The little sports shop at Scheidegg sells only ski gear in winter and the shop-keeper had to search in his storeroom for pitons. He had given me a lift two years before when I was hitchhiking to the Eiger for the first time. We told him our intentions. It felt a little better that someone knew. We did not expect a rescue if we were in difficulty, but last time it had felt very lonely on that mountain, with all this life going on down below and ourselves completely anonymous, not in anyone's mind high up on that awful wall.

'Good luck. Come in for a drink when you get back.'

'Thanks, we'll need it,' and we plodded once more through the snow towards the bottom of the wall where the ice steepened.

We climbed further than on our first attempt, sixteen rope-lengths, nearly 2,000 feet, before we started looking for some place to spend the night. We were both more optimistic. Our knowledge of the mountain helped us to avoid the false lines we had tried the first time.

We were at the top of a bank of snow, at the foot of a vertical step of rock over 100 feet high. There did not seem to be any possibilities of a safe place to stop where we were and Dick started testing the rock wall inquisitively, feeling for hand-holds and foot-holds, looking for a line up it in case we should need to climb it before nightfall to see if there was a better chance of a place above in which to spend the night. He was making exploratory moves when his feet gave way beneath him and his legs disappeared from sight. He pulled himself out of the soft snow, glanced into the hole he had left and looked at me, grinning with pleasure: 'Guess what I've found – a cave.'

To us it had looked as if the wall of rock rose straight out of the snow, but the bottom of the wall was undercut and the bank of snow had concealed a hollow beneath the overhang at the foot of the wall. We crawled in through the hole, hollowed out the cave further and made ourselves at home. When we had finished we had a level floor, large enough for us both to lie down on comfortably, there was a place for the stove, a crack in the roof to drive pitons into from which we hung our gear – it was palatial. We were safe from any avalanche and secure against the worst storm. Had we found this on the first attempt we might have been able to stay on the mountain.

We could have been anywhere. Warm in our sleeping bags, there was none of the discomfort of a big mountain. So cosy were we that we overslept. Dick, relying on an innate sense of the time, was equally fooled by the peacefulness of our eyrie. Outside the day was clear.

The wall above was not easy. Both of us searched along the bottom for a point of departure upwards. I tried one line, climbed up fifteen feet and then there were no holds for hands nor cracks for pitons. A coating of snow concealed much of the rock and baffled further progress. I retreated, hands numb from scraping holds clear of snow.

Dick tried to the left. A few feet up he drove a piton into a crack. An hour later he was not much further. He had fingerless gloves on beneath his mitts. On this sort of climbing we needed our fingers clear, but he could only move for a few minutes without stopping to blow warm breath onto his senseless fingers. He edged slowly leftwards; my feet froze; two hours had passed; eight thousand more feet to climb; the third hour and my body was screaming with the cold. I could not let my tongue say anything; at times I thought Dick was going to come back and ask me to try, but I would have been as slow; the whole situation was impossible, it was midday and we had not climbed even a hundred feet. The tempo of Dick's movement quickened; he was still slow and deliberate, each step was controlled, he let the displaced snow or ice stop falling from the holds each time he settled his crampon points onto a lip of rock. It is better climbing rock without crampons, but there is no better way if the rock is iced over. The deliberate movements were more constant by the end of the third hour and then he shouted that the worst was over. There was still a lot of rope left; he could have gone further but I knew he would be exhausted. As Dick hammered in pitons and secured himself I tried to shake some life back into my stiff limbs. At no time did the futility of our efforts seem as great as when battling with this wall so low down on the whole climb.

I had the security of the rope above me and I needed it. I could hardly feel anything in my fingers, and lacked the confidence to move when I could not be sure of my strength to hold on. It was typical of Dick's persistence, his utter refusal to admit to discomfort, to give in to what he saw as weakness, that he should have pressed on for three hours, painstakingly warming his fingers before every move. It had been too difficult for him to climb wearing his sack. In the middle of the pitch he had taken it off, hung it on a peg and now I untied one of the ropes from my waist, tied the sack to it and while I warmed my fingers, Dick pulled in the rope. With help from Dick pulling gently on the other rope it took me half an hour to reach him.

By evening we had gained the bottom of the Difficult Crack. This pitch, eighty feet in length, is a key link in the route up the lower part of the climb. It is not exceedingly difficult, but in summer it was wet and unpleasant. This time we found it dry, with little ice in it, but by the time we were ready to start up, the night had come.

There was no place to spend the night below the crack; from summer we remembered that above there were some broad ledges. We needed to reach those so I dumped my sack and led off by torchlight. The crack is in the back of a corner; I groped over the walls of the corner for any little knob of rock, or flake on which to pull myself up. I hammered in a piton and felt more reassured. Dick, anxious in the dark below, called up from time to time to ask how it was going. I was slow, but I was progressing.

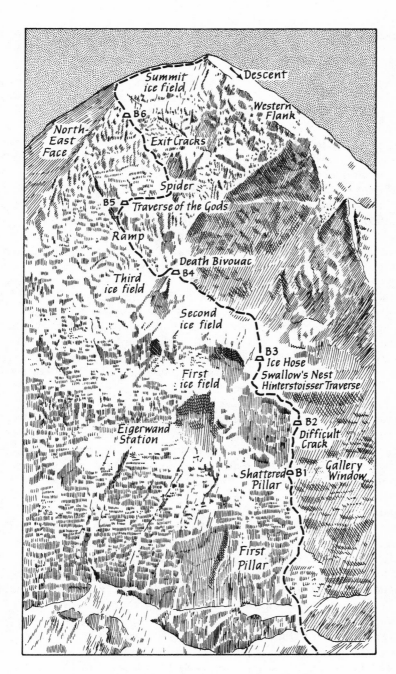

Labels in image:
Descent
Summit ice field
Western Flank
B6
North-East Face
Exit Cracks
Spider
B5
Traverse of the Gods
Ramp
Death Bivouac
B4
Third ice field
Second ice field
B3
Ice Hose
First ice field
Swallow's Nest
Hinterstoisser Traverse
B2
Difficult Crack
Eigerwand Station
Gallery Window
Shattered Pillar
B1
First Pillar

1. The line of our ascent on the North Face of the Eiger.

In spite of myself I felt a thrill at the performance of climbing in the dark. At half height the difficulties eased and I knew it was only a matter of time before I would be able to relax.

Dick climbed up the rope, using a prusik clamp, which slides up the rope but not down, I could hear his scufflings, his grunting and groaning in the dark and the beam of his torch sometimes flicked upwards. When he arrived we dug into the snow and ice, cutting out a platform for three hours before being able to settle down. It was nine o'clock before we were in our sleeping bags and making the evening meal. We thanked our luck that it was another still, clear night.

We had climbed seven rope-lengths this day, only a few hundred feet vertically. Above us the dark bulk of the rest of the wall towered massive and uncompromising. I wondered at our chances. I wondered what sort of people we would be at the end of this; if after days and days of such sustained, punishing effort we would be a little deranged, a little disturbed. Neither of us had gone through anything that was as long as this was likely to take whether we succeeded or not. We just had to keep on, we expected to reach the ice-fields the next day, but for the moment we could not complain, we were warm, we had food. Our fingers were sore from contact with icy rock, from the constant numbing and warming. The lights of the hotel at Scheidegg station made a pool of green far below. I thought of the holiday-makers in the bar, or just finishing their evening meals, in the warm glow of Swiss accommodation in winter, and wished that I did not feel the compulsion to do what we were doing.

I stared into the night until sleep took me.

The third day. A quarter of the way up the wall. Some of the links with life below had snapped; no longer were my thoughts escaping to fantasies of a warm shower, or a pint of beer in a cosy pub, or sleep in a large bed without wearing boots. The furthest my thoughts strayed was to the evening's halt on a ledge, in a bivouac I always promised myself would be better than the last, and the height of luxury would be the first steaming mug of soup.

An old rope was in place on the 120-foot stretch of rock called the Hinterstoisser Traverse after the brilliant young climber who had first found the way across this key pitch but who had not been able to lead the way back during the enforced retreat of his team. The ensuing tragedy in which they had all perished was that described in the book I had heard read out in the seminary which had first brought the Eiger to my attention. One by one the climbers had died, leaving Toni Kurz alone to explain the events to the rescue party before he too died only a few feet away from safety. Since then parties attempting the climb had made certain that their retreat was assured by leaving a rope in place on that crucial section.

Dick led off, climbing horizontally leftwards. The old rope was frayed,

1. The North Face of the Eiger as seen from Kleine Scheidegg. In winter there would be much more snow and ice on the face. (Photo: Swiss National Tourist Office)

2a. Dick at the first bivouac which we later had to vacate owing to the avalanches pouring down from above.

2b. Dick on the Hinterstoisser Traverse.

3a. Dick coming past the Swallow's Nest, a traditional bivouac spot, but in winter blanked out by snow.

3b. Dick traversing along the band of snow at the top rim of the enormous Second Ice Field.

4a. The van on the dirt road of eastern Turkey on the way to Dunagiri.

4b. Dunagiri seen from Changabang. The South-East Ridge is that outlined by the meeting of the shadow and sunlight. The glacier basin is that down which Joe wandered in delirium. Dick descended the other side of the horizontal ridge coming out of the mountain.

its central core was exposed in places due to the erosion of the winds. Huge icicles and, in parts, sheets of ice hung from it. I could see Dick trying to climb relying solely on the rock, but the rope, rotten as it was, hung temptingly close. As the climbing became harder and harder, his hands more and more numb, he nervously tested his weight on the rope. I had him safeguarded on our own ropes and would hold him if he fell but he was a hundred feet away from me in a horizontal line and he would fall in a long bruising arc.

'Watch me here, Joe.'

I watched; he meant me to take extra care that I had the ropes held tight, and then he had done it. He crossed the last twenty feet in a frantic scuttle, looking as if he was willing himself to float.

We bypassed the Swallow's Nest, a niche, secure from all stonefall, on the edge of the first ice field. Now it was blanked out with snow, but we did not want to stop there. That had been our first bivouac when we had climbed the face in summer; this time we had taken two and a half days to reach it.

The first ice field was silent, though in summer as we slept in the Swallow's Nest stones had droned past most of the night. Without the apprehension of being smashed by rocks falling from above, we tiptoed up the right-hand edge of the ice-field to the steepening runnel of ice snaking its way up through rock.

It was too long and steep to climb carrying my rucksack; I left it with Dick. As I wound myself up to face the difficulties of climbing the column of pure ice, testing the hold of my axe in the ice, testing the purchase of the front points of my crampons and massaging the stiffness out of my calf muscles, an alien drone broke the stillness. A distant speck, small as a fly, came towards us growing larger and larger – a helicopter. It hovered a few hundred feet away from us. We could see the occupants, cameras or binoculars masking their faces, and I could not move. From stage fright at realising I was a performer in a gigantic vertical arena my feelings turned to resentment that our very private world should become the focus for the curiosity and pastime of others. I could not concentrate until it was gone, could not rid myself of the thought that those visitors, anonymous and safe in their plastic bubble, would have had the most perfect outing if they could only have seen one of us fall.

Somehow I regained the concentration that had been dented after three days by that bizarre visitation and worked my way up the wall of ice. We used to lead out four rope-lengths each, between four and six hundred feet of climbing. In this way the mental and physical strain of leading is concentrated into one section, and as second on the ropes one can then enjoy a spell of mental relaxation and less physical strain. So it came about that I had all this uncompromising ground to lead between the First and Second

Ice Fields. In summer there had been no ice, just water-worn slabs, on which we had felt insecure, though the climbing was not difficult. It was different in winter. Though the angle of the rock became easier, bands of hard ice stretched across the slabs of rock. My crampon points scarcely bit into the brittle ice, and they grated off when they touched rock. I hammered in a piton and felt safer with my rope passing through the karabiner attached to it. I attempted to climb without my crampons, trying to step on the rock clear of ice with the rubber of my boots, but there was too much ice, and the rubber skated treacherously at its touch.

I moved further left, beginning to feel thwarted; it was no better. I had been trying for an hour. Crampons back on. Still no good. Insignificant in the midst of that huge wall, I was defeated.

'Dick, I can't do it.' It was hopeless and depressing.

'Try without your sack,' he shouted back.

I fastened my sack to the peg and tried again. It did help not having that weight pulling me out of balance. I was able to climb six feet higher.

At chest height there was a sloping ledge of rock with a band of ice an inch thick across it. I drove the points of my ice axe and hammer into the ice. I felt them jar against the rock beneath the ice but they held. I pulled up on them, contorting myself to raise my leg and stick my crampon points into the ice as well. The crampons slipped on the rock before they reached the ice, my foot fell and I was holding on only by the points of axe and hammer. I placed the crampon on another lip of rock and again it slipped and this time I saw the pick of the ice hammer levering itself out of the ice. I lunged, pressing my shoulder onto the hammer to keep its pick in the ice, I twisted my body, fear removed the pain from my aching, weary muscles and I flung my foot upwards beside the axe. The crampon points bit into the ice and I pushed myself upright and into balance. The moment was over, exhaustion overtook me, I shook nervously and waited a while before moving to the easier ground now within reach. The far eastern wing of the mountain was catching the rosy glow of the evening – I had no idea how long I had taken on that pitch.

Our ledge that night was only a foot wide. We slept with nylon slings attaching our chests and legs to pitons in the rock against which we pressed. We hardly spoke to each other by this time. There was no outside stimulus for conversation; we each performed the role we had to; we were working steadily if slowly; after all these years together Dick was still an enigma to me. I had ceased to worry about it. I struggled momentarily with sleep to stare at the constellations of stars and wish I had more knowledge about them and the energy to figure out which was which.

Normally we tried to wake before dawn. We slept fully clothed, only crampons, boots and sunglasses did we take off, but the morning ritual of re-fastening boots, attaching crampons, sealing clothing against the wind and blowing snow took half an hour. We had both somehow disciplined ourselves to excreting only once a day and the most convenient time for that was in the morning. There was no need to undress, only zips and velcro flaps to undo and layers of clothing to be parted. To have undressed would have been to expose ourselves to the heat-stealing wind.

The fourth day was all ice and Dick started the day. The Second Ice Field is not steep and on ice each movement is similar and repetitive, but I was glad it was Dick to lead. This was the ice of winter, dark, hard, repulsive, a thousand feet before the next bit of rock, a thousand steps, kicking crampon points with toe-bruising force at the ice trying to make them stick there, hammering at the ice with the picks of axe and hammer to make them bite in as hand-holds. When I followed Dick my hands became numb and insensible as I hit them against the ice inadvertently in trying to get the axe to bite deeper. The shaft of the hammer was shorter and my left hand suffered more.

We were creatures of the mountain now, lost to our former lives, remote from the tourists far away, remote even from any more visitors that might come to stare. The starting for me is always the hardest; once under way I could almost forget the passing of the days.

We switched round leads four times on this everlasting day. Fourteen rope-lengths of climbing in all, with the last two hundred feet up, escaping from the ice field, too difficult to climb with the weight of my sack. I left it behind to haul up later and clawed at the rock with senseless, bleeding fingers. It was so cold that each piton, each karabiner stuck to my hand and took away a little more skin.

Our sacks were still heavy and we had begun to consider a change of plan. We were two-thirds of the way up the wall and to speed progress we planned to consume as much of our food as we could and make a dash next day for the summit. We stopped earlier than usual to prepare a good platform for the night – if we intended to rush to the finish we needed to be well rested. It took three hours to complete the platform and only then, so engrossed had we been with the work, did we notice the grey streamers of cloud sliding across the sky with the dusk.

If bad weather came we could not risk scoffing all the food at once. We reverted to our former plans.

We used the tent for the first time. A small wall of rock leaned gently over the platform, protecting us from any stones falling from above and holding the tent upright. This was the infamous Death Bivouac where the first two men to attempt to climb the face, Sedlmayer and Mehringer, had arrived in 1935 and died in blizzards to stand, frozen sentinels, for long after their attempt had halted in the storm. I felt no foreboding, unhaunted by any ghosts; my mind was preoccupied with our own practical problems. We needed to hurry now. For once I was impatient for morning, keen to start moving, to get as close as possible to the top before we were engulfed in the storm which was threatening.

I noticed Dick stealing secret glances outside, checking the weather. It preyed on both our minds. We did not need discussion. If the storm came we would have to decide whether to go up or down; this Death Bivouac was the last place from which it would be sensible to attempt a retreat, and once we left here the only rational way off the mountain was upwards. My hands smarted all night from the slowly suppurating cuts they had now acquired and sleep eluded me.

In the morning there was a grey expectancy in the sky but no snow was falling. I was slow from lack of sleep but we could move upwards through the Third Ice Field, more dark, splintering ice and the diagonal slash of the Ramp, scything leftwards towards the complex exit pitches. The Ramp was so long, so huge we were in it all day. We had expected ice in a chimney that had been pouring with water in summer but there was none and we felt favoured. The steep rib above the chimney was clean of snow; Dick tried to talk me into leading it in a sudden loss of confidence but I was as worried as he and I bullied him on.

There was some tension between us. Dick led another pitch and was perched out of the way on a ledge as I climbed up the gully of ice at the top of the Ramp.

'Joe, could you carry on, it will be too awkward to change over here?'

I really did not want to and grudgingly felt out-manoeuvred.

'Joe, could you take that ice piton out as well, so I don't have to go down for it?'

'Bloody hell, Dick, you ask me to take your turn leading, you ask me to take pegs out for you, do you want me to climb the bloody mountain for you?'

I felt self-righteous and I hated Dick's stupidity. I climbed off upwards. It mattered only for a moment. Five days on a knife edge, everything was close to the surface.

That fifth night was the worst up to then. All we had was a seat smashed from the ice and loose rock. We sat with legs in our sleeping bags hanging over the edge, and a sling of nylon round our chests to stop ourselves lolling forward as we dozed off. For the second night the sky was grey with a pregnant expectancy. I remembered that my first climbing partner, Stefan, was getting married on this day. I had had to write to say that I probably could not make it.

My rucksack hung from a piton beside me. I wedged my head behind it to stop it falling forward as drowsiness began to take hold of me. I dreamt there was a policeman with his notebook out taking down my particulars:

'Hello officer, what's this for?'

'I'm booking you for driving a piton too fast down this groove.'

'But, officer, I didn't know anyone else knew about this groove.'

'I often drive down this way myself.'

I woke to find that Dick had continued to lie down. His head was resting in my lap and his feet were wedged somehow behind a rock projection.

'You don't mind do you, Joe?'

'No, it's O.K.'

We moved on, in the semi-darkness before the dawn, feeling the pressure now to use every moment of light. There was no snowfall but the heavy greyness was still in the sky. I was shaky and unnerved as I climbed rightwards along the Traverse of the Gods. I knew from summer that it was sensational rather than hard but I was still apprehensive. Ice coated every hold. I had memories of my struggles on the icy rock below; beneath my feet the face curved inwards, revealing the whole of the rest of the climb.

This horizontal section took us back into the heart of the mountain to the last of the ice fields, the White Spider, the catchment area for all the rockfall from above, though now silent. The ice was the worst yet, more black glass and steeper than any of the other ice fields. It fell to me to scrape and claw my way up it for five hundred feet. The ice was so hard that no technique helped; only brute strength made any impression. I kicked with my feet and smashed with my axe, never feeling secure as the brittle ice splintered away from my crampon points or axe pick.

An old rope hung down to my right, remnant from some previous epic. I climbed out of my way across to it and unashamedly used it as a handline for fifty feet. When it ran out I had to return to the blank, dark glass and regretted ever sampling the security of that rope. I longed for some excuse to hand over the lead to Dick, to stand by whilst he felt some of the terrible insecurity. But we had reached the start of the Exit Cracks, the final obstacle on the wall, before it was his turn to go first for four lengths of the rope. My fingers, cracked and bruised with the hammering, raw with the cold, were bleeding profusely.

The most difficult pitch remaining, the Quartz Crack, was concealed by a huge bulge of ice. Stubbornly Dick butted away at it. Watching him I could see no way that he could get past, then the mass of snow collapsed, brushing him to one side, but he clung on and the rock above him was clear. He climbed up and leftwards out of the difficulty and into sunlight. For the first time in days we were leaving the shadow of the face and it was as if we were being welcomed and congratulated for the climb. Feeble though the rays of the sinking sun were, some warmth soaked through my clothes and suddenly I had had enough. There were only hundreds of feet left to the summit, not thousands, but I had no time for the painstaking precautions we needed. The rock was loose, treacherous beneath a thin covering of snow, not difficult but insecure. I grew impatient and careless, then the sun was gone, clouds swirled round the summit, a wind caught us when we reached the exposed upper slopes and snow began to fall. Dark was upon us before we were near the summit and all we could do was push a few loose rocks to one side and squat down with the bivouac tent pulled over our heads.

The threatening storm had broken, the wind tore at the tent, snow soon covered over bits of equipment we had strewn on the ledge.

We huddled together for warmth, battered by the wind through the tent. At first we crouched over the stove, slowly suffocating from its fumes until we had eaten and drunk. Then we wriggled one at a time into our sleeping bags, boots and all while the air without the stove quickly chilled. Ice formed on our beards and on the inside of the tent only to shake off and fall like snow as the nylon flapped furiously in the relentless winds. The cracked and festering sores on my fingers hurt all the more in the warmth of my sleeping bag as the salt of perspiration aggravated each cut. Dick confessed that he was suffering too.

A little voice in my mind kept whispering 'You've done it, you've done it,' but I did not want to listen until I was down off the mountain, down on flat ground. I held the fabric of the tent in my teeth to stop it flapping against my face and disturbing me with showers of ice.

It was a fitful night. We were two lost souls in a bleak, forlorn limbo, shuffling about to ease the cramps and aches of our constricted quarters.

At dawn we left, without reluctance, without food, racing now before the storm strengthened and we were stranded and lost in ever-deepening snow. I felt humbled and undeservedly favoured to look down and see the snow covering those last loose pitches we had scrambled up the night before. Only a few easy pitches on comforting soft, blue ice were left for us, and then we were on the sharp crest of the ridge leading to the rounded summit.

We were pushed and tugged by the wind, there was no view of distant peaks over the ridge, only heavy swirling cloud. Dick was there first; he flopped down in the snow at the highest point and pulled in the rope with which he was joined to me. It was 8.00 a.m. on Monday 3 March, six days after leaving the station at the foot of the mountain.

There was no time for congratulation, no time for the indulgence of regret at achieving a goal, the blasts of wind and stinging snow drove us on and down, sliding, scrabbling, gasping in pouring streams of avalanching snow. We had anticipated bivouacking but we were being allowed to escape. I held my breath, stayed tense and watchful. We kept checking with each other, trying to recall the devious way down, disguised now by winter, and then we were clear, free from the steep ground, free from the slipping and sliding, entering a gully which eased out onto level ground and from there it was only wading through deep snow, sometimes crawling, but we were safe.

It was the middle of the afternoon when we reached the small hotel on the railway line. There seemed to be something happening; a small group of people were outside, and then they clapped – it was for us. They helped us off with our rucksacks. Dick winced with pain as he tried to peel his inner gloves from his damaged hands and a girl took charge and cut the gloves away.

Inside, heads turned and stared, we were wild in appearance and with long icicles hanging from our beards. We sat down and the manager sent over beer and soup. An Englishman was sitting across from us reading a newspaper – '41 killed in Moorgate Tube Disaster' – on the juke box someone was singing 'I've got two strong arms, I can help'.

I left Dick at the table to go and buy the train tickets for our descent to the valley. As I walked away I heard the incredulous Englishman asking: 'You mean you only bought one way tickets?' and Dick, with his enigmatic smile that spoke of hidden strengths, not knowing what to answer.

THREE

It Could Be Worse

DUNAGIRI

I

We called in to see Frau Gertsch to pick up the key to the hostel.

'*Tous les gens parlent de vous,*' she said, knowing we understood some French.

'*Quels gens?*'

'*Les gens de la région; vous êtes merveilleux.*'

She was homely and reassuring. In the hostel she bustled about making the place as warm as she could. Dick and I shambled around aimlessly. Too late to obtain anything from the shops; no celebratory meal; the same rations we had been eating for the last month; we went out to the only bar in the village and sat silently over a drink, nothing to converse about. I lay awake most of the night, feeling lost on the spacious bed, still highly strung, physically weary but mentally alert.

'Joe, would you fasten my buttons please, my fingers hurt too much.'

Next day we left, back to England, to Manchester, to school and classrooms full of children most of whom, like myself, wanted to be anywhere but behind a desk.

At the same time as we had been planning to climb the Eiger in winter we had begun thinking of going further afield. Initially those people who went on expeditions to the Himalayas or the Andes had seemed a select group, eligible for a place on an expedition team by virtue of their great experience, proven ability and stamina. We could not see how people became eligible without having already been on an expedition and it seemed a double-bind situation. So without really knowing what we were taking on, we resolved to form our own 'expedition', and before leaving for the Eiger we had sent applications in to the government of India for permission to climb one of their mountains.

We had applied for permission to climb a beautiful mountain called Shivling in northern India, launching ourselves into our first skirmishes with the complex formalities of going on what inevitably we had to call an expedition. 'Expedition' was a grandiose title for what was no more than the climbing of mountains higher than the ones we had so far climbed but the remoteness, the greater degree of organisation needed, and the official approvals required, seemed to impose an identity which transcended our simple intentions. We wanted to climb bigger mountains than in the Alps, we wanted to climb a difficult route on a big mountain; we did not know about the time it would take to deal with the bureaucracies of the East; we did not know that to climb a mountain in any of the Himalayan countries wewouldhavetopayabookingfee.Thepeoplewhowentonexpeditionsseemeda small, tightly-knit group, and we did not feel qualified enough to expect admission into that closed circle which from the outside seemed to hold all the knowledge we needed. We could not understand what was different about going to the Himalayas, except that it was further; we did not know anything about the logistics of large groups and it seemed that the best way to climb would be as a pair, but since the mountains were so remote we decided to invite another pair to come along. It would not be much different from sharing a vehicle to go out to France and it would mean there were other people to lend a hand to us or us to them if an accident should happen.

Ideally, as a team of four people, a compact group, we could travel overland in a transit van, and climb a new and difficult route on the mountain we chose. Our ambitions were limited to peaks of around 20,000 to 23,000 feet, since we did not have the confidence to plan for anything higher, and at this height we hoped to be able to do what we knew best, routes of technical difficulty but without the need for fixed camps and massive organisation.

So we planned ahead, further than I had ever planned before. Always I had a certain reserve about planning beyond the next climb when so much depended on fate, but to go to the Himalayas, to go forward for us, meant making arrangements almost a year in advance. It meant also broadcasting our intentions, again something we were unaccustomed to. Not that we worried about competition, we just felt reservations about making claims that we were going to do a climb about which we felt not the least bit of confidence. In order to obtain permission, however, we had to present a confident manner and a positive approach in our application to the Indian government, and we had to present the same confidence to win the approval of the official mountaineering bodies in Britain.

But even organising a group as small as four had its problems.

One of the other pair we asked, a friend of Dick's, was doing a college course. He could only go during holidays, which would restrict us to climbing in the monsoon period, a most undesirable time of the year with constant heavy rains and snow, or to climbing in an area outside the Himalayan chain. Neither prospect held any appeal. We arranged to meet in Wales one weekend to talk it over. As the evening wore on with no sign of the other pair, Dick and I rationalised the situation.

'If they can't even turn up to discuss the expedition how reliable are they going to be on the trip itself?'

'Well, what shall we do? Just go as the two of us?'

'At least we would know where we stood. We probably won't need to buy a transit van if there's just two of us.'

'Would your car make it?'

Dick, who could not drive and was delightfully innocent of many of the practicalities of life, saw one vehicle as much the same as another.

'My old heap probably wouldn't get us to the Alps again. We'll have to buy an Escort van or something like that. Should be able to get one for about £150. You'll have to learn to drive, though. I'm not doing all the driving myself.'

So it was decided.

We could not have Shivling since it was in a restricted area close to the border; we could not have Changabang for some other reason. As beginners we were faced with the whole chain of the Himalayas to choose from and

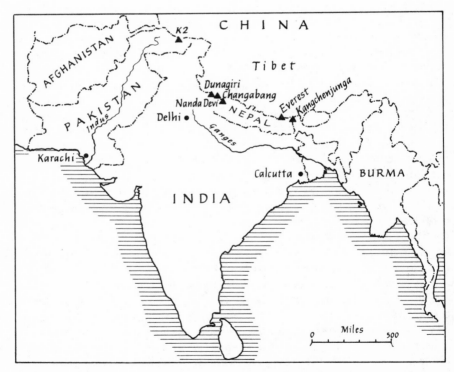

2. General location of mountains climbed by the author and other notable peaks in the Karakoram and Himalayas.

it was all academic, choosing a mountain out of a book, trying to piece together all that would be needed to reach that mountain and to climb it, and then pouring all energies into obtaining permission. At first I did not know where Kathmandu was in relation to Everest, which mountains were in India, which were in Pakistan or Nepal. Gradually patterns emerged and we began to know which mountains were where and what we were interested in.

Then more refusals came back. Two was considered an insufficient number from a safety point of view, all the mountains we were choosing were close to the border and for that reason out of bounds to expeditions.

It was discouraging carrying on with arrangements to go, buying the van, accumulating a few more items of equipment, when all the likelihood of ever going seemed minimal. Dick took up a teaching job in Manchester and started learning to drive.

It was a marvellous summer for rock-climbing, rushing away from school to climb in the long evenings on the crags around the city, sunny days in Wales and the Lake District. I met a girl called Muriel, full of vitality and dynamism, who caused me to wonder at how much I could lose by going off for so long on such an unpredictable venture.

To all but ourselves our 'expedition' was very definite. Then we met a Mrs Beaumont, whose brother had disappeared exploring a lake in Africa. In his memory a fund had been set up which disbursed small amounts of money to Manchester University students or graduates going on exploratory trips.

We had applied for a grant and were interviewed by Mrs Beaumont, now a trustee of the fund, a lively, grey-haired lady, driving a sports car and quizzing us in a motherly but encouraging manner.

'Did you say you were having difficulties with the Nepalese government? My husband has some friends out there. We might be able to help.'

She was kind, but it was with the Indian government we were having problems; the Nepalese had not even replied. We gave her details of our proposals and she left promising to chivvy them up in Nepal. I wondered if she knew where Nepal was, but expected little from it anyway since it was in India we were wanting to climb.

Dick went up to London for an interview with the Mount Everest Foundation to seek their approval and a grant towards the 'expedition'. The Mount Everest Foundation, or MEF, was set up as a result of the first successful ascent of Mount Everest in 1953, and all monies accruing from lectures, book and film were invested to provide a fund from which other expeditions could receive some financial support. The committee of the MEF is made up of eminent members of the mountaineering and scientific fraternity and approval by this august body carries some weight with foreign governments.

The interviews take place in the council room of the distinguished premises of the Royal Geographical Society on Kensington Gore. A huge polished table runs the length of the room and on one side are ranged the mostly grey- or white-haired dignitaries who conduct the interview with the applicant who sits alone across the table.

Dick had never learnt how to present an appearance of being anything else but himself.

'Why are there only two of you for this proposed expedition?'

'What if one of you sprains an ankle and needs helping down off the mountain?'

'Who have you consulted about your plans?'

'What are your plans? What mountain do you intend to climb?'

At the time we intended to try a steep and difficult ridge on Changabang. A frail-looking, white-haired gentleman at the far end of the table, who seemed to have been asleep, opened his eyes and asked: 'Why don't you try Kalanka?'

'It looks too easy,' replied Dick without hesitation or embarrassment. Later he discovered that the white-haired gentleman was Eric Shipton who had explored and climbed in the area since long before either of us had been born, and still knew it better than anyone.

Then Mrs Beaumont rang us. 'The Indians aren't happy about there only being the two of you but we've twisted their arms and they are sending you a letter to say you can choose one of three peaks. So don't go and fall off otherwise there'll be hell to pay.'

And it was all definite. Expeditions are one hurdle after another, this major one was over. We were given the choice of Devisthan, Mrigthuni and Dunagiri, all three in the same region. We chose Dunagiri, the highest of the three at over 23,000 feet, and climbed only once before, in 1939, by an expedition led by André Roche. We wanted to do a new route on it, and from pictures decided that a steep buttress, the south-east ridge, looked excellent for our purposes. The other two mountains were lower and not as interesting.

Then came more problems, and more costs. We had to have a Liaison Officer, whom we had to equip and feed. In the letter of information we were told that he was to assist us with the selection of porters, purchasing provisions and advise us on the climate and acclimatisation, snow conditions, risks and the feasibility of climbing the mountain.

It was nonsensical. We were going to the Himalayas because we felt capable of climbing there, not on a course at a climbing school; we did not want someone imposed on us who almost certainly would not know as much about mountaineering as we did ourselves, and on top of that we were being asked to feed and equip him.

One hurdle after another.

The days of summer sped by; I was climbing better than ever before – never with Dick, somehow we knew each other too well, needed a relief from each other in Britain – was also very much in love, and I could not help but feel that I was committed to something which could take away all this happiness. The pleasure of climbing rock is the pleasure of the gymnast, whilst the mountaineer is more like a marathon runner. The life of a lover of necessity is one of togetherness and voluntarily, I hardly knew if I wanted to or not, I was abandoning that for a solitary life on a mountain. Naive as I was, I did not know if it was normal to worry that we might not come back.

We bought an 1100cc Ford Escort van for £170 and had it checked over by the A.A. The engineer's report was discouraging:

> Considering vehicle's age, recorded mileage, faults evident, a below-average example of the model. Urgent attention required to engine, suspension, brakes and corroded bodywork. This work will prove expensive and its economic justification should be thought out initially.

> In its present condition, in my opinion, the vehicle is not roadworthy for the journey I am informed was proposed for the vehicle. The best way of using this van to reach the Himalayas is to drive down in it to Heathrow and fly.

We had some work done on it but could not afford to do all that he suggested. We could only trust to luck.

We were going for a post-monsoon attempt on the mountain, the season after the end of the summer rains and before the start of the winter snows. School ended and we packed ready to leave.

There was something of the boredom as before an exam. I had been involved in the preparations for too long and, ready or not, I just wanted to start. I used to wake up to immediate consciousness – no more the slow, lazy surfacing to see what a new day had to offer – it was as if I had just turned away for a moment, everything was there waiting to be attended to. Letters, phone calls, equipment, medicine, insurance, vaccinations, maps, itineraries, food and on and on.

I lived with my two friends Don and Jenny, who never murmured about the constant phone calls, mounds of equipment and food, early morning calls from the postman with yet another parcel.

On Monday 4 August 1975 Dick passed his driving test and on Tuesday the 5th we left for India.

At 8.00 a.m. Dick was sitting at Jenny's sewing machine finishing his cagoule for the mountain as I packed the van. We had never made any estimate of how much would have to go into the van; it was the biggest vehicle either of us had had anything to do with and we had not thought to question its capacity. We had even been considering selling a place in the van to someone for the overland journey. The van sank lower and lower on the suspension as we loaded everything in. There was not a bit of space spare when we had finished. The leaf springs bent back over on themselves in an inverted ∩.

We discarded one or two bits of gear, closed the door on the house, started the van and lurched forward out of the driveway. The exhaust grated on the ramp of the drive as we entered the road at the start of the 6,000-mile journey.

We called in to see Ken Wilson, editor of *Mountain* magazine, and an authoritative spokesman on world mountaineering. Not known for being indifferent about any subject on earth, he favoured us with his enthusiastic approval: 'I like it, I really like it. You guys just going off, chucking your gear into the back of a van and going to the Himalayas. It's got to be the shape of things to come. Great. Go for it.'

He gave us the news he had just received that Messner and Habeler had climbed one of the highest mountains in the world, Hidden Peak in the Karakoram, as a twosome. As always in comparison to people who seemed more proficient we felt self-conscious at pitting ourselves against a similar objective.

The drive became a job like any other. Up at dawn, breakfast; driving by 8.00. Lunch. Finish at 5.00 p.m. The smooth tarmac and order of Europe changed to ruts and chaos as we drove further east. No one seemed to obey rules; it was all observation and luck.

Dick had recorded some classical music to play on the car's cassette player during the drive. Mine was mostly rock music. By the time we reached Turkey, the hot air streaming in through the wide open windows, the classical music lost out. The noise of car, wind and road drowned the subtleties of Dvorak, Beethoven and Mahler. It was Dylan above all who, with his nasal, insistent drone, won the day.

Dick had organised the food. Frugal to the last, our diet for the journey was to be sandwich-spread on bread for as long as we could obtain bread, home-made muesli with powdered milk, an omelette made from egg powder, and at night sometimes a tin of meat with whatever vegetables we could find. We were passing through countries each with their own particular cuisine but in the interests of thrift, if it served a final goal, Dick could discipline himself to put up with anything. We differed radically on this. Always I felt the spendthrift, the wastrel, the hedonist in his company. Always, without expressing a word, he managed to instil in me an uncomfortable sense of guilt and self-consciousness about any deviation from the spartan diet he had calculated as meeting all our calorific needs even if it did not meet the needs of the soul.

I tried to explain my point of view by telling him how much regret I would feel if I was to die in the mountains, to die whilst doing something so arduous, uncomfortable and painful as mountaineering and knowing that all the time I had been off the mountain I had led a spartan life as well.

I never knew whether the enigmatic smile concealed puzzlement or philosophical acquiescence. Dick continued contentedly munching chupattis covered in sandwich-spread when we could no longer get bread.

The wild, amiable disorder of Istanbul gave way to deserts and a breakdown. It seemed to be the coil that was at fault. We were unable to speak the language and met with incomprehension at every garage. The van limped on for two days until we met a Turk who had worked in Germany and arranged a replacement for the faulty part.

Then we met the savage, unsmiling rush of Tehran. Dick still had a studied air of concentration when at the wheel, betraying that he was not so familiar with driving that it was second nature yet. Not long after entering Iran on the open road in front of us a goat strayed from a herd and wandered across the road. A second goat began to follow and Dick, at the wheel, not calculating that the goat had only to walk a few steps before being full in the path of the van whilst the van had to travel twenty yards to get past, put his foot down to try to squeeze through the gap between the two goats. He hit the second goat square on and it was flung backwards into the ditch.

We stopped the van. The goat-herd rushed up, shouting and gesticulating at us and the injured goat, making chopping motions at its neck with the hoe he held. We had heard that it was better to knock down a man than an animal in some of the eastern countries; we had visions of languishing in gaol, trying to pay off an impossible fine. The van was not damaged.

We could not communicate at all, and being in the middle of a desert had the blessing that we were not immediately surrounded by a curious mob.

'What shall we do, Joe?' Dick looked bewildered.

The goat-herd turned his attention from us and saw more of his herd wandering across the road into the path of an oncoming lorry. He ran at them, shouting and shooing them out of the way.

'Let's go.'

We jumped into the van and drove for two hundred miles before stopping.

'I thought he was going to chop its head off at first,' said Dick.

A few days later, leaving Mashad, the last town before the eastern border of Iran, at the busiest time of the morning Dick seemed to be trying to imitate the apparently effortless weaving in and out of the traffic that some of the cars were doing. Not realising that it was a deft play between accelerator, clutch and brake, he seemed to be trying to achieve the flowing movement simply by turning the steering wheel from side to side. He hit a car a glancing blow and stopped.

'What shall we do?'

The car was caught up in the stream of traffic going in the opposite direction.

'Keep going.'

We left behind the cunning, plausible con-men of Iran and met the wild-looking, amiable rogues of Afghanistan, fierce with their ancient rifles and huge knives tucked into their waist-bands. Each rest-house we stayed at was like a miniature fortress, with an enclosed courtyard where we could sleep beside the van which contained more than a life's fortune to any of the local bandits.

We met people of all nationalities journeying east: a couple in a little Citroën 2CV, with wire mesh across the screen as protection against flying stones; a French-Canadian who smoked a lot of hashish and became very argumentative about independence for Quebec; a Belgian and a Frenchman, partners of the road, and Willie from Dundee, a dustman until he was fifty-five and his mother had died. With no more responsibilities he had set out for India, something he had wanted to do all his life, and he was heading for Varanesi where he had heard you could stay in the temples and get fed. He was worried that he did not have enough money to get across some of the borders, having heard that everyone had to have a minimum amount.

To all of these travellers we seemed to have a more tangible purpose in travelling east; to some the van was a wondrous machine when parked in their midst, with stereophonic music drumming out of it. To me these people seemed to have an enviable, carefree existence, wandering at will, with no burning ambitions eating away at their insides.

We crossed into India, out of the deserts into the lush greenery of the end of the monsoon, along roads that were forever lined with people walking, walking, from no definable source and towards no obvious destination.

After three weeks on the road we reached Delhi and telephoned the office of 'the friends' who had pleaded our case and obtained permission from the Indian government.

The office of J. D. Kapoor was an oasis of cool out of the enervating heat. He sat filling his armchair, holding court, with meek servants being summoned and dismissed at the touch of a concealed buzzer.

'Well, it was very lucky you see, it turned out that this fellow Chakravarty works for a firm on the floor above this. I just went up to see him and told him you were excellent climbers. The best in Britain and so we got permission.'

'But you have never met us.'

'Ah, I was given my orders. Mrs Beaumont instructed me.'

He beamed hugely as at a joke.

We stayed in a guest-house, costing 7 rupees per night, approximately 30p. There were three rooms, each holding about eight people. We intended to stay only one or two nights but we were there two weeks.

There was some problem over the Liaison Officer. He was not available when we arrived. We made a daily visit to the Indian Mountaineering Foundation headquarters in the Ministry of Defence. Munshi Ram, Assistant Secretary, laboured there over another expedition application, surrounded by unstable stacks of yellowing records whose tattered edges waved in the draught from the endlessly creaking fan on the ceiling.

We would sit sweating in the heat for a couple of hours, clearly being expected to understand by our being allowed to wait there that they too were as nonplussed as us and by sharing the waiting they were somehow trying to show us they were trying their hardest. Still nothing happened.

'Mr Tasker,' in a sing-song voice, 'I think he will not come today now. He will be here tomorrow. Please come back tomorrow.'

The bureaucracy could not cope with an expedition without a leader. There were only two of us but they wanted one of us to be 'Leader'. Dick asked me to do it. He did not feel comfortable adhering to what he saw as a pointless formality.

We suspected that the delays we were experiencing were due to the tacit disapproval of our two-man expedition; on top of this we had come overland on the 'hippy-trail', we wore jeans like hippies and stayed in the cheap sort of doss-house where hippies generally stayed. In Britain there is no class difference amongst climbers, a homogeneous group which does not make judgements on the basis of dress or financial standing. In the east, in the countries where worn and dishevelled clothing is not a sign of disregard for the importance of superficial or material symbols of merit but an indication of material poverty, the westerner who through choice abandons his potential wealth and voyages like one from the lower classes is looked down upon and is not taken seriously. The well-dressed in India are at pains to demonstrate their distinction from the lower classes and it was almost an insult to them that they had to have anything to do with us who did not act as visibly worthy ambassadors of our highly privileged country.

The days slipped by; we sat in the guest-house watching Mr Sony, the morose but friendly proprietor, de-lousing the beds, and we could do nothing. We suggested that we be allowed to go up into the mountains ourselves and the Liaison Officer could join us when he arrived in Delhi, but that was vetoed. Dunagiri, the mountain we had come to climb, was only a few miles from the border and the area was militarily very sensitive.

One day an English lad, Peter Roberts, came to see us. He wanted to go trekking in the mountains and Munshi Ram had suggested he join us. One way or another the authorities were determined to increase the size of our team. Peter was not a climber. He was on holiday in India with his girlfriend, in a Volkswagen minibus, packed with tins of food and goodies from Britain. He was a down-to-earth, humorous chap and we had no objections to his coming to Base Camp with us. He would be welcome company, though his intention to leave his girlfriend to fend for herself for six weeks or so seemed strange.

J.D. and his company came to our rescue again. With many muttered imprecations he shouted questions down the phone and within two days things were moving. Six weeks after leaving Britain, the van was toiling up the steep, winding road along the Rishi Ganga, up the pilgrim route, with Inder Kapoor, an athletics teacher, as our Liaison Officer.

We parked the van in Joshimath, at the Neelkanth 'Motel', run by Bhupal Singh, an amiable man of Tibetan appearance. He had been a trader until the border with Tibet had closed and he had opened this rest-house for the pilgrims on their way to the sacred shrines of Badrinath, a further day's journey by bus. Neelkanth was a mountain visible from Badrinath, but I asked him what had made him call the rest-house a 'motel'. He explained with amusement, in imperfect English, that his brother had been to Europe once and the name had taken his fancy as being more impressive than a plain 'hotel'.

He seemed a most honest and reliable man, so we left the van in his charge when we set off for the mountain, climbing up from the road, a few hours by bus from Joshimath, on the six-day trek towards our Base Camp.

II

On the second day of the walk to Base Camp I developed toothache. Dick and I had hired from the villages of Lata and Reni, where we had left the road, ten porters to carry food and gear for ourselves and Inder. Peter hired another three to carry all the tins of delicious foodstuffs he was bringing along out of his supply. We made the long, steep climb up from the side of the road over two days to a camp-site at 11,000 feet, and then I was almost incapacitated with toothache. I pressed on with the rest of the party next day up to Dharansi Pass and along the high plateau at 13,000 feet but the throbbing pain in my gums made me feel sick. The porters were sympathetic; one gave me a piece of root produced from a dirty rag secreted about his person. I pressed the root against my gum; Dick, with implicit faith in things of the earth which he did not have in man-made medicines, felt sure it would work. Neither root, nor aspirin, nor anything else made any difference.

That night, after a long descent down three thousand feet from the plateau, I consumed antibiotics and extra-strong painkillers. By morning I was delirious, my lower jaw numb and swollen.

I was asked questions, asked to make decisions, but I was in a daze; through a blur of nausea and searing frustration I could not think and Dick took charge. He told me to take a porter and go back to Joshimath where there was a Military Camp and possibly a doctor. He would continue to Base

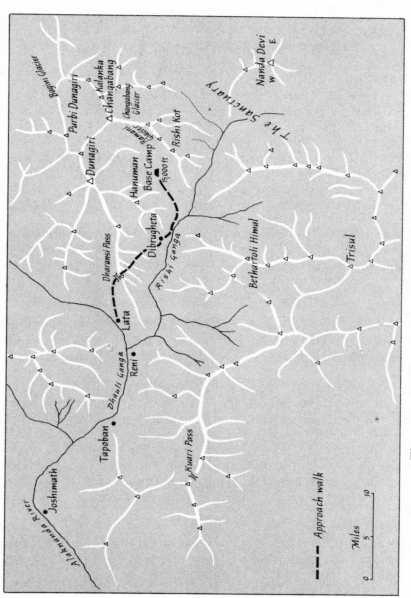

3. The approach and area surrounding Dunagiri and Changabang.

Camp with the rest of the porters, and he and Peter would wait for me there. He put his hand on my shoulder and squeezed it as I was leaving, in a gesture which spoke volumes of sympathy he felt but was unaccustomed to expressing.

'Take care, Joe, you'll be all right. Good luck. See you soon.'

More ill than I could ever remember I climbed back up the 3,000-foot rise to the plateau we had crossed the previous day. Bijay Singh, the porter, took my rucksack. I carried nothing but still could hardly move. It was midday when we reached the top, but I could go no further; I felt dizzy and at each rest I fell into a doze. I could not imagine how I had ever dared presume to climb in the Himalayas. I impressed on Bijay the need to halt.

With the long-suffering patience of people accustomed to hardship he set about making a shelter as best he could. There were no trees. He stretched a piece of polythene over a wall built from rocks and made a fire from some roots he collected during a long search over the plateau. I crawled inside to sleep with a miserable apology.

I woke periodically to know it was raining and Bijay was sitting crouched over a fire, another square protecting him and the fire from the downpour. A couple of times he handed me tea, then I woke to find it was night and there was a bundle of sackcloth beside me; that was Bijay; it was still pouring down. I writhed all night, dreams mingled with bodies and tattered thoughts.

By morning the fever was over, and the sky clear. Bijay shepherded my dizzy steps across the plateau, over the ridges and down, after glimpsing the frozen, magnificent sentinel of Nanda Devi, which only seemed to mock from afar.

In Joshimath I visited the army compound. The dentist was away and I was partially glad when I saw the pedal-operated drill and rusty instruments. To the doctor, a man from the plains, I was a distraction from the boredom of this posting in the mountains, where alcohol was forbidden due to the proximity of some sacred shrines. He diagnosed an abscess beneath the tooth and prescribed penicillin injections. An orderly performed the injection, fishing the syringe out of a glass of murky water and squeezing it hard into my arm before realising that there was a blockage in the needle.

From the damp, bug-infested room of the Neelkanth Motel in the utmost depths of depression I looked out onto a beautiful valley. There was warm sunlight, and cool shade, the comical proprietor of the Motel clucked his sympathy; the tough, hard life of a mountain village went its busy course, and everywhere I looked there were the elusive hills. I calculated that Dick and Peter would have reached Base Camp by this time but for me the nine months of planning, preparations, frustrations, setbacks and advances had ended in a dark room whose walls sweated and were stained with the damp oozing from the toilet and wash room above. I asked myself over and over if I could ever rise from this bed of pain to reach 23,000 feet. I felt as if nothing, not anything, could touch me, nothing could ever affect me again, after coming so far to be turned back at the last moment. I was completely numb, a wound cauterised. I had never realised that climbing meant so much to me. Twice daily I trailed up to the compound for more injections and more discouragement from the doctor.

In front of myself I could never again maintain that I was caught up in this game unwillingly. I knew now what I wanted to do. Willingly would I accept the hardship and fear, the discipline and the sacrifices, if only I could be given back the chance to climb that mountain.

Then the course of treatment was completed. My jaw was still painful and swollen but the sickness was over. I was admonished to return to Britain but my excuse was that Dick was at Base Camp and I would have to let him know.

I raced back up the hillsides on my own, sleeping out with a polythene sheet against the rain. I was driven like a man possessed. I continued to take the antibiotics we had in our medical kit as advised by the doctor, the pain had become a dull ache and I nurtured a quiet hope that by taking the tablets for as long as they lasted I might be able to climb the mountain.

I looked with new eyes and new pleasure at Nanda Devi, 25,645 feet high, the biggest mountain in India. It no longer seemed to mock, but was the beautiful 'Seat of the goddess Nanda' which had attracted so many of the famous pioneers to attempt to climb her and which had finally succumbed in 1936 to Bill Tilman and Noel Odell. The route to Dunagiri lay partly along the Rishi gorge, which comes down from the so-called sanctuary of Nanda Devi, but branches off up a side valley towards the Ramani glacier and the cirque of peaks comprising Rishi Kot, Changabang, Dunagiri and Hanuman.

On the second day, in a clearing, I came across a ribbon of coloured plastic tied to a bush and a note pinned to a tree.

Joe,

Hope you're in good shape. From here the track winds up the steep grassy slope to the right of the crag facing the clearing. I can't make it out from here but Hart Singh assures me it will go. We will leave markers.

There are 2 tins of pilchards under the flat stone next to the cliff 3 ft from this tree.

Dick

Towards mid-afternoon, feeling satisfyingly fit now, I crested a ridge and caught sight of two figures coming my way. I was dumbfounded. It was Dick and Peter.

Dick reached me first. He was mightily pleased to see me in much better form than the ailing figure he had said goodbye to some days before.

'Peter has decided to go back. Couldn't stand it at Base Camp. Found it too lonely. I don't think I'm very good company for him. I think he missed you making fun of him and chatting.'

Peter was apologetic and disillusioned, feeling that he had set himself a goal and found himself inadequate. I knew, however, that the mountains themselves, though beautiful, are barren, and that Dick, who is so self-contained that he seems not to need other people, would have daunted the gregarious Peter with his self-sufficiency and silence. I was daunted myself by Dick's reserve but I knew what to expect.

We camped together for the night telling stories, laughing and joking around a fire. This was what Peter had expected to find in the mountains with his two friends, not solitude and not the single-minded, self-abnegation and devotion to one sole aim to the exclusion of all else. I could see twinges of regret in him that he had decided to leave, but if he had stayed he would have been lonely. He could not understand what was wrong. He had longed to see Nanda Devi, to camp near its base and wander about in the mountains, but it had all been different when it happened. The mountains were perfect but he felt isolated; there was no enjoyment or sharing of the experience.

Next day I carried his rucksack for him back along the track, up steep slopes. I was bursting with energy now. Random flickers of pain in my jaw kept my enthusiasm in check but I was more and more sure that I could go on the mountain. Peter told me of the loneliness he had felt at the Base Camp, in a bleak, misty plain, with only the taciturn Dick for company. How they had spent two days in their separate tents in the rain, suffering a little from the altitude, and how they had hardly spoken in that time.

We parted in good humour, each of us with a clearer understanding of our goals and of ourselves, and I hurried back to join Dick, who was clearing up the camp.

Together we reached Base Camp the following day, Dick showing me the way and pointing out features with a proprietorial air as if he was taking me round his country estate. We could see little, a heavy mist filled the small valley where nestled the tent which was our Base Camp, and we were completely alone.

III

Dick had already walked up from Base Camp to the vantage point from where Dunagiri could be seen. Our tent was on a level grassy plain, enclosed by long hills of loose rock and earth. These were moraines, the residue heaps from the passage of glaciers over bedrock in millennia past.

To the east the 20,000-foot mountain Rishi Kot formed an outlying buttress to the rim wall of peaks surrounding the so-called sanctuary of the revered mountain of Nanda Devi, home of the goddess Nanda, and the highest mountain in India. To the north a steep mound of rubble concealed more peaks, and to the west was the rounded summit of the peak of Hanuman, the monkey god.

I climbed for an hour up the narrow valley of the water course running down into our camp, feeling the excitement mount as the bullet-shaped tip of Changabang started rising into view. At the same time as I reached a position to see the full length of the peak, Dunagiri came into view at the head of the valley to my left. We had first aspired to climb Changabang – it was a magnificent spectacle, symmetrical and sheer. Secretly Dick and I cherished the hope of climbing Dunagiri and then, if we coped well enough with that, climbing a long ridge which offered the only possible way up Changabang from the west.

Dunagiri did not look as fearsome. It resembled mountains we had looked at in the Alps, and having looked at decided on the line to follow and then climbed. At the west end of the mountain an ice-fall and buttress led up to a long, low-angled ridge which culminated in the summit. This was the way by which the mountain had been climbed once before and was a possible means of descent for us if we reached the top by a more difficult route.

Across a wasteland of moraines and ice, immediately in front of me and leading directly up towards the summit, was a steeper buttress and ridge, which, forming the south-east spur, seemed to offer a direct and more difficult line, with a steep barrier of rock 800 feet high some 1,000 feet below the summit. We had come to find difficulty, we did not want the low-angled ridges by which we knew a mountain could be climbed; we wanted the uncertainty of a difficult route. Further right than the south-east spur were big walls of rock which looked featureless and improbable. The obvious line for us to attempt seemed to me to be the south-east spur.

I returned to Base happy, now that the mountain had resolved into definite shapes and features. Dick had also picked out a line and we seemed to be in agreement until, discussing it in more detail, it transpired that he was thinking of the huge walls of rock to the right of the south-east ridge. The lurid reds and orange of that rock indicated that it might be loose and in the end Dick agreed that for our level of knowledge about the Himalayas and limited experience at altitude we would be better on the south-east ridge which looked more probable. Sometimes Dick annoyed me by what I regarded as unrealistic suggestions, and we finished the discussion with my feeling somewhat uncomfortable at having yet again advocated a more cautious plan than Dick had been pressing for. The same question perennially bothered me whether I was more realistic, more balanced in my

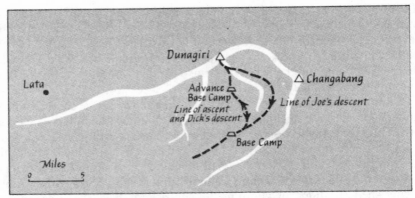

4. The ascent and separate descent routes of Dunagiri.

judgement than Dick or whether I was more timid, lazy and cowardly than he would ever allow himself to be.

We built a wall of stones in an arc against a huge boulder, made a roof over this with our remaining sheet of polythene and stored all our food inside. This was our Base Camp shelter, for we dismantled the tent and carried it up to a spot only two hours from the foot of the mountain with all the food and gear we would need on the climb.

We were concerned at the amount of time we had lost in reaching this point. It was the last week of September and lest we got caught in the first snows of winter we did not dare spend time acclimatising and getting fit on smaller mountains. We moved up and occupied the tent with the intention of starting out early next morning on the climb.

We wrote a note giving the date of our departure for the mountain and expected arrival back, and placed it in the shelter. It was not that we anticipated any visitors coming this way, for the valley we were in was a dead end, surrounded by mountains and high ridges. There would be no villagers passing through on their way to market, nor any chance passers-by. We left the note out of knowledge that if we disappeared on the mountain, the definite date of our departure would clarify once and for all the likelihood of our being found alive or not if in months to come a search party should be mounted as relatives and friends in England grew anxious.

It snowed in the night and I welcomed the reprieve. During the day Dick sat inexpertly practising tunes on a flute which I had known him attempt to play for several years. Driven off by boredom and the irritation of the repetitive practising of scales and nursery-rhyme tunes I went back down to Base Camp for a book to read. There I discovered that in our brief absence some creature had invaded our shelter, gnawed into various packets of food and scattered outside innumerable of our boiled sweets. I blocked up the entrance as best I could and returned with a tin of meat and some tinned fruit for the evening meal from the store which Peter had abandoned when he left Base Camp.

Next day it was clear. We hoisted heavy rucksacks onto our backs, sealed up the tent and left for the gullies of snow and ice leading up onto the southeast spur. In spite of the understanding of myself and my true intentions which I had come to when my illness seemed likely to rob me of the mountain, all the usual doubts and hesitations still niggled away inside. Dick, as ever, seemed untroubled by such thoughts and was eager in his preparations.

There were several of these gullies over one thousand feet long all terminating near where the spur became a rock ridge. We chose the most difficult and the most direct because we were new to this game and did not think about conserving our energies for higher up.

We climbed together, each of us with a rope coiled over a shoulder. There was no need to use rope at first until unexpectedly the rays of the sun touched the top of the gully, and rocks, loosened from the ice by the sun's warmth, bounced down towards us. We escaped out of the line of fire onto the steep side walls, tying onto the ropes and moving one at a time.

I did not feel attuned to the rhythm of the climb at first; I was too aware of myself, aware that we were treading new ground in a practical sense and strange ground in terms of what we were accustomed to. Already we were above the height of the highest mountain in Europe, higher than either of us had been, with more than another 5,000 feet of climbing before the summit. It was silly but we kept checking with each other to see how we both felt. There was a slight breathlessness and our sacks were heavy but that was little different from what we had already experienced.

I was leading at one point when I saw a bulge in the ice above. I intended to stop when I reached it to let Dick go ahead as he was carrying most of the pitons for hammering into ice. When I reached the bulge the ice was running with water and would not hold any pitons. I had to lead on. Dick would have known that my stopping was only an excuse, and we came onto the crest of the ridge in the late afternoon at 19,200 feet; only 4,000 feet to go.

We made room for ourselves for the night on some shattered ledges, settling into our sleeping bags without using the bivouac tent. The petrol stove would not work properly; it spluttered and flared constantly, taking long hours to melt snow and heat water. We witnessed a breathtaking transformation of the milky white walls of Changabang's granite through deepening shades of gold and orange to red as the beams of the setting sun played on that mountain, then finally lifted away to leave a colourless twilight. The night was spoilt for us by the malfunctioning stove.

Our progress was satisfactory. The vertical interval of the route we had chosen was the same as the North Face of the Eiger. It did not look as difficult so we had estimated we would take four days to reach the summit and allowed ourselves two days to descend. Our food and fuel was calculated accordingly. Six days' rations and a litre of fuel, the same as for the Eiger in winter.

The shallow ridge of rock above had appeared, from a distance, discoloured, indicating poor rock, though not too steep. We pulled onto ledges covered in loose blocks, sometimes skirted difficulties and at times had to climb steep towers of granite that reared up out of the camouflage of the surrounding rock. Sometimes whoever led had to leave his sack behind and haul it up afterwards, sometimes difficulties disappeared once we were at grips with an apparently problematical wall. The weather stayed fine, the strangeness vanished and I felt at home solving the vertical problem we had taken on.

We took photographs because it had become an ingrained habit, though sometimes I wondered for whose benefit I took them – as a record, for a magazine or because I liked photography. I no longer knew, it had become more natural to use a camera than to leave it hanging as superfluous weight.

Though I felt more at home I was not relaxed; the climbing seemed just like the hard work of the Alps only more tiring. We passed 20,000 feet, ticking off the altitude mentally by checking with the altimeter. There was no problem with the climbing except the effort needed. It was not that I did not want to do it, my brain was active and alert, racing ahead, but my body had trouble putting thoughts into action. I felt well but it was as if lead weights were in my legs; it was fine at each halt. I would not relax, no matter how well we were going, until the whole thing was over.

I do not know how many rope-lengths we climbed each day, sometimes we made 1,000 feet in height. Dick had an idea that this was pretty good; he had read that on Annapurna Mick Burke and Tom Frost were very pleased to have fixed 1,000 feet of rope.

Some time in the afternoon, without words, there was a consensus that we should stop and prepare the bivouac for the night. It was dark by 6.00 p.m. and we had to be ready by then. At the least we had to find a ledge on which we could, ideally, lie down, though more often we spent the night in a semi-reclining position. Sometimes we had to clear a ledge of loose rocks or dig one out of the snow.

The second bivouac was on top of a prow jutting out from the ridge. It was windy and flakes of snow were in the air so we used the small tent, without poles, which we had with us. Dick woke to find he was hanging half outside the tent and off the edge of the ledge. He was ill pleased and blamed me for having secured the best place on the ledge for myself.

The summit was still a long way off. I had ceased to think about it, ceased to think far ahead at all. I had learnt on the Eiger not to look to the end of the punishing effort, otherwise I would go out of my mind with impatience.

I was looking to the comforts and consolations at hand; making sure the bivouac was as comfortable as possible; relishing the piece of fruit cake saved for the end of the evening meal; lingering over the mugful of hot cocoa and savouring its warmth as it slipped down seemingly to the tingling ends of my toes as I sat ensconced in my sleeping bag.

But like this, one loses sense of time and somewhere we lost a day, somewhere we spent a night that we cannot account for. More rock and ice and a granite wall. I thought we had bypassed the 800-foot barrier below the summit but we had not. That great cliff was still waiting for us when we climbed out onto a corniced ridge which ran directly into it.

Though there was some daylight left, and Dick wanted to press on, there were only steep slopes ahead and the snowy shoulder on which we stood was flat and would provide by far the most comfortable bed. Dick capitulated and we dug a square hole a foot deep into the snow, in which to lie with some shelter from the wind. We settled down with muttered comments from him about not sleeping near the edge of the ledge that night though we were on the flat top of the rounded shoulder and we could hardly fall off it.

We had a tin of sardines or pilchards for each night as part of the meal, but to cut down on weight Dick had disposed of the cardboard box and thrown away the little opener which makes opening the tin so easy. I tried to open the square tin with his Swiss Army knife and had trouble at the corners. The tin bent in my hands, tomato juice and morsels of fish squirted out as I mangled the tin using brute force to tear into it and cursed Dick for his counter-productive scheme for lightening our loads. He cursed me in return for the mess I had made of the tin, and my lack of dexterity with a knife, which I took as a comment on my life which relied more on gadgets than his.

We had been on the mountain for three or four days. Mostly the weather had been fine. The snowfall, cloud and winds had not lasted long. The rock barrier was the only real obstacle remaining, once up that the summit slopes fell back in an easier angle and, though our food might be running low we expected to be able to descend rapidly. We relied upon the south-west ridge to provide an easy descent.

A ramp of snow ran diagonally leftwards into the centre of the wall. There was an area of bare rock, then above that snow and ice on the rock indicated that the barrier was no longer vertical.

Dick led for four rope-lengths up to and along the ramp. It was my turn to lead when we reached the bare rock.

The ramp of snow faded to a thin sliver of ice which squeezed itself vertically upwards into a bay in the rock wall, and then the bay closed to form a narrow chimney split by several cracks and clefts.

I left my rucksack behind and climbed upon crampon points in the ice until the ice was no more. Crampons were now useless, the rubber sole of my boots would have held better on the granite, but I did not dare take the crampons off. I could see the fingers of more ice reaching down from above the block which closed the chimney and up there I would need the crampons to be still on my boots.

I hooked crampon points onto the edges of cracks, hammered pitons into the cracks and wedged chock-stones of aluminium into wider cracks; I used anything I could to pull myself any bit further upwards. A huge flake of rock frightened me with its hollow sound, it seemed only to be stuck in place by the ice behind it, but I needed to pull up on it; I was high in the chimney, sweating, thrown out of balance by the steepness and beginning to feel the surge of panic as I tried to move on without obvious means of reaching safety. I could stand with my legs straddled across the chimney, feet braced against opposite walls, crampons scraping on the rock as my muscles began to ache with fatigue. To go on I needed to launch myself over the block which jutted out above me, launch out with no security, with little possibility of reversing any move I made, in the hope that out of sight above me there would be holds to grasp once I committed myself to moving.

Eighty feet below, Dick peered questioningly upwards asking what it was like. I did not want to break my concentration to answer.

I hauled myself on my arms out of the chimney, out round the great block, my crampons scraped and sparked on the granite walls. The lead weights seemed to be fastened to my back now, and I did not have long before my hands would uncurl their grip and I would fall. I thrust one cramponed foot at the cleft where the block met the wall and pushed upwards. Everything suddenly flowed smoothly, I was in balance, there was a small ledge to step onto, the much prayed-for stroke of luck. I was safe.

'What's it like?' came up from below.

'O.K.', and I smashed my fist with a sob of relief and pent-up feeling against the rock.

We had to sit all night on an uncomfortable promontory of ice in the upper part of the rock barrier; most of the day had disappeared into that difficult pitch. It was a relief to stop anyway, physically I was drained, and the next day we expected to reach the summit.

It was not to be so. On anything but an easy snow slope time just slips away. We dug another bivouac site the next night a few hundred feet below the summit; this time there were definitely no more obstacles.

We were slow with the altitude, stopping every few steps to gasp for air, we were tired mentally and physically. The sunsets and sunrises had become empty spectacles; it was a cold, uninviting beauty. Somewhere deep inside there must have remained the spark of determination, when it

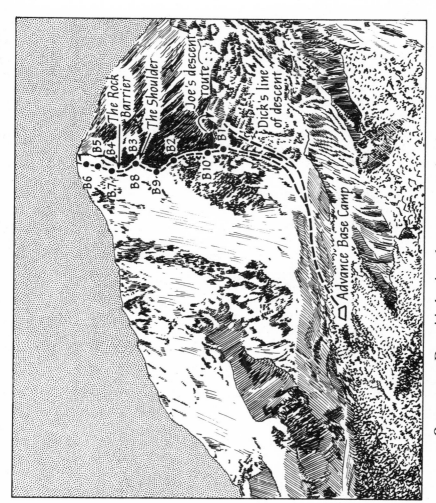

The Rock Barrier

The Shoulder

Joe's descent route

Dick's line of descent

B5
B4
B6
B7
B8
B3
B9
B2
B10
B1

△Advance Base Camp

2. Our ascent up Dunagiri, showing where we separated on the way down.

was all suffering, all lung punishing effort, all mental and physical fatigue, to keep on; not to question the sense, not to have considered retreat.

We climbed out of the rosy glow of sunrise to a small cliff of ice beneath which we left our rucksacks. To descend the south-west ridge we would have to come back to this point. An easy slope to the left of the ice cliff ran up to the summit.

For once I was ahead of Dick when it was only a matter of plodding. Normally he can drive himself on when I give in to the need to rest. We both still held our axes, using them to lean on, but they had short shafts for steep ice and the slope we were on was at a very shallow angle. Bent double, like old men, we advanced to the highest point of the summit dome.

When the mountain sloped down away from me in every direction I crouched down and turned round. Dick had stopped fifty yards away, he was lying prostrate on his back staring vacantly into the sky. Eventually he pushed himself to his feet and made his way up the last slight incline.

We grinned as best we could. Dick was apologetic and alarmed that he felt so exhausted.

To the east the splendid pyramid of Nanda Devi poked through the clouds, the rounded summit of Changabang and more pointed summit of Kalanka barely pierced the blanket. These mountains had been our constant companions for days. From the summit we looked for mountains to the west but there was nothing of any size. The cloud layer beneath us ran disappointingly clear to a uniform horizon.

From where we were we had a clear view of the south-west ridge down which we had intended to descend. From our vantage point it now looked complex, precarious and formed from insubstantial flutings of snow. We were so tired that if we tried to climb down it we would run the risk of making mistakes from lapses of concentration and falling through a deceptive cornice of snow. And so it was decided. After a good night's sleep we would descend the way we came; it would necessitate abseiling down the upper barrier of rock but from then on it would go more easily. At the very most it would take us two days and though we only had a little food left we thought we could spin it out for that time, since we would be gaining strength as we descended to thicker air with more oxygen to help us along.

We turned to go back to our rucksacks. I felt only the tiniest bit of satisfaction that was anything other than relief at not having to step upwards again, and no compulsion at all to linger on the top.

IV

We slept comfortably in a hollow beneath the cliff of ice where we had dumped our rucksacks on the way to the top. We had had time left to go some way down but we reasoned that the slopes as far as the top of the rock barrier were uniform and would take very little time to descend. We would best utilise the time by resting in readiness for making a big effort next day to get down as far as possible.

We used up the last of the fuel. It had lasted about the length of time we had calculated it should. The food we apportioned out, keeping a little fruit cake, a tin of sardines, a few boiled sweets and some squares of chocolate for the next night.

The ascent had taken longer by two days than we had planned for and now we had to descend with no fuel and a minimum of food. I wondered what had happened to my usual caution and aversion to effort which would normally have made me seize on the unexpected difficulty and time it was taking as a short-term excuse to go down and rest, postponing the final effort until a later date when we could return refreshed and with more supplies.

I mentioned this to Dick, in self-mocking pride that for once he had not had to sustain my flagging enthusiasm with his own relentless drive.

'I can't understand why it didn't occur to me to suggest going down before we came into the rock barrier. It should have been obvious then that we would be cutting things fine. Not like me, is it?'

And Dick replied: 'No, but it occurred to me that it would be more sensible for us to go down then, and come back later, but I thought you would be suggesting it at any moment so I just carried on and you never said anything!'

Without fuel for the stove we could melt no snow for water and without liquid we would deteriorate rapidly. We needed a minimum of eight pints of liquid each day to avoid rapid physical deterioration, and though we were surrounded by snow we had no means of melting it. The total food we had left amounted to no more than a snack, hardly enough to sustain us, but even if we had had more we could not have swallowed anything without liquid to wash it down.

Our situation was serious but we pinned our hopes on being able to descend more rapidly than we had climbed up. We regarded the rock barrier as being the most difficult stretch, but knew that we could abseil down that and any other awkward places below. Without the constant struggle upwards in thin air, against the force of gravity, with heavy loads on our backs, we calculated that it should not take us more than two days to reach the bottom, where we would find water and food at our tent. We would be very weak by then, but we were confident that we could do it, and we left at morning to overcome the worst obstacle, the rock barrier.

Great gaps in time exist from those days. We only reached part way down the rock barrier next day and nothing remains in my mind of all that we did before evening came and we had to chop out a precarious ledge in some ice. The ledge was a foot wide. It was a struggle to work ourselves into the bivouac tent as shelter against the gusts of wind and showers of snow. With my head swathed in the folds of nylon I heard the clatter of the pan lid falling as Dick shuffled into position. I thought that it didn't matter as there was no fuel for the stove and we could not use the pan anyway. Dick told me that the pan and the stove had gone too and still it did not seem to matter. On the contrary, they had all become surplus weight once the fuel ran out and we had not had the wit to discard them anyway.

We ate nothing, not having the wit either to realise how weak we were becoming and that in a short while our throats would become too parched to swallow even the morsels of food which did remain. We were too cramped on the tiny ledge and too exhausted to scrape about in the bottom of our sacks amongst the wrappers and empty food bags on the chance of finding something edible. Sleep was a merciful oblivion when it came.

We left that bivouac and continued to abseil down. I can remember only that it was difficult to find somewhere to drive the pitons from which to hang the ropes. As we slowly descended the weather deteriorated, clouds covered the sky and the bitter wind brought more snow. We spoke little. Any word was a curt passing only of essential information, talking took energy. We needed no words to perform manoeuvres which we had rehearsed on every climb we came down from. We were mute collaborators in a performance for surviving, Siamese twins and yet strangers, muffled in now ragged garb smattered with snow.

We came out of the rock barrier some distance to one side of the snow ramp by which we had entered it some days ago. An expanse of hard, blue ice separated us from the shoulder on the ridge where we had spent a night on the way up.

We pulled the ropes down from the anchor point lost now in the mist. Dick coiled one rope and placed it over his shoulder. He fastened himself to two barbed pegs driven into the ice and stood on a tiny step he had scraped out for his feet. I had made ready the other rope and having tied one end to my waist harness started across the hard, brittle surface of the ice slope with Dick paying out the rope as I moved across in a horizontal line.

There was an initial area where snow covered the ice and my crampon points bit in quite well, then I was on the bare, uncompromising ice itself. After days of use, the points of my crampons had become blunted. I kicked at the ice with all the force I could muster, trying to embed the metal spikes in far enough to hold my weight, but my legs had no strength and my movements were listless, like those of someone in a nightmare trying to move faster.

My arms struck powerlessly at the surface with axe and hammer but the ice flew off in tiny fragments and the picks skated wildly away from where they had struck. Somehow I had to cross another seventy feet of this ice before I was safe.

Dick seemed unaware of my predicament. I felt the rope tighten on my waist, pulling me off balance, as something prevented him from paying it out, then he spoke:

'Joe, can you hold on while...'

My patience snapped and I shouted at him in desperation: 'Can I, hell? This ice is terrible,' so that he would know I was in trouble.

I was weakening fast. My calves ached unendurably. I cut a small step out of the ice with my axe and stood on it while I hammered in an ice peg. I passed the rope attached to my waist through a snap-link in the peg and moved on with a little more reassurance. The dreamlike state persisted. Dick became a vague silhouette eighty feet away through the mist and driving snow. I kept making the motions of driving in axe, hammer and crampon points, moving imperceptibly further, but my adhesion was only tenuous. Wearily and inevitably, but with surprise, I fell, banging down the ice to be stopped twenty feet below the ice peg, dangling from the end of the rope.

I had stopped, and I had no thought for the danger of the situation. Four thousand feet of mountain stretched away beneath me, and one six-inch spike of metal had held in the ice, taking my weight on the rope which I had attached to it. My brain filtered out all but the essential. I needed no concern for myself, I knew I was safe, but I called out to my partner, 'Are you all right, Dick?', concerned at the shock he must have had in stopping my fall and the strain he would be feeling in holding my weight still.

'Yes, I'm all right,' he shouted back in a tone which said, 'It's you that's fallen off, are *you* all right?'

I was more surprised that I had actually been held on an ice peg than frightened and unnerved by the experience.

'Dick, I can't climb across this, I'll tension across from the peg to where the ice is better.'

I had fallen to an area of even harder, steeper ice and with even less strength than before I could not kick my crampon points far enough into it. Dick held my weight on the rope which ran through the karabiner on the peg. In delicate balance, not thinking that the peg might have been loosened by my fall, I edged across, leaning against the pull of the rope, clawed with the points of my axe and hammer and pushed with the tips of my crampons. Fifteen feet, ten feet remaining and then I reached the white, snow-covered, softer ice.

'How much rope, Dick?'

'Forty feet.'

I advanced to where a rock buttress came down into the ice and drove some pitons into a crack. They were really secure. I knew that Dick, as fatigued as I was, would have an equally hard time crossing the ice.

The wind was hurling the snow into my face, inside the hood of my anorak and around my neck. After an age Dick still had not moved.

'Dick,' I screamed into the mist, 'what's the matter?'

My throat was dry and sore from thirst.

'Just getting the pegs out. Coming now.'

I drew the rope in, feeling him moving, though only vaguely seeing. I wondered what it would be like to hold onto the rope like this if Dick fell. My hands were in thick mitts, matted with ice, I was shaking with cold and hardly able to stand upright. Without warning Dick swung off, tumbled down the ice and came to a halt dangling from the end of the rope, much as I had been some time before. It was not anything terrible to hold his weight. The rope still ran through the karabiner on the peg that had held my fall. I just felt the uncomfortable strain of holding a weight I must not let go.

'Are you all right?'

'Yes.'

From the position he was now in, the rope would not be long enough for Dick to reach me. If he climbed up to release the rope from where it ran through the ice peg he would still be stranded in the middle of the dreadfully hard ice. Without the safeguard of the ice peg to take some of the strain, if he fell, all his falling weight would come onto me. I was no longer strong enough to be sure of being able to hold a fall which came directly onto me.

'Dick, you'll have to take the rope you're carrying and join it to the one you're tied to. That will give you extra length so that you can have a back-rope from the ice peg to reach here. Put another ice peg in where you are while you tie the two ropes together.' The effort of shouting all this exhausted me further.

He hammered in an ice peg and fiddled about uncoiling the rope he had been carrying over his shoulder. I could not quite see through the wind-driven snow and cloud but I could sense that something was not right.

'How am I going to get this other rope to you?' he asked.

'There's no need to; just tie it to the rope you were first tied to, I'll take it in till the knot comes to the top peg, then tie yourself into that second rope; that should give you enough free rope to reach me here using it as a back-rope on the higher ice peg.'

'Well what's this ice peg for here?'

Somehow Dick was not thinking straight.

'That's so you don't fall off whilst you're doing all this.'

I was not annoyed or even impatient, it was simply essential that all this be done in the shortest possible time. There was no sarcasm in the way I spelt out all these basic manoeuvres as if to a novice. It was urgent that there be no misunderstanding and that we reach the bivouac spot, on the shoulder only minutes away from me, and get into our sleeping bags out of the cold. This time he was doing it right. After those minutes of waiting which stretch into hours, Dick started to move. Then he stopped.

'What's the matter?'

'I haven't got the ice peg out.'

'Stuff the ice peg.'

'I'll get it tomorrow.'

'All right, tomorrow.' Anything to keep him moving. 'But please hurry,' I pleaded. I was freezing and beginning to panic at the desperation of our situation. Carefully he arrived.

'Good lad.'

'That's what comes of being hassled,' he spat at me as he came alongside, waving a foot. The crampon dangled loose from the boot and I gathered that somehow he blamed me for it.

We were both suffering from an advanced state of exposure and we did not know it. Dick's lack of comprehension of the simplest instructions, slowness of reaction and irrational behaviour were classic symptoms of sustained exposure to extreme cold which not only dulls fatally the central core of the body but affects the functioning of the brain as well. I should have recognised these tell-tale signs and taken control but I too was so affected that I could not think beyond my own misery and felt he was only being abnormally perverse.

After twenty feet the angle of the snow slope eased off into the almost horizontal shoulder on the ridge where we had dug a shallow hole against the wind on the way up. I vacated the stance I had been in for some unconscionable time and hurried down the easy ground towards the hole. The rope came taut before I reached the chosen stopping place and I waited for Dick to free himself from the pegs and follow me. He started hammering the pegs loose. I waited and froze. He hammered and hammered. He was only dimly discernible. The cold was terrible.

'Joe, one of the pegs won't come out.'

'Stuff the peg. Leave it.'

'I'll get it tomorrow.'

'All right, tomorrow.'

At last he moved. He sat down for a rest. We moved on again at opposite ends of the taut rope.

'Another fifteen feet . . . I'm almost there . . . I'm at the bivouac, Dick.'

Another step into the slight hollow remaining of our previous hole. I flung my sack to the ground, sat on it and started to pull in the rope. Dick stopped again. After the normal interval for a rest he was still there. All I craved for was sleep. Not food, nor drink, only sleep; but there still seemed to be so many things to do before we could settle down. I sat holding the rope.

'Joe, you look after yourself...'

I could not catch the next words, they were garbled in the wind and mist. Then I heard: 'I'm strangling myself. Got to sort the rope out.'

I realised he must have got his legs caught up in the rope, but he was nearly with me, only thirty feet away. He had reached the rounded crest of the shoulder, whose broad, almost flat top was nearly fifteen feet wide. He was safe now, so I left him to untangle himself while I made ready the hollow for us to spend the night.

I pulled out the bivouac tent, put my piece of foam mat inside, sleeping bag on top of that; duvet jacket on, crampons off, boots off, inner boots slackened, a quick photograph of Dick through the airhole of the tent, and I snuggled down into my sleeping bag. In seconds I was asleep.

'Joe, do you want something to eat?' Dick's voice came from outside through the blue folds of the tent. I had no idea how much time had passed, but there was a dimness, as of twilight, outside.

'Is there a piece of cake left?' It was the only thing with any moisture in it, and I hoped that the moisture would help the food slide down the dry and inflamed tube of my throat.

A small morsel of cake appeared through the entrance. I bit into it and a filling fell out from one of my teeth. It was too much effort to eat. I put the cake to one side and fell asleep again.

'Joe, do you want any of those sardines you've got?'

'No,' and in the unspoken language of the intimate rapport we had developed this meant that the sardines did not get opened. We had to do things together. If I did not eat my half of the sardines at the same time as Dick we would have the problems of carrying round the half-empty tin. It did not occur to me that I could eat them in the morning, or that they would be frozen anyway and could be easily carried.

After another unmeasured period of time, I woke again; it was dark and Dick was still not in the tent beside me.

'Dick?'

'What?'

'What are you doing?'

'Nothing. It's clear out here now. It's a three-quarter moon too. Really beautiful.'

The thought never came to me that he needed help, that his mind was waning with his strength. I thought it was only his everlasting toughness and resilience which enabled him to sit out and look at the stars when all that I could think of was the oblivion of sleep. I did not know that he sat out there possessed of a strange excitement and intoxicated by a silvery landscape illuminated by the rising sliver of moon.

I simply thought that I was with a person who was tougher and who had more mental reserves than I would ever have, and I fell back to sleep.

It was morning, but the sun was not yet out, when next Dick woke me.

'Joe, what do you think of these?'

I struggled to find him through the folds of the bivouac bag. He was sitting up, half outside, and he held out his hands. At any time Dick's fingers look fat or plump, now as he thrust them towards me, they emerged from his fingerless gloves swollen and BLUE; solid, hard BLUE.

'Jesus Christ, do they hurt?'

'They're . . . I'm not sure'.

'Can you use them?'

'I think so.'

I was lost. It was up to him to express pain and disquiet, or to complain; he just seemed to be commenting on an extraordinary phenomenon.

There was another four thousand feet of mountain to descend before we were back on the glacier, back on level ground, and able to walk or crawl in relative safety back to Base Camp. We had by this time been without water for two days, what little food remained was virtually impossible to swallow without any liquids. It was in trying to chew some chocolate the previous night that Dick had realised that there was something wrong with his hands. He had discovered a couple of squares of chocolate when he had finally settled into his sleeping bag and sat up while eating them. Suddenly he became aware that he had finished the chocolate and was nibbling at his own fingers, which were dark, hard and unyielding as the chocolate had been. The ends of his fingers were senseless and frozen.

He told me how the discovery that his fingers were frostbitten had not worried him at the time and he had woken to think that it had all been part of a bad dream, until he had pulled his hands out of his sleeping bag to check.

Both hands were the same. It must have happened when he took his gloves off to hammer in the ice peg and tie the ropes together, but he had said nothing about the cold then, and after a while his hands had probably gone numb so that he stopped feeling any pain.

We usually waited until the sun rose from behind Changabang and warmed us a little before we started to move. There was no longer the ritual of melting snow, making some tea, having breakfast, which had been the normal introduction to the day, not for the two days past. With so little intake of liquid and food we also had had no cause to delay over the intricate process of relieving ourselves, for there were no solids or fluids passing through our bodies at all.

I led most of the abseils that day. We had thought we would be able to scramble down easily but the mountain was steeper than we remembered it. All day I prepared anchor points, hung the ropes in position, pulled them down to us when we had both slid to the end and looked for the next anchor point to repeat the procedure. Dick seemed to be ill as well as afflicted by his frostbitten hands, but he was nonetheless apologetic.

'I'm sorry you're having to do everything for me, Joe.'

'That's all right, I want to get myself off this mountain as well.'

I went down the ropes to the end of a rock rib and on further down a slope of snow to within sight of some more rocks. Dick came on down and stopped at the top of the snow slope.

'What time is it, Joe? Is it too early to stop?' he shouted down.

In the unspoken language which held most of our communication now, I knew Dick was really telling me he had to stop for the night. I was surprised; it was only 3.00 p.m. and it was unlike him to give in to himself.

'Is there a good place up beside you?' It was understood that he would not have suggested stopping without having spotted a convenient site.

'There's the start of one; one and a half places here to sit down, and one there. We'll have to dig them out.'

'It had better be really good for me to climb back up there.'

It was only fifty feet back up an easy snow slope but I had to rest many times, I had to stop and pant hard for breath before I reached Dick, and experienced a wordless disappointment when I saw the two tiny, inadequate hollows on either side of a prow of rock. Futile to criticise; the decision had been made.

I hacked at the snow and ice, disloging a rock which gave a little more space. Dick, round a corner from me, was similarly preparing his place for the night.

'This is going to be a hanging bivouac,' I complained out loud.

'Sounds grim,' said Dick, and I presumed he was better off round that corner.

'What's your place like?'

'All right.' I could visualise him sitting in comfort.

Into the rock I hammered a couple of pegs. In a horizontal line with them I drove in an ice peg and further along thrust my ice axe into the snow. From the rock pegs I hung my rucksack into which I slipped my foam mat and sleeping bag, and with great exertion I inserted my legs into the sleeping bag, attached my waist to the ice peg and my chest to the ice axe. Though the ledge was only a few inches wide, the rucksack held my legs in place, and the nylon loops attached to the ice peg and ice axe held the rest of my body against the side of the mountain. I was ready for sleep.

Dick was fiddling about with something round the corner. I asked what he was doing and he said that he had found a candle in his bag and was melting some snow. Drink was the one thing we craved above all but I thought he had dropped the pan days ago, and of course we had long since run out of petrol even if the stove had not been dropped too. He said he was using his mug. The mug was made of plastic, and from the other life, before this climb, I was sure that I had a memory that plastic melted in flame, but I thought that maybe I had been mistaken and that perhaps plastic did not melt after all. We had been on the go a long time; I could easily be wrong. No water appeared and I dozed off.

From the lethargic sleep of exhaustion I became aware that it was snowing. I pulled my hood further down over my face so as not to be disturbed by the cold flakes, and hoped that the snow would be sufficiently dry due to the extreme cold that it would not make my sleeping bag any damper.

Dick disturbed himself from whatever his arrangements were to reach round for the bivouac tent which was hanging unused by my feet. It did not surprise me that he did not allow himself to be affected by the lethargy which had prevented me from rigging up the tent.

I dreamt of various things, but mostly of food; hot steaming pans of vegetables and casseroles of meat.

Dick was up first, before the rays of the sun had reached us. He thrust the opened tin of sardines at me. There were three left in it, a good tin, some only had four. The volume was probably the same but it seemed as if you were getting more.

Forced into movement, I grumbled accusatorily as I packed things away: 'This was a lousy bivouac. What was yours like?'

'All right.'

He was away well before me, hands in pain or not, prospecting the rocks below for the first anchor point. I glanced round the corner enviously to examine the spacious platform I had visualised him sleeping on. There was a minute ledge six inches wide and at most two feet long. The ledge was marked with indentations of crampon points and I realized now why he had stirred himself to open up the bivouac tent. He had not been able to get into his sleeping bag at all but had spent all night crouched on the ledge, had not even taken his crampons off. He had needed the tent as a cover all the more when the snow started. I knew now why he was up so early; he needed to get moving to restore his circulation. 'All right,' he had said it was, 'all right'!

Neither of us had any idea of how many days we had been descending. Dick had recovered from the state of illness of the previous day and now it was only his hands which hindered him apart from the gradual wasting away which was common to us both. But I lapsed into a state of weakness from which I was losing the will to emerge. I felt that I could so easily sit down and rest forever. I felt no regret for the life that was slipping away, no regret for the way of life back home and people I would be leaving behind; I only wanted the suffering to come to an end. I now, in my turn, relied on Dick. If there was one person I had ever known who would go on until he dropped in his tracks it was Dick. I did not think I had the strength any more to get down off this mountain but I felt I had just a little strength left with which I could follow Dick's example. I forced myself to imitate his movements and resolved to do so until the end took me.

At midday I asked him to stop for a breather; putting one foot in front of another even downhill was wearying. He scrambled about in the bottom of his rucksack and produced a polythene bag which had the remains of a portion of muesli in it and a boiled sweet. In spite of the dire straits in which we were, we still carried with us all the rubbish of food wrappers and empty bags from the time when we had had food. We had kept the rubbish deliberately, not wanting to litter this barren wilderness, but now our reward was finding once-overlooked or spurned remnants of things to eat from when we had had plenty. Dick's mug was blackened and misshapen but it had not been destroyed by his attempts to melt snow the previous night. He mixed the sprinkling of oats with snow and ground up the sweet into the mug. The result was a slightly flavoured, slightly more moist slush than the snow from which it originated, and it momentarily relieved our dry and burning throats. We were surrounded by tons of snow, but it was no use to us without the means to melt it. Sucking snow or ice only very briefly alleviated our parched mouths. It took too much body heat to melt even a trickle of water in the mouth and the cold caused our mouths to crack and chap worse than before. We needed a minimum of several pints of liquid each day to avoid physical deterioration and for some days now we had had only a few mouthfuls of snow.

Both of us remembered the lower third of the spur, the region of the lurid, discoloured rock, to be loose, but fairly easy. It was for this reason we had decided to descend this way, expecting to get down it speedily. It all took so much more time than we could ever have imagined in a nightmare. Huge, loose blocks lined the way, threatening our every step. In our fatigue we were a danger to ourselves. We were both stumbling, trailing our legs and arms along, stopping to sit down at every opportunity.

'How many more abseils do you think it is, Dick, to the Col?' The Col at the top of the snow gully was the end of all our ambitions. From there we reckoned we could descend without using the rope.

'About three or four.'

'Do you fancy stopping for the night?'

He looked at me strangely: 'I thought you were serious for a moment.'

'I was, but it doesn't matter.'

We did another abseil, so long and steep and devious that I could not see Dick as I slid down the ropes, hanging free away from the rock. I wondered if he had fallen off the end of the ropes. He was sitting behind a rock. It was quarter to four.

'How many abseils now, Dick?'

'Not more than two.'

'You know we won't make it to the Col before dark and we can't descend that gully with the torch broken. Do you fancy stopping here and finishing the descent tomorrow? I'm knackered.'

'What's the matter with you?'

'I dunno, all the spit's been knocked out of me.'

We were on a shelf of shale and loose rock. We each levelled out a ledge and collected snow in polythene bags. These we were going to take into our sleeping bags to try to melt some of the snow by our own body heat in the night. I was in my sleeping bag first as Dick was still working away at preparing his ledge. We would both be able to stretch out full length here.

'Could have chosen a better place,' he was muttering, and then, as I was sinking into the torpor of rest, he spoke up.

'Joe, do you want to see a crystal vein?'

'What's a crystal vein?'

'One of the wonders of nature,' he said in the tone of reverence he used for mountains and things of the earth.

I was cosily established in my sleeping bag, my leg muscles were slowly relaxing for the first time that day, crystal veins were unnecessary to me and I had no energy for rising to look at one.

'No, it's all right.'

It seemed as if we might survive after all. We were a little more relaxed with each other that night and chatted briefly.

'What do you fancy doing next, Joe?'

I knew he was thinking about that ridge on Changabang. I did not know whether to believe his persistence and again I questioned myself as to whether I was more realistic and logical or whether I was inadequate and cowardly beside his undaunted determination.

'For me Dunagiri has given me everything I hope to get out of climbing for this year, and apart from that your hands are in a bad way. You'll have to get to hospital as soon as possible with them.' This last was absolutely true, but saying it to Dick, it somehow seemed like a lame and invalid excuse.

'I suppose you're right,' he said, as if it were a new thought.

I vowed never again to get far away from the basic essentials of life. Comfort was what I promised myself forever, total self-indulgence, never far from warmth and liquid and food. A life of ease, a life of luxury, was what I wanted and I would never put it at risk again.

In the night we woke several times to press moist snow from the polythene bags into our mouths to alleviate the dreadful sensation of burning. I dreamt of food again, dreamt that I was skivvying in the kitchens of a big hotel and could help myself to all kinds of choice morsels.

Dick dreamt that there had been an accident round the corner and that a helicopter was coming in to pick up the injured. He woke me to ask if I had heard the voices.

'No, but if you do see anyone, ask them to give us a hand as well.'

We were sleeping on the east side of the ridge so that we caught the first rays of sun. Some of the snow in my polythene bag had melted and I had resisted the temptation to swallow it all at one gulp. We found more bits of oats among the dirt in the bottom of our rucksacks and a few boiled sweets, overlooked in a pocket. We shared another of the snow mushes Dick had invented, and this one was quite moist.

I felt fortified enough at the knowledge that we were almost certainly going to live now, and that by the end of the day we should be in safety with food and drink, so that I found myself able to consider someone other than myself. Dick handled everything tentatively, and I knew that he was in constant pain from those black finger-ends. They were a strange sight, incongruously dark where normally there was white flesh, and it was not the surface blackness of a bruise or blister but blackness deep as the bone. It was as if alien growths had come out of him which he needed to be rid of but which were part of his own flesh.

I tried to convey some sympathy by a question:

'Are your hands painful, Dick?'

'It could be worse.' And that was all he said. There was no complaint, no looking for sympathy, and I did not ask again.

Dick was away again first. We had got into a routine in which he would put in a peg or arrange a loop of nylon round a rock spike and put the rope into it, then I would tie the knots and afterwards would pull the rope down to save more suffering from those terrible hands. He had started taking some Ronicol tablets which improve circulation and help prevent frost-bite, though it was perhaps too late. He was taking Fortral too to kill the pain.

Pulling the ropes down after an abseil was exhausting; sometimes the rope caught on every little projection and flake. Somehow I had lapsed into letting Dick do all the thinking and leaned more and more heavily upon him psychologically; I did the physical tasks and he did the brain work. I was the hands to his mind. I felt as if all my climbing life had been a preparation for this; a constant rehearsal so that when this need arose every movement came automatically.

Descending on the ropes had become such an unrelenting chore that we could scarcely believe it when the last one was completed and we could scramble down over large terraces to the shaly slope and new snow leading to the top of the gully we had chosen to descend. This was a different gully from the one we had used to gain the ridge. It was just as long but looked much easier. Only another thousand feet down to level ground and back to the camp.

For all that it looked very easy I did not feel that I had the strength to hold myself upright, flexing my knees over and over again for a thousand feet downwards. The other side of the Col looked to be an easy slope and much shorter, leading down to an upper branch of the Ramani glacier. The glacier appeared flat and free from crevasses. To descend to that glacier would mean a longer walk back to Base Camp but it would be a quicker way to reach level ground on which to walk upright.

I mentioned my thoughts to Dick but he was not interested. Suddenly he was anxious for his hands and he preferred to descend the gully, on his backside if necessary, to reach the tent at our Advance Camp where there was food and a stream.

So we parted. In the back of my mind, as I stepped off downhill, I could see the pundits muttering about the folly of separating like this in the mountains, and I could see the wise, grey heads of the Mount Everest Foundation Committee wagging their disapproval in an attitude of 'We told you so; it was too much for the two of you'. If anything should happen to either of us there would be never-ending recriminations about our splitting up and dividing our forces. I was talking to myself; they would just have to understand; I was pleading that there was not enough elastic left in my legs to bend them and straighten them up after each step so many times descending that couloir.

I called after Dick.

'Will you be all right on your own?', a pang of doubt surfacing in me.

'Yes, will you?'

A sense of cheerfulness grew inside me as I moved rapidly down the gentle angle of the snow, and imagined myself only a few minutes away from being able to walk erect like a human being and from finding a rivulet of water on the surface of the glacier. Still five hundred feet above the glacier I noticed a rocky band cutting across the snow slope below me. I reached it and looked over the edge to discover that it was a cliff fifty feet high with no way of avoiding it. Numb with shock and horror I collapsed, defeated.

On the crest of the ridge there was now no sign of Dick. It would take me days to climb back up to where I had last seen him, I felt so weak. I had no pitons, or lengths of nylon, no gear at all save the rope, my axe and hammer. I took off my sack and scrambled backwards and forwards searching for a projection of rock, anything to which to fasten the rope. The rock was all broken, shattered and insecure.

I discovered a crack in which was lodged a small rock. I picked it out and wedged it back into the crack more securely. From my hammer I detached the thin line by which it was fastened to my waist, and made a loop with the nylon round the rock. Through the loop I threaded the rope and was gratified to see both ends reach the ground below the cliff.

I slid down the rope and retrieved it. After that I made no further pretence at walking. On my backside I slid down the remaining slopes of snow and shale to the edge of the glacier.

The crevasse, where the more level ice of the glacier met the steeper slope I was on, was covered in snow, its existence marked by a shadowed depression. I could not judge whether the snow covering the hole would hold my weight when I stepped onto it. I hesitated, staring at the concealed crevasse, wondering whether it had a benign or hostile personality, whether it was going to swallow me up or allow me to pass safely over it.

I advanced at a crouch, waving uselessly in front of me my short-shafted ice axe; it was too short to probe the snow. I crossed the crevasse at a run and felt elated on reaching the other side, as if I had won a great victory. I took off my rucksack and sat on it to celebrate the achievement on the edge of the great white desert stretching out ahead which I had to cross.

This desert was flat, absolutely flat and glaring white. The snow was crisp under foot and firm; I took it for granted until I sank into a soft patch and the surface broke at every step. Then it was firm again. I walked towards a bend in the glacier where it swept round a small peak towards Changabang and the valley down to Base Camp. Changabang looked nearer; much time seemed to have elapsed. I stopped, sat on my rucksack and glanced back to the slope I had left. It appeared to be only a hundred yards away. I never looked back again.

Every so often I stopped and sat. It became as much of an effort to raise my rucksack from the ground and put it back on my shoulders as it was to walk. I needed to rest frequently, so after a while I just flopped down into the snow without taking the rucksack off. A brilliant sun burst down out of a clear blue sky. It was all so silent.

At one point there swam into my vision, insidiously and suddenly like a shark, a sharp undulation in the snow which marked a hidden crevasse. I trod warily lest it came any closer, but it swam by harmlessly.

It was folly, utter folly to wander about alone as I was on this glacier with the danger of falling into a deep crevasse, concealed beneath the surface snow, and of dying there, lost without trace. The decision to come this way, to separate from Dick, had been the decision of a mind deranged from thirst, hunger, cold and physical deprivation. Had there been the two of us, we could have stayed roped together and proceeded cautiously, well separated in our tracks, so that if one of us fell into a crevasse the other could hold him on the rope and effect a rescue. But now was no time for regrets. I was committed and there was no way back.

My only remaining sunglasses were a very cheap pair and had become hopelessly scratched, so my clear vision was limited to only ten yards. I strained my eyes frequently, peering ahead to check my course; the glare on the snow from the sun was too painful to allow me to leave aside the sunglasses.

I was nearing the bend where the glacier turned sharp right into the main valley back towards Base Camp when I remembered spotting from on the mountain, some crevasse shapes in this region. Two of them drifted into view. I skirted them on the left and was congratulating myself on my escape when dimly, and so bizarre that I was startled, there appeared, down to my right, at the centre of a concave bowl, a circular crevasse hole. I had never come across a circular crevasse before and could not judge its size, whether it was large or small, or how far away it was. I circled uneasily round it, watching lest it did something unpredictable; I was drawn, mesmerised, irresistibly, into its vortex. I continued circling until out of the corner of my vision I glimpsed some rocks on the glacier far away. My brain registered that rocks on glaciers can mean water and the trance was broken, my gaze snatched away by the distant rocks.

A great flat table of rock sat on a column of ice. The water formed by the rock absorbing the heat of the sun and melting the ice around it had run into a pool at the bottom of the column. A crust of ice covered it, untouched as yet by the day's heat.

My axe, short-shafted and useless as a walking stick, had dangled on its strap at my side or caught between my legs, not really knowing its purpose on the glacier. Now it asserted itself and in a few blows had broken through the crust of ice.

From my pockets and the bottom of my rucksack I scooped up a dirty palmful of oats, from when we had had muesli, two squares of chocolate and two boiled sweets. I had nothing else. I mixed half the oats into a mugful of water, ground up the sweets and chocolate and settled back against a rock to savour this heavenly mixture.

Liquid, cold, wet and liberal spilled into my mouth and out of the sides. I spooned up from the bottom of the mug the thicker sludge and then several spoonfuls of the thinner liquid from the top to spin out the delicious concoction for as long as possible.

I was aware that there seemed to be an American family standing a few paces away staring at me. A young boy said to his father, with a note of distaste: 'Why is he making such a scene about that mixture as if it was something great?' The whole family wittered on in silly chatter. I rose to refill my mug; it came as no surprise to find there was no family there at all; they were only in my mind.

Changabang loomed above me; the south-west ridge which Dick and I had contemplated climbing looked magnificent, and fearfully hard; far too difficult for us, I thought, and the incredible, ice-smattered precipice of its west wall was so smooth it made me think of a cinema screen on which there would never be any actors. I took a photograph, thinking that someone might want to attempt to climb the mountain from the west some day. The photograph was not for me. Dunagiri had done for me. I had had to drive myself to limits I never wanted to reach again and I was certain that I would never be going to any mountains again, let alone the Himalayas and something as awe-inspiring as that great wave of rock with ice dripping from its crest that was Changabang. I drank more mugfuls of water and settled back for a rest, sheltering myself from the sun with my down jacket.

After the second mugful of liquid and the last of the 'mixture', I knew I was saved. All that remained was graft, sheer hard work for several hours. I knew I could do it, knew that much as I disliked hard work I was capable of doing it. The long years of self-discipline in the seminary had left me with the knowledge that I could put up with things I did not like for a long time. There were no more major obstacles. I would make it eventually.

At 1.00 p.m. I left, reckoning that five hours of daylight should be enough for me to reach Base Camp. Various other people, apart from the American family, were with me now, all wandering along near me and watching with interest.

When I reached the long, low ridge of rocks along the edge of the glacier I recalled Dick mentioning that he had seen a rough track along the rocks. I left the glacier, stumbling over the boulders, into holes and against mounds. I did not usually decide to rest, it just happened. I could not force myself to keep going for ten minutes, nor even five minutes with the promise of a rest for an equal length of time as I had been walking. I would just find myself reclining after perhaps fifty yards with my rucksack resting on a rock, appalled at the thought of settling it onto my back again.

It occurred to me several times to stop where I was for the night, but the mountain wall near which I was walking was continually spilling off rocks and although I felt in harmony with nature, with the mountains, with the world, with those falling rocks, I knew as an instinct that I could not stay near where they were coming down.

I could hear the American family complaining about my being slow and wondered why they did not offer to carry my rucksack for me, for it was that which was slowing me down. They never offered and for some reason there was a barrier of silence between us.

I could hear the down-to-earth comments of Maurice about this escapade. He was a worldly-wise transport driver we had met in Iran. He had advised us to set fire to our van if it broke down and collect the insurance.

Old Willie was with me too, the dustman from Dundee. 'Be careful lads, but you'll be all right,' he was saying.

Then the comments of the Americans made me think again of my sack and like the resting there was no decision. I left my sack and the rope by a rock, building a cairn of stones to mark the spot. There was nothing in the sack I needed, since there was a sleeping bag at Base Camp. It was 4.00 p.m. and I set off anew, trailing thoughts and fantasies like streamers in my wake.

Vaguely I knew where I was, I could see Dunagiri now, that old adversary appearing from behind the small peak I had been skirting round. I could not quite locate the exact spot which I was searching for to give me my bearings until I tumbled down a rocky slope and into a grassy bay. It was the head of the narrow valley running straight down to Base Camp.

It was only another half hour to Base Camp, all downhill to home, and Dick too, if he had not stopped off at the tent of Advance Camp. I wondered what his purgatory had been and hoped that he was all right.

When I reached Base Camp there was no sign of Dick, so I presumed he had stopped off at the tent where there was also food and running water. It got dark before I could find matches. I gorged myself on cold tins of fruit and rice pudding, relics from Peter's brief sojourn. I ate indiscriminately, discarding part-eaten tins as my teeth hurt with the cold of the contents. I settled down into the shelter we had made from rocks with a roof of clear plastic.

I could not sleep. Beside me I kept a pan of water and by touch alone I found other foods and sweetmeats to nibble at. I glowed with the ecstasy of life. Thoughts fizzled round my mind, ricocheting and bursting with sparkling trails. I stirred myself to leave the bliss of the sleeping bag, feeling an insistent nagging in my bowels. And suddenly I was running out of the shelter, tearing at straps and zips but too late. Embarrassed, I found I was coated in faeces; my body had not known how to cope with food after so long without. I had no energy left to undress. I closed the zips and returned to bed.

I lay on the grass soaking up the morning sunlight expecting to see Dick arriving at any moment. He was never one to stay in bed. I knew he would have been up at dawn. Lazily I made drink after drink, ate wantonly and scoured the narrow cleft of the valley down which I anticipated his arrival at any time.

Doubts began to gnaw at me. It was a couple of hours at most from Advance Camp. If he had stayed there the night, had food and water, he would have been fit enough to get down by 9.00 a.m. It was impossible to imagine Dick lying in bed enjoying a rest and a long lie-in. By 11.00 a.m. I was very worried. I began to visualise him lying at the bottom of that gully with a broken leg – I could not bear to let myself think of him as dead.

I resolved to leave by noon with a rucksack of food, fuel, stove, clothing, everything he would need to survive lying at the foot of the mountain until I had had time to race out to the nearest village and bring help to carry him down. Mentally I was reconstructing a scene of what I feared to have happened.

I glanced up every time I packed another item into the rucksack, hoping and hoping, gripped round the heart by a black foreboding. Then I saw him, or saw movement which had to be him, and I tried to run, but it was a breathless hobble and I met him part-way up the valley. I pulled his sack off his shoulders and put my arm round him.

'What's the rush, Joe, what are you so excited about?'

'I thought you might have had an accident, I was really worried. You've been so late coming down.'

He looked as if the thought of anything untoward happening had not occurred to him. Then I noticed he was carrying a stick I had taken up to Advance Camp. I had picked it up on my way in to Base Camp and had become attached to it.

'I see you've brought my stick down.'

'Yes, well, I slipped in the bottom of the gully and I seem to have sprained my ankle. I've been using it as a walking stick.' Then I realised he was limping.

We sat on the grass outside the stone-built shelter and I plied him with drinks. He told me how he had been up at daybreak but his boots were frozen. Once out of the boot his ankle had swollen up, and he could not get the boot back on until the sun came and thawed the boots out. Then it took him an hour with his frostbitten fingers to get the boots fastened, and he had been slow once he got moving as his ankle was painful.

'What was it like getting from the gully to the tent?'

'Horrible. I couldn't decide which way to cross a really bad area. Then I heard your voice telling me which way to go and it was the right way.'

He was very anxious about his hands. The fingers were black at the ends now and I could sense some of the dismay he felt at the thought that the thing he held most dear, climbing, would be curtailed if some of the fingers had to be amputated.

I cut away the tattered remnants of gloves which still clung to his hand, cut away loose, dead skin from around the blackened ends and cleaned up each finger, sprinkling them with antibiotic powder before dressing them with light lint and finger bandage. On top of the dressed fingers on each hand I eased a large silk glove.

We had some antibiotic tablets remaining and Dick started to take a course of these to discourage infection. We were not sure if it was the right thing to do but it was all we could think of.

He wanted to leave next day to get to hospital as soon as he could. I knew now he was in pain. The keys to the car and our money were up at Advance Camp. Late in the afternoon, I left to go back to the tent. I had little strength left for such an effort but also I was reluctant to break the relief

5a. Dick approaching the couloir up which we climbed to gain the crest of the ridge running into the rock buttress.

5b. Joe approaching the shoulder (third bivouac) with the rock barrier visible in the background. (Photo: Dick Renshaw)

6a. Joe on the shoulder, site of the third bivouac. Nanda Devi is in the background. (Photo: Dick Renshaw)

6b. Dick on the snow band, entering the bottom of the rock barrier. The sharp snow ridge in the background is the site of our third bivouac (the mark in the snow) and the 'hole in the snow' which we were making for on the descent from the rock barrier.

7a. Dick approaching the summit of Dunagiri. Our ice axes were too short to be of much use as walking sticks.

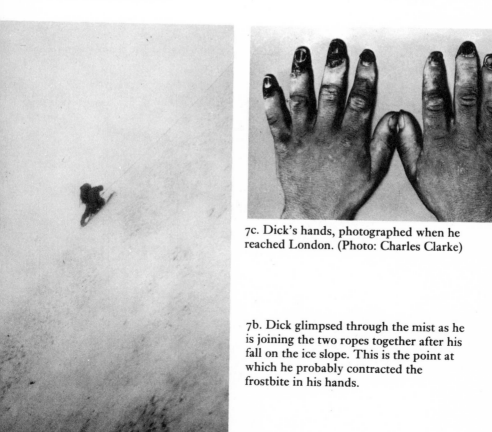

7c. Dick's hands, photographed when he reached London. (Photo: Charles Clarke)

7b. Dick glimpsed through the mist as he is joining the two ropes together after his fall on the ice slope. This is the point at which he probably contracted the frostbite in his hands.

8a. Dick at Base Camp after his return, outside the rock-built shelter with its plastic roof.

8b. Vera and the American girl guarding Joe's baggage at Ljubljana station where the train broke down.

of being together again, and the spell of being considerate to each other in a way we had not been before. We were like lovers after a quarrel, seeing depths of feeling in the other person previously unsuspected.

It was night before I returned. I brought back with me the tent and everything else I could carry to save my going back up again. I still did not have full control over my movements and my mind roamed free as I picked my way back across the outlandish badlands, apprehensive and unnerved under a full moon, until I came upon the familiar grassy valley down to home.

Dick chose to sleep away from me that night so that he would not disturb me with his restlessness and groans of pain. He left next morning after I had changed his dressings, hobbling off with a long ice axe which we had brought for the Liaison Officer as a walking stick, and promising to organise and send three porters in to carry out all the gear. I was to gather it up and pack it all ready for their arrival.

I had no way of checking the passage of days. Each day I tried to write a sentence in my pocket diary just to note that a day had passed, but I had no notion what the date was. Sometimes I was not sure if I had noted a day's passage or not.

The fastest I expected the porters to arrive was in four days. On what I thought to be the fourth day I noted: 'Porters didn't arrive.'

Fifth day: 'Porters still not here.'

I finished reading the few books we had brought with us to pass the time. I set off one day to walk back up towards Changabang and take some photos, but my feet were very painful and my throat still extremely sore. I did not go as far as I had intended. I bivouacked out and took some photographs by moonlight, and returned next day after collecting the rucksack I had dumped several days before.

I sat outside the shelter.

Sixth day: 'Still no porters.'

I had no sense of loneliness during this period. I was not alone because I had been rejected by other people. There was a purpose in my being where I was, and if that entailed being on my own too, it was tedious but did not arouse any anxiety or self-questioning.

I spent hours trying to trap some unseen creature which had raided my food store in the night. It had eaten into an opened tin of delicious pork I was saving for the next day, and carried off the remaining piece of fruit cake which I had apportioned out as a luxury to enjoy at the end of each evening meal. My dealings with the creature lasted several days. Fragile as my mental balance was, I began to feel in a state of siege. My toothbrush also disappeared.

I was lying on the grass, staring into the sky, when I thought I heard a voice. I jumped up and scanned the lower entrance to the valley, imagining the arrival of a loveable trio of hillsmen come to my rescue. There was no one. Out loud I abused myself for hearing things.

I jumped up again when I thought I heard voices a second time and still saw nothing. Six days of solitude, I thought, and I was talking to myself and hearing things. I ignored the chattering which I thought I could still hear. Then I saw some figures descending the rocky hillside from a different direction to where I had been looking.

There were only two of them. They were expecting a third. I made them welcome and offered them food to eat. There were several tins which it was pointless to carry all the way back. They opened them all and gorged themselves, wasting a good deal.

The third porter did not arrive. I had to abandon some of the gear and re-pack the loads, promising extra money by sign language.

The two porters seemed related. One was strong and capable, the other was thin, more elegantly dressed and started asking for things straight away. When we set off the next day, the thin one could not carry very much. I was very weak myself and had all that I could take in my sack. The strong one shouldered more from his partner, but whined demands for gifts of clothing.

It was a demoralising progress. We lost time with constant complaints from the thin one; he indicated that he felt dizzy on the track along steep hillsides and could not carry a load. I began to build up a resentment for these two. I softened when the thin one hurried up from behind and handed me the crash helmet which had fallen from my sack and tumbled down the slope.

They stopped frequently to smoke and inevitably we did not get far. We had to stop in poor camping places beside the track. Next day it was the same halting progress. They started the day smoking hashish and did not seem to want to move at all. I hassled them on but we had to camp at the foot of the steep slope I had had to climb when ill with toothache.

In the night it snowed. Six inches of snow fell on the tent and was thigh deep on the slope up to the pass before we reached the top. The two porters insisted on abandoning their loads; they could hardly keep their footing under the heavy weight. They buried them under a rock somewhere in the middle of that vast, uneven hillside.

At the top of the slope, on the plateau, conditions were worse. It was no longer steep but the cloud was thick and the falling snow flakes were dense. I tried to go ahead to break the trail, since I had better footwear, but I had no idea what to make for. The plateau steepened and became a series of ridges. The strong porter shouted unintelligibly and pointed at an indistinct rock feature. I tried to follow his directions. He grunted again but did not wait this time, going off ahead himself. Sometimes I saw him pause and peer into the swirling mist. A darkening in the mist denoted some rock on the mountainside, and taking his bearing somehow from what he saw, he would surge forward again. I hated this tedious, exhausting battle, in a direction I was unsure of and for a length of time I had no way of guessing. The direction he was following went across a more and more precipitous series of ridges. I could only guess that he had herded sheep or goats this way and was familiar with every contour and every rock, even when covered in snow. We came over a final ridge and started to descend. I could not guess how he had found this point, and it was dark by the time we started on the descent.

We stopped by some huge boulders and dug out two hollows in the snow beneath them. We had no tent, but I was still carrying my sleeping bag. I was passably warm, but could hear the two porters chattering all night, wrapped only in a blanket which caught the falling snow in its folds. I shared with them a tin of meat I was carrying and some sweets.

At first light we started down. His mountain sense deserted the porter and by following his directions about how best to reach the village he lived in we became entangled in dense thickets and caught up in thorn bushes. My clothes were in shreds by the time we came into the village in early afternoon.

The two porters disappeared. Someone gave me some tea and chupatti. The headman came over with a villager who could speak some English. I had almost written off the chances of retrieving the gear, now that the first falls of winter snow had arrived, but the villager announced with grand gestures that he would lead men to recover it. I agreed a fee and the headman suggested that a goat be sacrificed to offer up thanks for our safe deliverance from the mountains. I was touched by the gesture but checked first who would pay for the goat. A bony finger pointed unwaveringly in my direction. The headman, by gestures and cast-down looks, showed his sympathy for my partner, Dick, whom he had obviously met. He made sorrowful gestures of chopping at the ends of his fingers, indicating his view of what would happen.

I visited the doctor at the army camp who had treated my tooth.

'Poor fellow,' he said. 'I told him he would have to have them chopped off. They are quite gone.'

I could imagine how traumatic such comments would have been to Dick and how he must be questioning still the chances of his ever climbing again if his finger-ends had to be amputated. I did not know where he would be by this time, but I journeyed on to Delhi when the abandoned gear was eventually retrieved.

I became ill in Joshimath with severe stomach pains which kept me prostrate and helpless in that same room in which I had nursed my toothache so many weeks ago. When I drove down the Ganges valley, and across the plains of northern India, I could not stop to eat, as food only made me more ill.

In Delhi I rang J.D. and he told me that Dick was in the military hospital. I met him there, lying in bed in a spacious and clean ward. Thankfully he had as yet had nothing amputated.

He looked grubby, and he explained that the nurses seemed reluctant to give him a bed bath as would be normal in Britain. We guessed that it was a taboo of the Hindu religion for a nurse to wash a man's body. He could not wash himself for fear of getting contamination into his fingers.

They put him on a drip feed of a glucose solution. It was designed to promote recovery of his tissues. He had lain for some hours after the needle had been inserted, feeling his arm growing heavier and fatter as the solution fed into it. The arm became so heavy that he could not raise it. He called a nurse. The needle had been wrongly inserted and the fluid was building up in his arm rather than being absorbed into his system.

Painful as it was to his sense of thrift, he resolved to take a plane back to Britain to get treatment there. For me the prospect of spending another three weeks driving before I got back seemed like entering a long and endless tunnel.

V

I advertised in the Tea Rooms of Connaught Circus, in the centre of Delhi, a place much frequented by travellers, a place in the van back to Britain for $150 or £70. I had very little money left and on my own had not enough for the petrol. The van was discovered to have a fractured piston when I was having it serviced ready for the return journey. There was no piston available to replace it and even had there been it would have cost far too much. The mechanics welded up the piston and I left with my passenger, a New Zealander called Donald, on his way to Cardiff to play the violin in an orchestra and taking the overland route in order to see something of the countries on the way.

It was November, cool at night but pleasantly hot in the day. Donald appreciated the amenities of the van, the books he could read while I was driving, Dick's classical music and a tent at night.

I was wise to many of the ruses and pitfalls of the road after having travelled along it once. To drive up to the Khyber Pass we were asked to pay a toll. We had no Pakistan currency left. I offered dollars, the officials refused, there was no foreign exchange counter. I promised to pay at the border where I could change money, we were allowed to pass and not troubled again.In Afghanistan I had learnt the Urdu numerals from one to ten. It helped to keep check on the petrol pumps and of how much we were charged. A favourite trick was for the pump attendant to say how much was owed and once the money was handed over, by very deft sleight of hand, the notes somehow were changed to ones of lower denomination though of a similar colour. Being strangers to the currency it was usual to suspect oneself of making a mistake and to pay the extra demanded. It was the eagle eye of Dick that had spotted this trick and thereafter I enjoyed the predictable confrontation each time we had filled up in Afghanistan and paid the exact amount only to be confronted by a so-plausible request for more, from an innocent and hurt-looking attendant, appealing to the policeman who gazed on the scene impassively. Donald came to think I was very shrewd and cavalier to stand up to all these tricks, but it was simply a matter of experience.

We reached Kabul at evening and drove down a street towards the resthouse which Dick and I had stayed in. As I pulled onto the main street I was flagged down by a policeman. He pointed to a sign and someone from the crowd that soon gathered explained that we had driven down a one-way street in the wrong direction and were being fined $20. Donald said he did not remember any such sign at the other end of the street. I protested that I could not be expected to read Urdu. I was told that $10 would do. I insisted on seeing his superior officer. The policeman squeezed into the van with us and we drove down dark alleyways to the walled enclosure of the police station. I refused to drive inside and left Donald in the van with instructions about going to the British Embassy if I did not appear in an hour's time.

The superior officer looked as if he had been summoned out of bed. An interpreter came in too and they both sat on the opposite side of a dusty table in the dimly lit room. The traffic policeman explained his case in Afghan. My 'offence' was explained to me by the interpreter.

My cash was concealed in a money belt under my shirt. I asked if they would take traveller's cheques, knowing they would not. I could not pay the fine until I went to the bank next day and changed some money. They demanded my passport. I needed it for changing the traveller's cheques in the bank. It was like a game of chess. I offered my International Driving Permit as guarantee that I would come back next day. They knew as well as I that it was worthless as such a security. Stalemate.

'Have you got no cash?'

With a dramatic gesture I flung my loose change of mixed currencies onto the table. It was worth only a few pence, and I pulled my pockets inside out to illustrate my lack of any more.

With a wave I was dismissed. The officer had grown bored with the game. I left and drove back into town with Donald. Later we checked that street-traffic was flowing both ways and there was no sign of any kind at the other end.

We had trouble with the van in trying to leave Kabul. I had to buy a new dynamo costing £40. It would not start in the bitter cold mornings. I had to hire a taxi to give us a tow. One demanded an extortionate $20 in payment. I disagreed. He drove off with the climbing rope which I was using for the tow. Three times we tried to get on our way, each time we came limping back. Ominous screeching sounds came from the engine before it started and for a while afterwards. Gradually I came to terms with the idea that the van was not going to make it back to Britain. Donald was very decent about it. I returned his money and he lent me £90 as now I was flat broke.

It is difficult to leave some countries if it is stamped in your passport that you entered the country with a vehicle. This is to prevent a black market in motor cars. In Afghanistan it is possible to make a gift of a vehicle, if it is in working order, to the government. This I resolved to do. Providing the engine was warm, no unhealthy sounds emanated from it. I reckoned I could pass it off as in working order.

A Turk in the rest-house I was staying in was appalled that I should be so generous to the government. He had some involvement with a bus company, Akel Tours, which ran coaches all the way from Kabul to London, and he promised that in return for the van he would give me a seat on the bus and fix all the formalities about transferring the vehicle onto his passport.

It took two days of bribes and official fees to complete the arrangement, but it was done. I only hoped he did not want to start the van before I left. I went to the main hospital in Kabul and sold a pint of my blood for £5. It felt like manna from heaven. The easiest money I had ever made. Things were beginning to go right at last.

There were fourteen items of baggage when I packed up everything out of the van. All my gear, Dick's gear, the tents, a huge and heavy kitbag of gear from an English climber who had asked me to take it in the van since he was returning by public transport and did not want to carry that weight about. I was charged the equivalent of an extra seat for all the baggage I wanted to bring with me.

The coach was only half full when we left Kabul. There was plenty of room to stretch out and relax, the gear all packed beneath the floor and someone else to do the driving. A bus all the way to London was the answer to all my prayers. I had parked the van in a courtyard. The Turk was mightily pleased with his acquisition, but I never saw him try to get it started. I felt a criminal thrill of relief at my escape when the bus pulled away.

The journey has become a blend of sunsets across deserts, long hours gazing into space day-dreaming and tragi-comic interactions between the random companions of the bus. It was some time during that journey that

I started thinking of that impossible wall on Changabang. It was far away now, distance and time softened its features and inclined its precipices to an easier angle. It certainly seemed an interesting wall to examine. I found I was trying to guess at how it would be in the middle of the wall; whether it was as smooth as it appeared or whether its size dwarfed every feature and that in reality it was a huge staircase. On the other hand, I had been told that the meaning of the name 'Changabang' was 'slippery' or 'smooth'.

Somewhere along the road I met some friends from my home town of Teesside. They told me that some mutual friends were going to Changabang the next year. The news made me suddenly eager to get back to Britain to see what they were planning. I presumed that they were aiming to try that wall on Changabang.

I chatted to Donald on the bus, trying to reassure him that he had not seen the last of his money, and that I would pay him back as soon as I reached Britain. I had none at home either but from somewhere I would borrow it.

At first we were sitting just in front of the back seat. Behind us I could hear a conversation going on in a harsh, strange language. I glanced round to catch sight of the people talking and to guess at their nationality. There was only one person visible. I presumed the other was lying full length on the seat.

The bus journeyed on through the night. We had been assured that there were always two and sometimes three drivers to relieve each other so that there was no need to halt. The bus was empty enough to have a seat each to lie on. The guttural chattering continued. A broad-shouldered, blond-haired youth appeared to be having an endless conversation with himself. I lay full length on the floor of the coach sleeping soundly. Objects fell to the floor around me and I presumed they had rolled off seats. I was woken by someone protesting: 'Sven, stop throwing things about.' Sven was the lad who had been talking to himself, and we began to realise that he was affected by something more than a heavy intake of hashish or opium.

At the border we had to empty the bus of everything. I was preoccupied with my fourteen pieces of luggage, having them checked by the customs official. The Afghan border post is a clay-daubed brick building in a dusty compound surrounded by desert. Without any hitch it can take two hours to complete the formalities. There was a commotion beside the bus. Two Americans were asked to help. Sven was lying inside the bus, stark naked, and refusing to leave. The American couple dressed him and carried him from the coach. He was limp and they supported his sagging body. He straightened up, his arms outstretched, and in clear English pronounced: 'I am the light, the light who has come to save the world.' He turned to his two helpers and told them he was all right now and they could leave hold of him. They let go and he crashed face down, arms still outstretched, into the dust. The ragamuffin soldiers of the Afghan army stood linking hands with each other, completely bemused. The Americans took complete control of Sven then and shepherded him round the numerous offices, getting his baggage checked for him.

When we left that border post we were all united on the coach by a common concern – Sven. The Iranian border post was five miles distant across no man's land. There are exhibit cases there of some of the means by which people have tried to smuggle drugs through Iran with a photograph of each individual involved and the heavy sentence each one received on being caught. It is an effective and alarming deterrent. We were all convinced that Sven's behaviour would immediately rouse their suspicions and that all our belongings would be gone through meticulously and the coach would become one of the vehicles we could see behind a wire fence with holes drilled through panels and the roof cut open.

By a miracle it did not happen. The police accepted the story of Sven being sick and the promise that he would be taken to his Embassy in Tehran to be repatriated. There was even little problem with all my baggage. I had to carry it all through the inspection room piece by piece and on my own because few travellers in the east will take the risk of holding any luggage which might contain drugs.

In Tehran there was no Icelandic Embassy. It was a holiday and the Danish Embassy would do nothing. Sven continued with us.

The coach filled up. We could no longer stretch out and sleep. We journeyed day and night in the same position. It became clear that we only had one driver. The American girl stood over him insisting that he stop after he had been driving almost continually for four days with only brief rests in Mashad and Tehran. This time he had driven thirty hours without stopping and was swaying over the wheel, causing the bus to swerve on the road. The scene became ugly when he produced a knife but some hours later we stopped by a small hotel and slept in beds for the only time on the whole journey.

Sven seemed to be losing more and more control of himself as the journey went on. It became clear that he had soiled himself and the stench from his clothing wafted down the bus. A Swedish couple took charge of him and washed him down at one food halt. Thereafter they took him away at every opportunity to oversee his toilet.

A couple from the Channel Isles told me their tale of woe about how this was the final blow to a holiday which had been their lifetime ambition. For years they had planned to visit Kathmandu and had paid their money for the coach all the way from Istanbul. In Herat, in Afghanistan, the driver had refused to go any further, thrown everyone off the bus and told them to get to Kabul to see about getting their money back. In Kabul they were told they would have to go back to Istanbul to sort it out and it was only as a favour that they were allowed to travel on this coach as their tickets had been bought from a different company, Viper Tours. The incidents with Sven were the last straw. They confided in me as someone of their own nationality who could understand their point of view. The only consolation they could find was that Sven was not violent.

The days and nights filed past the windows. At one period, in the dark there were commotions up towards the front round where Sven was sitting. The interior lights came on and I could see Sven erect, turned towards the passenger behind him, one of the Swedes. Sven was hitting him hard. A couple of other passengers jumped up and dragged Sven off. I noticed the arm of his seat had gone. The lights went off and we carried on.

The commotions immediately prompted the lights to come on. This time they caught Sven upright, his fist raised, drawn back ready to strike. The Swede was stating plainly, pleadingly: 'No, Sven, you must not beat me, this is the last time.'

Before he could be held, Sven lunged towards the Swede, who cringed back, but the driving fist opened into a spread of fingers and stopped short. Sven smiled, the tension snapped and the whole coach applauded with relief. He did not use violence any more.

In Turkey he had to be rescued from irate tea-stall owners whose rows of waiting glasses full of the black Turkish tea Sven had gleefully upended.

I last saw him being shepherded about Istanbul by the Swedes as I tried to sort out getting back to Britain. The coach was not going any further than Istanbul. Sammy, an oily Levantine, protested he had been trying to inform the Kabul office by phone for the past fortnight that he had not been sending buses to London for a month. It was a struggle to extract part of the money back; he maintained that the van must have been a private arrangement with the Turk in Kabul since I had no receipt. In the end I prevailed and shunned his offer of a coach to Munich. The Channel Isles couple tried to extract money for their aborted journey. They had bought their ticket from him but since at the time he was working for a different company he maintained he was no longer responsible for the actions of that company.

In the Pudding Shop near the Blue Mosque, which Sammy also seemed to own, I met a friend from university days. He was flying back next day to London. How I envied such mobility! I booked a seat on the Orient Express and the American girl said she would accompany me; she had had enough of buses. She was on her way back to America to marry a fiancé she had not seen for nine months.

In the railway station I was having problems getting all my baggage onto the train. Suddenly a white-haired lady waded into the confrontation spouting Turkish and the problems disappeared.

'They try it on, you know,' she said to me in English.

'Where are you going? We can travel together.'

So we made a trio: Vera, at sixty, returning from one of her solo excursions round Turkey, the American girl, going home to get married and myself, with hardly any memory of how I came to have so much baggage, nor where I had been.

We crossed a frozen eastern Europe with a compartment to ourselves. Vera vetted all who tried to come in. She let a ruddy-faced Yugoslav join us. He was seventy, he said, and pointed out of the window at his farm as we passed it. He plied us liberally with slivovic from an earthenware bottle he carried.

'I thought that's what it was,' whispered Vera, 'that's why I let him in.'

We had to vacate the train at Ljubljana when it broke down. When we boarded another six hours later we had no seats and the three of us reclined on top of my luggage spread down the length of a coach. Each border meant a passport check and baggage inspection. Dick's flute, shiny tubes of metal in a black case, roused most suspicion.

In Paris there is no connection between the two stations on opposite sides of the city. I persuaded a taxi driver to take me and all the baggage. He charged a franc for each item and tried to convince me that I had sixteen pieces.

At Dover I had to have porters to get the gear through customs on a trolley.

'How much do you want?'

'Treat us like a gentleman should, sir.'

In London Ken Wilson collected me from the station and all I could talk about was the journey. I phoned my parents to say hello, Don and Jenny to see if they could put up with me as a lodger again, and Muriel to see if she still wanted me. Ken scowled his displeasure at having his phone taken up for so long. It was not the cost – I was paying for the calls – he just felt out of touch with world mountaineering for as long as his phone was occupied.

FOUR

Figures on a Screen

CHANGABANG

I

Changabang had wormed its way into my subconscious; the days on Dunagiri were days of continual exposure to the subliminal presence of that stupendous mountain. It had been a thing of beauty beyond our reach, a wall of difficulty beyond our capabilities, it had been the obstacle which blocked the sun's warming rays in the early morning and the silent witness to my delirious wanderings. For days it had hovered on the edge of my vision and when I returned home it re-emerged on the periphery of my imagination.

I had candidly dismissed as impossible the chances of climbing the mountain from the west, certainly with a small team. The calculations and evaluations which I took to doing on the journey back were simply mental exercises; the team which had permission for Changabang were not after all going for the west side, which I had taken to be the most compelling objective. I do not know at what point my mentality changed from working out ways and means of climbing something like the west wall of Changabang as an academic exercise to the positive frame of mind of asking myself how I was going to do it and with whom. There was a period when it was a lonely dream whose substance I was unsure of. I projected a picture of that west face onto the sitting-room wall to a friend looking for a mountain to climb. I showed him the mountain and pointed out the wall without expressing any intentions, hoping for some critical appraisal to give me guidance by which to judge how much grounding in reality my dreams had.

The mountain had been in my mind and in my life for too long by this time for me to make a detached judgement on it. I did not know whether the idea of climbing it was a perfectly reasonable one or a fanciful dream with no basis in fact. I could not put a proposal to Dick. He was receiving treatment for his frostbitten fingers and it was uncertain as yet how much he would have to have amputated. It was too early to plan with him for another major climb.

From being a plaything of my imagination, returning to Changabang had become not only a positive wish but also an ambition to be fulfilled urgently, and my thoughts turned to the practical necessities. I needed a partner and we needed permission.

My days were free at this time. I had found work for the Christmas period in a cold store, working nights to load up wagons with frozen food for distribution during the daytime to freezer centres. It was a convenient occupation. I earned enough money to pay off the debts accumulated over the Dunagiri expedition and had had to make no long-term promises to obtain the job.

One day I called in to see Pete Boardman in the office of the British Mountaineering Council where he worked. During this visit to Pete, who was sitting with the attitude of a wild animal, caged by his desk, I mentioned Changabang and its impressive western facet. I was sounding him out for a sign of interest in it as a desirable objective.

I had first met Pete on a climb in the French Alps. The meeting was implanted in my memory by the circumstances of the encounter. He and his partner, Martin, had slipped past Dick and myself in the early hours of the morning as we stirred ourselves from a chilly bivouac. All that day we climbed as separate pairs a few hundred feet apart. We spent similarly unpleasant nights on inadequate ledges sitting out a prolonged storm and retreated together next day to escape the snow. We shared the work of rigging up abseils and pulling the ropes down to use again. We were almost down from the steepest part of the mountain. I was standing on a tiny foot-hold a few feet below the other three; there was no room for me beside them. Martin was pulling the ropes down when I saw the three above me duck. Instinctively I pressed myself close to the mountain, heard the rush and sensed the mass of an enormous block falling past, brushing my rucksack and tearing my axe free. The rope had caught on and dislodged the block. By a miracle we were all safe.

That was in 1971, apprentice days in the Alps. Subsequently I had bumped into Pete a number of times and saw him more often when he moved down to Manchester from his post as an Outdoor Pursuits Instructor at Glenmore Lodge in Scotland. I knew he had done good things in the Alps and wanted to do more; I knew he loved rock-climbing; I knew of a trip to the Hindu Kush he had gone on from university in 1972; I knew of course that he had reached the top of Everest whilst I was away on Dunagiri. But it was not these things which made Pete in my eyes the right person to ask about Changabang. It was not the record of achievements that I saw in him but the attitude of mind that I sensed. With some people it is not necessary to have climbed in their company to know that they are of the same inclination and share the same spirit as oneself.

When, in the December of 1975, I talked to Pete of Changabang, I could see that there was a conflict within him caused by his role in the massive machine of the Everest expedition, which, after the successful ascent, was still at the focus of attention. With lecture tours and frequent public appearances taking up all his time, he felt that he was living a life far removed from his basic wish simply to climb.

He was interested, as a climber, in the fantastic mountain I had described to him, but he was doubtful if he would be able to escape from the office for a second year running on something which would not court and carry with it the publicity which inevitably surrounds an ascent of Everest, thereby lending prestige to an expedition which climbs it.

Most importantly, however, he was keen on the idea of climbing the west face of Changabang, and the dream began to take form in reality.

Unexpectedly he received the blessing of his superiors and without further reservation took to his heart the whole project. He came to see the few pictures I had of the mountain, and I was conscious of my failure to take more. His questions were specific and practical: where was the line I thought possible? What height was the wall?

I had been enthusiastic in my effort to inspire him with the idea of the climb but I had never been so detailed in my analysis of what line we could take. It was the concept of climbing a seemingly impossible wall that attracted me, but faced with Pete's practical questions I felt vague and unconvincing and the project sounded implausible.

I pointed feebly to patches of ice and shadowy lines, indicating that it was not a completely featureless face we were looking at. But Pete was not sceptical, his questions did not express doubts but real interest and a growing fascination with the idea. He was not convinced of the likelihood of us climbing it but he too was interested to give it a try, to go and see what would be possible. It was the reassurance that I needed, the affirmation that I was not out of touch with the real world, unless Pete was equally mad.

We sought the comments of others whose opinions we respected and when they told us it was a preposterous idea and that we did not stand a chance we were suitably awed and said we would like to take a look anyway and see what the best way to climb it would be. But our dedication must have been equally awesome and inspiring as Doug Scott rang me and asked to come. He had seen the west face himself and told me that it was beyond the bounds of possibility, but he wanted to give it a try.

I had never thought of going with more than two and given the chance I realised that I was lacking in the confidence to perform alongside someone whose high reputation in the climbing world made me feel distant and dwarfed. Succeed or fail, I preferred to do so unobserved. In Pete I sensed a kindred spirit. The expedition was to be our own very private folly.

The expedition to Dunagiri had cost £1,600. One-third of that we had received in grants and the rest we had raised ourselves by working as teachers. The van had proved more expensive than anticipated and this time we decided to fly, the cost of travel being cheaper if the extra time available for working was taken into account. The overall cost we estimated as being slightly higher, approximately £1,800 due to air freight charges and the extra heavy equipment which we were taking. To raise money we had to speak about our plans with a conviction I did not feel. To counter the arguments about the impossible difficulty we were taking on, we said that we had to rub noses against it before we could give it up. To justify the risks we were said to be taking by going as a twosome, we evolved the theory of being contained in our own self-sufficient cosmos in which we had everything we needed for survival and without the errors and misunderstandings possible in relying upon others.

From the Mount Everest Foundation and British Mountaineering Council combined we received a total grant of £650. From the Greater Manchester Council we received £200, since we were both based in Manchester and the expedition was seen to be a credit to the city. We made up the remaining £1,000 or so from our own pockets.

I worked the unsociable hours of night shift in the cold store, and climbed badly at the weekends. I divided the days between sleeping and preparing for the expedition. To make it possible to go off on another expedition I seemed stuck in a dull routine which neither exercised my mind nor encouraged the forming of any satisfying relationships. I was alone. My relationship with Muriel had not survived the long absence of Dunagiri. I lived only for myself. Sometimes the life I was leading seemed empty and pointless without anyone to share it; it had all the trappings of adventure and variety but I wondered what purpose it all served if it was only for myself. Sometimes I wondered if it was only because I thought I would lose face amongst my peers that I kept on riding the merry-go-round I had stepped onto. Sometimes, in the deepest recesses of my consciousness, I wondered if there lurked the secret hope that permission would be refused and we would be given an honourable reprieve from our self-imposed trial. But the doubts and self-questioning did not take a form active enough to hinder my efforts to overcome the objections raised on all sides against our plans and to bring into being the expedition. Our friends in India once more pleaded our case to the Indian government, which at first expressed complete opposition to an expedition of only two people going to attempt a route as difficult as the West Face of Changabang. Finally they relented in their opposition and I felt anew the onus of responsibility and of the trust which those friends of Mrs Beaumont had in us.

Gradually the chaos of preparations was channelled towards a departure date; the team from Cumbria which intended to attempt the south face of the mountain agreed to take two heavy boxes of food overland in the truck they had bought, thus saving us the cost of some of the air freight. They were friends and would be on the mountain at the same time as us but completely out of touch. Our approach to the mountain would be the same for two days, and from there they would take a divergent path to swing round in a long arc to the other side of the mountain from us. Our two base camps would be only a few miles apart but separated by a huge and difficult ridge linking Changabang to other mountains. To reach one base camp from another would necessitate a major climb or a trek of two or three days.

I came to know Pete more and inevitably to compare him with Dick. There was a rivalry between us in our climbing, there was a mutual weighing up and assessment of each other. Pete's progress in life seemed to have followed a straighter course than mine. From obtaining a degree in English, he had gone on to take a teaching certificate in Outdoor Pursuits, and then to intruct at Glenmore Lodge in Scotland, one of the most prestigious instruction centres in Britain. His current job as National Officer for the British Mountaineering Council involved him in countless meetings about safety standards, access rights to climbing areas and a host of other topics related to mountaineering. He conducted himself in this job with a calmness and diplomacy which I believed I could never have found the patience for. I did not even understand the issues involved. As an active climber he had perhaps the most respectable occupation related to the sport that any of his peers would contemplate holding. As such he seemed to feel a certain self-consciousness about his role when in the more anarchic milieu of the everyday world of climbers. He constantly expressed amazement at the more outrageous escapades of those around him and, with an ingenuousness which disarmed everyone, sought tuition in the fantastical world in which he believed all but he were at home.

We all live with preconceptions of those around us and Pete saw me as belonging to the indefinable community of 'the lads', who seemed to be more at home with worldly affairs than he felt. He looked to me to introduce him to girls, amongst whom he always professed to be shy and with whom he sought only to make gentle conversation. But beneath the gentlemanly politeness and urbane diplomacy there was unsuspected forcefulness and determination when it came to mountains. He might be diffident about asking for a lift or borrowing a book but he had no hesitation in taking the lead on a difficult climb. As with many people, he showed more self-confidence when contending against himself than when meeting the challenge of interacting with people on a daily basis.

His girlfriend had returned to Australia when she had overheard him by chance discussing with a friend the possibilities of climbing Changabang, before ever he had mentioned his plans to her. She took as callous lack of consideration what was in reality the forgetfulness of an over-full schedule

of meetings and travel and endless debates and repetitions associated with
his work.

I was the demon who was drawing him away and I was under appraisal
by his own close circle of friends who were concerned at what he was taking
on. I sensed the unease of Pete's parents too when I called in with Dick
to visit him at home and look at more pictures of the mountain. Pete
pleaded ignorance of the workings of his new slide projector and with a
confident assumption of my mastery of things practical I rapidly proceeded
to set it to work. A fuse blew and molten plastic dropped from the projector
onto the table. Having shown myself to be impetuous and clumsy within
minutes of arrival, I felt more strongly the scepticism of Pete's mother and
father whom I was meeting for the first time, and I was aware of their
frequent, wordless glances towards Dick, who had developed the habit of
keeping his still blackened finger-ends out of sight under his arms. I could
imagine as if it was written up clearly that they were asking themselves what
I would do to *their* son on this trip we were planning. The irrational guilt
feelings I had over Dick's injuries and my own lack of damage surfaced
easily.

Pete and I persevered with our preparations. From all that we could
judge, there were no ledges large enough for a tent on the central steep area
of the mountain. We planned to use hammocks to sleep in. Neither of us
knew how seriously to take ourselves. We knew of no one who had tried
to use hammocks on so high a mountain and in cold such as we expected.
The question arose constantly – if the mountain was so hard, what chance
did we have? It was like the game of 'chicken' – each person runs as close
to a chosen danger as he dare and loses points by the extent to which he
bales out before reaching the danger. Neither of us ever let himself express
doubts in front of the other.

We tried out hammocks in the cold store where I was working, spending
three particularly miserable nights in temperatures akin to those we expected to experience on the mountain. The hammocks were altered and
improved in accordance with the lessons we learnt in the cold store, but to
what extent we believed in what we were doing or were taken in by our own
hyperbole is hard to say.

There was a certain credit attached to going ahead with plans to attempt
'the preposterous'; there was a seductive temptation to believe in the pre-
expedition proclamations and pronouncements put out by journalists
hungry for copy and based on our own brief prepared to explain and justify
our intentions. I would rather have slipped away quietly to succeed or fail
in private but we needed to explain ourselves in order to obtain permission
and receive the blessings of the official bodies and we needed to justify
ourselves to show we were worth supporting and had made a careful
assessment of what we were doing. However it seemed to anyone else, I was

too much aware that ahead of us was a test greater than any that either of us had ever undertaken to be able to obtain the slightest satisfaction from the approval of anyone. Rather, I was daunted by the faith which was shown in us.

I called home to visit my parents, who had come to accept my departures to the mountains as being more important to me than a mere whim. I knew that they had received a certain amount of satisfaction when for a brief spell they were able to describe me as a teacher in the months before I went to Dunagiri. However many doubts and anxieties they felt, they had never expressed any dismay that I should graduate from university only to spend my time odd-jobbing in order to pursue more fully the urge to climb mountains. Initially, climbing had been incomprehensible to them and they had expressed their anxieties in advising me to take up a more normal sport, but they became accustomed to my coming back and saw this bizarre pursuit taking me to many places, making me many friends, and giving me a rich store of experiences. I came to rely upon the moral support and the confidence I felt in knowing that they were interested in what I was doing and would help in any way they could.

They were never deluded, however, over the dangers which we ran in the mountains and I tried always to ease the pain of worry. One incident revealed to me the apprehension with which they listened to the news whilst I was away. When Dick and I had set off to climb the Matterhorn we heard that two Englishmen had been killed on it the day before. I rang home as soon as we got down to Zermatt under the pretence of saying hello and lightheartedly telling them we had climbed the mountain. I was not over-reacting and my mother probably guessed why I called. 'That's where two people were killed, isn't it?' and I tried to pass it off as if it was as remote from us and as unsensational as a road accident hundreds of miles away.

Always I tried to call home just before leaving to say a last goodbye which none of us admitted to being a possible final goodbye. Always I like to call home as soon after I return as feasible to take them some gifts from the places I have visited, to share with them some of the tales and experiences, to let them know that it was not all danger and to try to give to them something of the quality of my life which I believe to be enriched by visiting such distant places and climbing such difficult mountains. I want also to give them proof by my physical presence that I am really alive.

II

We left for India on 22 August and it was the first time I had been in an aeroplane. I could not help but think of the weeks I had spent on the road the year before and how effortless this was by contrast, and no more expensive, boarding a plane to arrive in a few hours back in the steamy heat of India at the tail end of the monsoon. I had not thought I would ever be back and yet, less than twelve months later, as normal as if it were a weekend outing, I was returning to Delhi, where nothing seemed to have changed. The streets still thronged with teeming crowds of people, the vendors in the bazaars still tugged insistently at our sleeves as we walked past, and Mr Sony still sat outside his guest-house where Dick and I had stayed. His guest-house was full so we booked into another one nearby. This was just as cheap as Mr Sony's and was frequented by impecunious travellers on the hippy-trail. I felt as if I was introducing Pete to a side of India he had been cushioned from when he had passed through Delhi on the way back from Everest and stayed at the luxurious Inter-continental Hotel.

Nothing seemed to have changed at the GKW offices either. The staff greeted me with recognition and J. D. was holding court, as ever, behind his enormous desk with several attendants on hand making notes and running off to carry out his instructions.

Perhaps the single attribute of J. D. for which I most respected him was that he took us as we were. In a country where big means beautiful and wealthy and where small and casual means poor, J. D. did not register any reservation or diffidence to us. He made us feel that he had all the time in the world for us and that no obstacle was too great for him to sort out if we needed his help. He was a jovial Hindu who joked that he should come with us as a way to lose weight and alleviate his blood pressure. He had no conception of why we wanted to climb mountains, nor of what it entailed, but it was he more than anyone who, for a second time, had ensured that we were granted permission and given the opportunity to bring our dreams to reality. He wanted no thanks, and was embarrassed at a gift. 'It is my duty,' he protested. 'I was asked by my colleagues in England to do this for you.'

He ushered us on our way by train and ramshackle but sturdy bus up out of the heat of the plains to the Swiss climate of Joshimath. It was pleasing to meet again the acquaintances of the year before, Bhupal Singh of the Neelkanth Motel and Yasu, a sturdy youth of the hills. We delayed there with some of the friends who would be on the opposite side of the mountain, waiting as they were for their truck, with our two boxes of food. It was amusing to note the formation of a sub-group even out of their small team of six. Their leader was of the same age and background as they, but leadership had endowed him with a charisma which went beyond any rational explanation. The group of three who had come on ahead by bus had the definite air of charges who had escaped supervision, having been given an unexpected holiday through the delay caused by landslip some distance back along the road.

We retrieved our boxes when their truck arrived and slipped off ahead with fifteen porters and our Liaison Officer, Flight Lieutenant Palta.

We reached Base Camp in four days, a journey which for me was

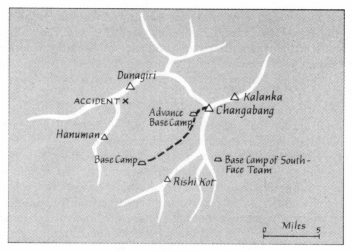

5. The route up Changabang.

nostalgic with memories of struggling out through deep snow less than twelve months before. Pete found it a delight, having read much about Garhwal, the Garden of the Himalayas. He showed an interest in flowers which set me to photographing them as well. He also expressed a patience and interest in our Liaison Officer which I did not feel. When I declaimed vociferously against the ignorant bureaucracy which imposed upon us an extra person who increased our costs, did nothing we could not have done ourselves and, having had a month of training in a climbing school, expected to be asked to climb the mountain with us, Pete deflated my arguments with an irritating placidity and spent time discussing with Flight Lieutenant Palta his views on life, religion and politics.

Our trip did not coincide with the image he had held of expeditions when he had volunteered his services; his attitudes appeared structured by notions of class or caste and his judgement of our expedition was influenced by his preconceptions about what was a fitting manner in which to live in the mountains for people of his and our standing.

I did not have any inclination to justify the manner in which we were doing things, and did not have any time for the diplomacy which enabled Pete to go along tolerantly with Palta's misguided notions that a month's tuition would fit him to climb a mountain we dreaded to confront after years of experience.

I felt a trace of reproach from Pete when Palta announced to us that he was so disgusted with the food we had brought, so disillusioned with the duties which we expected of him in sitting at Camp whilst we were on the mountain, that he wanted us to send him back to Delhi as soon as the march-in to Base was over. I was cold-humoured enough to think that it would be nothing but a relief to have only problems with the mountain to contend with rather than the extra problems of keeping a superfluous attendant happy and I resented all the formalities which we had had to go along with, all the façades we had to put on in order to achieve our simple ends.

Palta left with our band of porters and I walked up with Pete to look at Changabang from the vantage point at the head of the small valley, showing him the mountain as if it were a cherished possession.

The totem from my dreams of the year past confronted us, every bit as difficult, as impossible as when I had first seen it. A year thinking about it had done nothing to soften its severity, nothing to prepare me for facing up to it again in actuality. My resolve was very fragile at the moment when we stood gazing at the smooth monolith of granite, over five thousand feet high, smeared with ice. If it had been Pete who had brought me to this place, I would have shrunk less from the prospect of taking on the mountain; I would have assumed that he was either out of his mind ever to have contemplated such a thing or that he knew something I did not – either way he would be the fall guy. But Pete had come relying upon my judgement, trusting to my mountain sense, and faced with the climb I had enthused about I could not betray that inwardly I was horrified at what was before us.

He may have been shy in his personal relationships, diplomatic in committees and amenable in behaviour, but faced with a mountain to climb, when it was mainly himself he had to contend with, he showed no compromise. Whatever doubts he felt inwardly, none were expressed. Perhaps we both kept up the façades we had developed over the past year, even now when there was no other party to convince. We did not decide on a line we would try to follow all the way to the summit; we did not consider how to reach the summit at all. We discussed a way of reaching the crest of a small ridge which ran into the steepest part of the mountain one thousand feet above the glacier. From there we would be able to examine more closely the difficulties. We did not look too far ahead, lest the scale of the whole should dwarf and frighten us so much that we would hesitate to make the first step.

A lone Austrian, Hans, had trekked up to our Base Camp at the same time as us, upsetting all our Liaison Officer's credence in his role as a guardian of his country's border security. Hans enjoyed walking amongst and photographing mountains, apparently content with his own company, and wandered on when he had observed enough of one place. He left our camp after a couple of days and we were completely alone for the trial ahead.

III

We spent a week carrying food and equipment up to a camp close to the foot of the mountain. It was a four-hour walk from 15,000 feet to 17,000 feet, back along the route I had staggered down in my delirium from Dunagiri. The loads we carried weighed between thirty and forty pounds, requiring quite an effort at that altitude but providing a useful chance to adjust to the more rarified air, and accustom ourselves to rigorous physical exercise. It allowed us also to grow familiar with the mountain, and to scrutinise at different times of the day each little feature.

We came to accept the idea of being alone with each other. Dick and I had gone onto Dunagiri almost straight away, so I had not noticed the isolation so much. I knew Pete less and there were many idiosyncrasies we each had for which we both had to make allowances. I noticed how Pete used to make copious entries into a diary, so many that I could not visualise how he could do or say anything without the awareness that he was going to record that action or word. I had found after Dunagiri the value of recording the days as they passed, in order to keep track of time and I made one-line notes in the form of a diary. Pete was sceptical of the value of this at all as an aid to remembering events. I countered this by his own tactic of quoting, for greater authority, from other authors, saying that Graham Greene had written that as an author it was not trying to remember things that was difficult but trying to forget them. I could only just remember this saying and Pete was dubious about its authenticity.

We dug a ledge for a tent on the crest of the ridge where it ran into the steepest part of the west face. Above was the inscrutable wall, the first few hundred feet of which was not vertical and looked feasible to climb. Reaching the crest of the ridge had opened up a panorama of peaks, diluting to some extent the sense of confinement we both felt on the glacier, surrounded by steep slopes of ice or rock. I did not mind so much as Pete, who verbalised his frustration at having such a restricted horizon. Perhaps it was that I had surveyed the mountains for so long on Dunagiri and now I could see them in my mind's eye. Pete had read about the mountains, knew more about them than I did even though he had not visited them previously, and felt cheated that he had not even glimpsed Nanda Devi, which was shrouded in cloud when we were walking within sight of it. Partly I was defensive over his complaints, as if he was comparing 'my' mountains with 'his' mountains, the mountains he had been to before; partly I was apprehensive that his complaints were the beginnings of disillusionment.

We worked from the tent for days, learning more about the climb and about each other. We made progress sufficient to postpone any basic questioning about our overall chances of success. As the wall steepened, we made slower but still steady progress, fixing a line of ropes up from the tent, adding more ropes each day as we pressed on further, and slipping back down those ropes each evening to the haven of the tent. The days were hard but, dressed up in a routine, acceptable because we only had to think a little at a time.

The rock was sound granite, not loose and unreliable as on Dunagiri. Runnels of ice clung firmly to the grooves in the rock. Deciding which way to go was complex, and solving the problems of each section was both mentally and physically taxing. At first I felt conscious of Pete's critical observation when I led a pitch. I noticed an assumption of superiority in his performance and an authoritarian attitude in his climbing techniques and manoeuvres which I put down to his days of instructing. When I paused, working out a move, or summoning up the nerve to commit myself to an unpredictable position, I imagined him champing at the bit and thinking he could have led the pitch so much better or faster than me.

It was when not actually climbing that I noticed his inadequacies. He always took longer to arrange things to make himself comfortable, always found I had something or contrived something that he had not, such as a pillow from coils of rope, or my boots pushed together, and he gave off an air of being badly done by. He was nervous of situations where I relaxed, knowing that we had done all possible to make ourselves safe and dismissing as pointless any further worrying. Pete ended up sleeping on the side of the tent nearest the edge of the ledge and he often voiced his uneasiness at the thousand-foot precipice inches away from him.

We fell into a pattern of defined roles. Pete stirred himself first in the morning and made breakfast; I lingered in sleep, hiding from another day, for as long as possible. At evening I busied myself with the main meal, while Pete flopped into the back of the tent, glad to rest immediately from the day's exertions.

The climbing was mostly a delight, exhausting but enough inside our capabilities to encourage our optimism. We shared the leads, each of us leading four rope-lengths at a time. The difficulties, however, were time-consuming, so we only managed more than four rope-lengths on the first day, and Pete had been in the lead all day. After that it became normal for one of us to spend the whole day out in front whilst the other spent the whole day paying out the rope and following more rapidly the sections once the rope was in place.

I spent an afternoon on a ledge six inches wide and two feet long, while Pete moved upwards, ever so slowly towards a barrier of overhangs. The mist came in and he was lost to sight, though no more than a hundred feet away. Hours went by and I had no thoughts left to fill the time. The wind was too strong to let words be heard. I tried to shout information into the

Bivouac

Ramp

Kalanka

Hammock
bivouacs
2 and 3

Overhangs

C2

Ice field

Hammock
bivouac 1

C1

Advance Base Camp

3. The line of our ascent up Changabang.

mist but heard no reply. There was little rope left to pay out and if he did not halt soon he would be stopped from moving further by the restriction of the rope. I could faintly hear scraping sounds of metal on rock and snatches of words shredded by the wind. I thought I could see a figure near the overhangs when the mist thinned momentarily. I untied the parts of the rope I was using to tie myself to pitons and spikes of rock, freeing a few feet more. Again the rope came tight but I heard the positive sound of a hammer firmly striking a piton and knew he was safe. It was late in the day, Pete arrived out of the mist, having anchored the rope to the piton at his highest point. He told me how hard and worrying it had all been up there in the mist, about the rock becoming increasingly steeper, the cracks getting fainter and how far he had had to go without any assurance of reaching a place to rest, tiring all the time, knowing that he was coming to the end of the rope. That was a worry and fear he was up to, that was when he came into his own, when facing difficulties he could solve by superlative skill and dangers he could ignore in the concentration needed to solve the problem, or put up with in the knowledge that he was committed to a test of skill which he welcomed. He was a different person when climbing from the one who slept uneasily by the side of a steep drop, no matter how securely he was tied in place.

It came about that the two most difficult pitches up to that point were in Pete's rota of leading. I spent three hours next day under the shadow of the overhangs, watching and freezing while Pete struggled, only feet away in the sunlight, to find a solution to the biggest problem we had yet met. The barrier of overhangs spanned the whole area above us. If we could not find a way through then we would have to start all over again. The previous day Pete had moved rightwards towards where the overhangs formed a notch at the top of the rounded corner where the wall curved out of sight. He had not seen round the corner, but had been forced in that direction by the impossibility of climbing leftwards or straight up.

Now he was exploring the unknown. I could see only the lower half of his body and hear his grunts and imprecations. He could not tell me more than that he could see the next few feet were all right, though difficult. The rest was out of sight round more steps of overhangs. I watched his legs twitch upwards out of my range of vision and heard him hammering more pitons in to aid his progress. I dabbled my own foot in the sunlight which touched the slab on which I was standing, a captive tied to the shadows, hoping some of the warmth would creep up my leg into my frozen body. I was disgruntled that it was my turn again to be second on the rope with none of the thrill of breaking new ground and not even warmth from physical exertion, but each of us had to accept a turn in this secondary role every other day. It had been absorbed into my subconscious many years before that physical discomfort was a valuable penance and I sometimes wondered whether our penances and frequent deprival of physical pleasure did indeed benefit our souls and make us better people.

I was frustratingly out of touch with what Pete was doing. No longer able to see any part of him, I became dissatisfied with his uninformative replies to questions with which I could not help pestering him. I longed to have a go myself, unable to comprehend why he was taking so long if it was, as he said, possible.

When at last I could move I was stiff with cold: I was clumsy and awkward in the contortions needed to follow the tortuous line of the rope through the overhangs and up to join Pete at the top of an icy ramp. Justifiably he was proud of breaking through that barrier, finding the vital link to bring us within reach of the vast ice field at mid-height on the mountain. Justifiably he expected praise and pragmatically I thought he had only done his job, much as he made breakfast and I cooked tea; another time it would be my turn and all I could manage was: 'Good lead, mate.' It was an enormous psychological boost to reach that ice field. We were halfway to achieving what we had thought might be impossible, and by the time we had skirted up its left edge and anchored the ropes to its top rim, our thoughts had changed to knowing that we could do it. The wall above the ice field looked equally hard and a huge tower looked more difficult still, but we had found confidence in the progress we had made and no longer had such doubts as we had started with.

It took almost a week of climbing every day to reach the top of the ice field at half-height on the wall. We had brought along a thousand feet of rope at Pete's suggestion to fix on the mountain. This was one of the results of his applying his mind to the problems of the mountain and based on his experiences of the value of fixed rope on Everest.

At the top rim of the ice field I stood drawing in the rope as Pete came up towards me. I had skirted the left edge of ice, which was green and hard, contriving a way up the little ripples in the smooth rock slabs at the side. It was a delicate tip-toe all the time on the verge of insecurity which I revelled in as each gamble of a move paid off. It was nothing like as strenuous as the pitches Pete had led earlier, but every few movements upwards had left me panting from the exertion. I watched Pete as he followed up the rope, retrieving all the intermediate anchor points, leaving only the main one at the bottom, since we needed to re-use the pitons and karabiners time and again. I held my camera ready with my eye to the view finder, composing the shot in the frame, waiting for Pete to move into a dynamic pose. The pose was not right but I took a shot in case something should prevent me taking a better one, and readied the camera again. He moved up, into a better position this time, I squeezed the shutter, but his head had sunk to his arm as he panted for breath, still not the pose I looked for, but it was real, showing the agony of climbing at altitude. Pete looked up, hearing the click of the shutter, and shouted: 'If you take another shot of me like this I'll come up there and thump you,' and the day turned black for me. I was sickened at what I regarded as a childish fit of temper; I wondered whether he only wanted photographs to be taken showing him in his best light; he already had pictures of me in similar pose. The fragile, often begrudging rapport which had held us together was for me destroyed; a sense of aimlessness and futility overwhelmed me; we were both far apart however well we had done so far with the climb. What little joy I had felt on reaching the upper edge of the ice field, our halfway stage, the confirmation that we could probably climb this mountain, all vanished. I felt empty and rebuffed. I looked forward no more to the upper part of the mountain, I simply wanted it to be over with.

Pete was repentant and I held back from catalysing the incident further, noting in my diary, 'This is no place for an argument'. I had had a glimpse of a Pete I had not suspected before, in whom there was anger so close to the surface, and knew that he too, despite the diplomacy and urbanity, was as subject to the stresses and strains of the mountain situation as anyone.

An element of non-cooperative, mute hostility arose in things which did not matter such as whose turn it was to make an extra cup of tea, but we were both aware of the strange circumstances in which we were living and of the inevitable tensions which were arising. It became a practice to defuse situations by putting a perspective onto confrontations by a comment relating back to normal life. 'Don't worry, it will be all right and won't matter when we get back down to the valley,' was a catch-phrase we both took to using.

Our days consisted by this time of several hours of tiring, anxious ascent up the hundreds of feet of the single line of rope we had fastened in place. Then hours of taxing climbing, with long, fraught abseils back down the rope, down more hundreds of feet, to the tent, at the end of the day. Under these circumstances we could not escape from strain; the high tension which sparked off arguments came from the same highly strung frame of mind which enabled us to keep up the concentration to solve the problems of the climb we had started on with such doubts. The magnificence of our situation, the beauty of the sun setting behind the cloud-wreathed Dunagiri, my old adversary, the deep blue of the sky on a cloudless day and the descent in the rosy glow of evening were all phenomena only partially observed, scarcely appreciated, in a corner of my mind and recorded by photograph for a time when I could view them in comfort.

We had not intended to make a line of rope all the way up the mountain, but thought we might have to prepare difficult sections first, fasten rope in place and then return for a mobile assault with the hammocks. All the mountain was difficult and we wished we had had more rope to leave in place. We added up all the lengths of extra climbing ropes we had brought with us and found we had nearly two thousand feet. We just managed to stretch this out to reach from Camp 1 on the ridge to the top of the ice field. From there we descended to rest and return with more food and the hammocks.

IV

Our stay at Base Camp was only overnight and we returned to the mountain next day. There had been a rumour in Joshimath that an American expedition was coming to attempt Dunagiri and would have a Base Camp near us. We had descended in anticipation of meeting them but there was no sign of anyone. The note we had left outside our solitary tent addressed to any passers-by was untouched. I re-wrote the note, changing the date of departure and expected date of return; I entered details of the point we had reached on the mountain. Of course there were no 'passers-by', our valley was a cul-de-sac ending at Changabang, but if we should disappear forever, without intending any melodrama, we were leaving details of our last location to avoid as many as possible of those uncertainties which make death in the mountains even more fraught for those one leaves behind.

For three weeks now Pete and I had known no other company. A little note from anyone who had trekked up to our camp would have delighted us; the discovery that we had new neighbours in the shape of another expedition would have let me feel that our partnership, though it seemed to us intense and jaded, had achieved much and was working well. Meeting more people would have brought more normality into our closed world.

We took hammocks back with us having, as we had suspected, spied no trace of a ledge wide enough to take a tent. On the way back we disagreed about the weather prospects. Pete had a similar drive to Dick, and seemed untroubled by any tendency to welcome an enforced delay in returning, so when we paused to contemplate the heavy cloud and snow flurries, he won the day as I knew that at least half of my proposal to defer departure was due to laziness. But bad weather did come in force. We were caught, late in the afternoon, hopelessly ambitious to regain the top of the ice field.

We had by-passed Camp 1, with loads much too heavy, and reached only halfway up the fixed ropes, before dusk and storm overtook us. It took three hours to produce one mug each of warm water with the stove perched exposed to the wind. Conversation was terse and to the point. We abandoned further wretched attempts at cooking in the wind and snow. It was time for the hammocks to be tried in earnest. We each attached a hammock by its single suspension point to the line of rope we had fixed in place over the previous week, and which we were now following back up the mountainside. Pete was suspended a few feet below me and I was pleased to notice that a large flake of rock protruded beneath me; I cherished the notion that if a falling lump of ice should cut through the rope whilst I was sleeping I might be caught on the flake or rock rather than fall all the way down.

The hammocks were the full length of our bodies. Three straps from each side were designed to hold a person securely in the hammock in a horizontal position. The straps converged on one point so that in such places as mountainsides where it is rare to find two convenient points to which to attach a conventional hammock, we could suspend the hammock from that single point. The material was nylon with a thin layer of insulating foam. We had brought synthetic sleeping bags to use in the hammocks, as down compresses too much under pressure and is then less effective against the cold. To cover the hammock we had a cape of nylon which draped over the straps and could be clipped in place with elasticated straps beneath the main part of the hammock. In the cold store we had found that we were crushed by the effect of our own body weights which tended to pull the straps together, so we had made some light alloy rods to hold the straps apart, but for our first night of using the hammocks in earnest we did not have the essential rods as they were up at our high point.

It was an awkward and uncoordinated night. Real mountain cold and discomfort made a mockery of using the hammocks. Inserting myself into mine was exhausting. I lay panting on my back, and struggled further to take my boots off. Any time my movements caused the canopy and the base of the hammock to part, gusts of snow-filled wind jetted in from the night. I tied my boots onto the hammock so as not to lose them and, still on my back, pulled my sleeping bag over my feet and along my body. I took a sleeping pill to deaden the discomfort and woke some hours later to find the foot of my sleeping bag hanging outside in the cold and my feet numb. The night stretched endlessly to that point in time when dawn would bring movement and the hope of warmth. Any change seemed desirable. Our situation could not have been worse. Snow squirted in through the slightest parting; I felt crushed by the hammock, and found breathing difficult.

I peeped out when a subtle lightening of the darkness signified dawn. The long journey through the night was over, but the world outside the red cocoon of my hammock and canopy was a world of wind, spirals of snow and heavy cloud. I shrank from the thought of moving into even worse cold.

It was not until 10.00 a.m. that Pete shouted from below: 'Are you getting up, Joe?'

'All right,' and I started the complex procedure of removing my sleeping bag and donning my boots whilst still lying on my back, in order to emerge fully dressed to face the day. Pete and I had conversed little during the last eighteen hours. His silence in the night I took to indicate his greater comfort over mine. He was calling again, so impatient I assumed he was ready and criticising my slothfulness.

I was closing the last zips and pulling back on my gloves when he shouted with real anger in his voice to ask why I was not up yet. I replied placatingly and pulled apart the canopy and hammock to step out onto the flake below. Pete was ten feet lower, still not completely clothed. He was bent double, his hands thrust into his groin, mutterings of pain escaping from his bowed hood.

'What's the matter, Pete, I thought you were ready?'

'I've been doing my boots up outside and my fingers have gone numb.'

He showed me his blanched fingers, holding up a hand as a palsied man might reach in supplication. He could not move his fingers easily, his face was taut with pain.

Immediately I forgave him his harsh words, my sympathy wiped away any trace of hostility lingering from earlier confrontations. I felt concern with no reservations, no embarrassment.

'How do they feel?'

He misread my concern for him as concern at the loss of a partner to climb the mountain.

'They're coming round now, but they're sore. Don't worry, it's not going to stop me.'

In doing up his boots outside in the wind he had lost sensation in his fingers, only realising that they were frozen when they failed to obey his thoughts. He winced in pain as the circulation returned and blood filled the damaged cells. His fingers took on a discoloured appearance. They were giving him pain each time he used them.

The incident served to focus our basic intentions in being on the mountain; whatever antagonisms might flare up, when it came to a real test of resolve there was no question but that we wanted to go on. I did not hesitate to let him see my concern, checking to make sure he could cope with each manoeuvre, packing down his hammock to save him bruising further his hands. It had needed an incident such as this to crack the shell of mute hostility which I had felt building up over the last weeks.

We made no attempt at melting snow for a drink, pressing on in the hope of finding a better place for the next night. We knew well that without a plentiful intake of liquid and food we would rapidly lose strength and would feel the cold all the more, but we were deceived by our memories of ascending these fixed ropes in a few hours and preferred to put off the task of melting snow until we had reached the top of the ice field where we promised to ourselves a spacious ledge with room to sit and a place to shelter the stove. But we had not reckoned with the slow pace imposed by our heavy sacks.

The morning cleared and encouraged us on, but it took all the rest of the day for us to reach the top of the ice field and by that time the storm had returned. There was no ledge to be found. I tried to climb further but showers of hail obliterated every foot-hold and hand-hold and we resigned ourselves to a repetition of the previous night's miserable performance. We managed again only one mug each of warm liquid and then struggled abjectly once more into our hammocks and sleeping bags. Then there were the tedious hours of waiting, marginally more comfortable, until dawn.

This was the end of a second day with little to eat and drink. Unavoidably we were slipping into a dangerous state of dehydration and starvation, but without a place where we could sit, and shelter the stove from the wind, we were helpless. Inside the hammocks we could not use the stove for fear of burning the fabric or spilling the contents of the pan over ourselves. Pete complained little about his hands.

Our values had become so debased that we only longed for a ledge to sit on, with room enough for the stove as well, not for a bed or our tent below. We only wanted hot drinks, not a feast. The next day we climbed 150 feet beyond the end of the fixed ropes and hacked some foot-holds from the ice. It was all we had time for before the day was gone and we entered the third night of misery.

It was a blessing next day to wake to the storm; it left no doubt in the decision. In three days we had made 150 feet of progress beyond what we had already done, we had scarcely drunk a pint of liquid a day and had eaten virtually nothing. We were both suffering from exposure and the chances of climbing the remaining 2,500 feet to the summit seemed minimal.

Retreat was welcoming; defeat was sweetened by the relief of escape from such physical distress. I did not think of it as a tactical withdrawal, I just wanted to get out of that misery, descend to warmth, drink and food.

On reaching the tent of Camp 1, I lay down inside, sheltered from the gusts of wind and lulled by the warmth of the sun which was beginning to make an appearance through the cloud. I was dozing when Pete arrived and he was furious to discover that I had fallen asleep without lighting the stove and melting snow for a drink. There was an implicit understanding that the first one back would always prepare a drink, which was the thing we most looked forward to all day. I knew I was in the wrong but made some feeble excuse about not having a pan and Pete indicated an empty tin I should have thought to use.

The ordeal of the night in the hammocks and days with no shelter from the storms endowed the mountain with a ferocity we had not noticed previously. Glancing back, as we hastened on down to Base Camp, we were as children looking incomprehendingly and nervously at a fire which has inflicted unaccountable pain. The confidence which had grown during the days of steady progress up to the ice field was now shattered; no longer did success seem to depend solely on perseverance. Above the ice field were areas of rock, steeper than below, and with no camp to work from we could not see how we would be able to guard strength enough to climb them.

We spent two full days at Base Camp and it seemed like a week. After three weeks of constant effort, these were our first rest days. We relaxed and ate, losing the furtive mannerisms of those who have come in from the cold. We chatted about home life, about the girls we knew, untouchable idols about whom we dreamed from our self-imposed monasticism. I photographed the ice crystals in the stream at dawn and sparkling droplets on the petals of tiny flowers. We talked about the mountain when the fear had mellowed and Pete suggested taking the inner part of a tent so that we could sit together on the mountain if we could dig out a ledge large enough. I dressed his fingers, now cracked and inflamed at the ends.

They were nothing like as bad as Dick's fingers had been the year before, but Pete was more prepared to admit to the pain he felt than Dick had ever let himself. This I found more comprehensible. His fingers did look painful and I could relate to someone who expressed his feelings of pain rather than subdued them in a stoic acceptance of misfortune. Dick had had no choice but to keep on moving if he wanted to survive. Pete and I were in a situation where we could decide not to go back on the mountain if we thought it too hard or if his fingers were too much of an affliction. At no time, however, did I hear him waver in his intentions of climbing the mountain.

It was implicit that we would try again. Inevitably we would miss our flights home and Pete would be so far overdue on his return to the office that he resigned himself to losing his job. We had come so far and we felt so close to knowing whether the climb was possible or not that we could not bring ourselves to walk away in order to keep to a timetable. Parents and friends would be worried too but we had no contact with everyday life, no external stimuli to alter a decision. The mountain was our main stimulus and it prevailed.

We packed to leave, altering once again the wording of the note 'to passers-by'. Then movement in the little valley out from Base Camp signified life, but it was not an animal, it was a person, and then two more. We were dumbstruck, more humans had reached our planet. They were two members and the Liaison Officer of the American expedition which we had heard about. Pete and I poured out a medley of questions, hardly waiting for their answers in the excitement of communicating with people other than ourselves. We did, however, gather something from their replies: Yes, they were attempting Dunagiri, by the original route of 1939. There were ten of them altogether. The Liaison Officer was sick and was being accompanied back by one of the expedition who had to return home. The other member was going back onto the mountain to rejoin the rest of the team. Yes, they had seen our note and when did we expect to go home now? Perhaps we could work together in summoning porters. Yes, their camp was nearby, about ten minutes away but out of sight in a hollow. They told us also the sad news of the death on Nanda Devi of a twenty-one-year-old girl, also named Nanda Devi. She was the daughter of an American climber who had been on the first ascent of the mountain many years before, and who had returned with her for what was intended to be a momentous ascent of a beautiful mountain by a beautiful girl with the same name. But she had taken ill on the mountain and had forced herself on until she had died. It was a disturbing story. We said our 'good lucks' and went our separate ways.

It had been an odd encounter, so casual when it could have been so significant. Certainly, had we been aware of their presence it would have given us some feeling of contact with the rest of the world, reassured us that we still had a place amongst humans. Both Pete and I had found the pair we had met puzzling. They were quite elderly, we thought, to be active climbers on a mountain in the Himalayas and their equipment was all new, as if bought for the occasion, with none of the individuality of tools that are familiar and well used. It was odd to walk down from an Advance Camp anyway to Base Camp carrying an ice axe and crampons, when most of the way was on slopes of rubble or earth. They struck us as people who like the mountains and buy the equipment recommended without a proper appreciation of when to use it. If their whole team was the same as the two members we had met, it emphasised the criteria that the Indian government used to judge expeditions. Age equated with experience and numbers with safety. They had had no trouble obtaining permission.

Pete voiced his puzzlement as we were on the way back up to our own Advance Camp, thus giving shape to an uneasiness we both shared:

'If anyone is going to have an accident it will be them, don't you think?' We knew, however, that these visitors in their turn probably shared the same view of our efforts on Changabang.

Our own unfinished task menaced every moment we were not on the mountain. We stayed a day at Advance Camp to prospect a possible route of descent. The strain of what still lay ahead imbued me with a depression which made me blame Pete for everything that went wrong. We both overslept and I blamed Pete for not doing his breakfast chores. I blamed him for the late start and late return, resenting the lack of time before I had to busy myself with the evening meal. I felt cheated of the moments I value in which to relax and savour the remaining life before the headlong momentum towards a confrontation with a mountain of which the outcome is uncertain.

Much of the anxiety was due to the apprehension inspired by our experiences with the hammocks. We tried to rationalise our fears, re-examined the progress we had made and the time taken, referred back to the previous year when Dick and I had spent ten consecutive nights on a mountain with much inferior preparation, as proof that we could do at least the same again.

9a. Changabang. The route takes approximately the left skyline. Camp 1 was on the small horizontal part of the ridge one-third up the left side of the picture. Kalanka is the snow peak to the right.

9b. Pete on the walk-in with some children from the village of Lata, just twenty minutes from the road.

10. Joe coming up the edge of the ice field, with the Ramani glacier curling past Rishi Kot into the Rishi Ganga below. (Photo: Pete Boardman)

11a. Pete coming up steep granite in the lower part of the wall. Camp 1 is the black spot slightly to the left of the ridge below.

11b. Joe at Camp 2 at 20,000 feet, with Tibet in the background. (Photo: Pete Boardman)

12a. Pete just three feet below the very pointed summit of Changabang which we did not have the nerve actually to stand on.

12b. Joe abseiling down to rejoin the ramp below the summit slopes. This was where Pete doubted the security of the piton. (Photo: Pete Boardman)

We were delayed at Camp 1 on the ridge by a thunderstorm and the strain was more intense. It seemed as if we were aware of every movement, every action and even every thought of each other. There were no arguments, few words, a mute passivity, clipped and curt, non-volunteering responses. For a month we had had to push ourselves to maximum effort and support entirely ourselves the full burden of the physical and mental strain. At no time could we take a day off to let someone else do the work and bear the strain, always the problem was waiting exactly as we had left it. We knew this was our last attempt. We had not food enough for another return. The heavy snow and relentless wind eroded our expectations.

The sky, however, cleared, the wind swept the snow from the mountain and we regained the scene of our ordeal in the hammocks, taking up with us the line of ropes from the lower part of the mountain. We laboured for hours, hacking at the ice, and formed a ledge just wide enough to lie on side by side. Here, at 20,000 feet, we made our Camp 2. We suspended the thin nylon of the inner tent by two corners, attaching them to pitons driven into ice and rock. It was a tight squeeze for us both to fit into the tent and stay on the ledge and one side of the tent hung off the edge. It was my turn to take the outside position. Only one of us could move at a time, every shift in position required consultation with the other person and it was a constant worry that we might drop or dislodge some essential item such as boots or stove.

The climbing above was more difficult and very much more sustained. We had disappointments at our slow rate of progress but we were solving a tangible problem. We spent days climbing up steep walls and icy runnels and hours zig-zagging round corners. We came to blank spots and strained blindly on the rope to reach other fault lines; we had moments of terror such as when a sharp edge part cut through the rope as I was climbing, and moments of joy at the end of the day as we swung down the ropes fixed as a life-line back to our cramped and tiny tent on the side of a mountain flaming red with the sunset.

The slowness was frustrating, but each advance added to a state of satisfaction. Each day we were exhausted and at no time were we far from the borderline with danger. Late one night, caught out by the dark, I detached myself in error from the rope and almost fell. If I had fallen, Pete would never have known what had happened. The days became almost routine. I was back first, Pete had lost his descending device and had to use a slower method on the long line of ropes. Back at the tent I would chop lumps from the ice, place them at the front of the tent, then slip inside to have them already melting for when I heard the clatter of Pete arriving and swinging across from the line of the rope.

It took four hard days to climb 1,200 feet above Camp 2, to a point from which we were certain we could reach a broad ramp of snow cutting across the face above and leading to easier ground and the summit. We rested for a day with bated breath lest the mountain should notice we were confident again of reaching the summit. We lay cosy in the sun-warmed confines of the tent, eating, sleeping, relishing the magnificent panorama through the entrance and the splendour of our airy perch 3,000 feet above the glacier. Without a hint of the strains from the previous days, I noted briefly on a piece of paper:

> Wednesday 13 October. Today we are both knackered and having a rest day. Can see smoke from the Americans' camp direction. They must be packing up. This expedition seems to have gone on for ages. Be glad to get it over with. Hell of a situation up here. Hope the weather lasts. People must be worried at home now.

Action and confrontation with the problem that had menaced us for so long was more acceptable than the ordeal of waiting. There was neither the constant whittling away of confidence nor the psychological demoralisation of being dominated by the whole problem. We had tackled it in parts and restored our confidence as we found the solution, no matter how difficult, to each one. There remained one stretch of a hundred feet before we reached the ramp and from all that we could judge there were no more obstacles between the ramp and the summit.

In the cold of the morning, before the sun reached round to the West Face, Pete led the way up that last pitch towards the ramp. He paused often to warm his hands, nursing fingers that were still painful. He reached the ramp as the sun pushed a halo of colours over the summit ridge. It was a sign of a change in the weather.

We did not follow the ramp, but climbed straight up, miscalculating the difficulty. It took until evening to gain the bottom of the slope leading uniformly up to the summit.

Bliss was the cessation of movement, shelter from the wind, food and sleep. We were deadly tired.

I ignored the strict demarcation of tasks in the morning and produced a warm drink before we left for the summit. We trailed upwards, moving together, linked by the rope. I was in front and never looked back. If the rope tugged at my waist I never knew whether Pete was moving more slowly or if the rope had caught on a fluting of snow. We crawled closer to the summit, the fatigue and exertion of altitude familiar and not disconcerting; dimly I was aware that at long last we were clawing our way to the top of the slope awesomely poised 5,000 feet above the precipice of the West Face. A few points of metal on our boots and metal tools in our hands were all that kept us there.

I tried to do the last twenty steps to the summit in one go but stopped short, panting for breath. I approached cautiously. The summit was a sharp crest dropping steeply away on the opposite side. Pete joined me and moved along to a spot which looked slightly higher fifty feet away.

The top was simply an end to the struggle upwards. Nanda Devi was clear for a moment long enough for Pete to satisfy his wish to see it. An advancing bank of cloud was bringing the bad weather heralded by the rainbow around the sun the previous day. No anthems played in my head; I only wanted to get down. The summit was just one stage in the process of climbing the mountain. I felt no ecstasy at our achievement nor pleasure at the panoramas on every side. The practical problems of descent and the further days of exertion needed before we would truly be safe prevented me feeling anything more than a relief that we had no more upward movement. For me the exultation and satisfaction could wait until we were back on firm ground. We looked for any remnants left by our friends in case they had reached the top but the snow was deep and we saw none. We were on the summit for less than half an hour, sharing some chocolate and taking photographs, then we started down as the first flurries of snow came and the valleys merged with the grey clouds.

I felt again the superiority in Pete's comments when he saw the piton I had driven in at the start of the long, steep abseil down to the ramp. It protruded for half its length and flexed as I settled my weight on it.

'You're not going down on that are you?'

I was curt in my reply, resenting the implied criticism that he could have arranged something different.

'Can you find anything better?'

He could not, and I sensed he was glad that I was going first. Foolishly light-headed, or with the trust that, having investigated every alternative, faith would add strength to the anchor point, I slid apprehensively down. Having done all possible, we needed now a little luck. The piton held.

It was twilight when we regained the fixed rope at the bottom of the ramp. The rope was our life-line and I felt reassured when I clipped into it and started the more mechanical manoeuvres to slide back down to the tent. In the thirty-six hours since last using this life-line, the wind had tossed it about in parts. It had been blown loose from one anchor point and I had to haul myself back onto course and refix the rope securely in place to make it easier for Pete. In the dark everything had to be done by touch and memory. My hands were stiffening with cramp by the time I was making the pendulum towards our tent. I hacked out lumps of ice as usual before tumbling into the tent and lying there, allowing myself to feel more exultation than I had ever permitted on the summit. Halfway down, halfway to safety, I waited for Pete to come jangling in.

Warm inside my sleeping bag, I revelled in the sensual ache of relaxation and started melting ice for a drink. The ice had melted, the water was hot and Pete had still not arrived. I turned the stove down, delaying drinking myself until I could share the pleasure.

I shook myself out of a doze to realise that the pan was still bubbling away and there was no sound of Pete. I peered out into the blackness. Nothing. I shouted. No reply.

I lay back, dredging up from my subconscious any sound from the last hour or two which might have been Pete falling, thus allowing the thought of accident to crystallise. Hopeless despair invaded me as the pan simmered pointlessly for the drink I had hoped to share and now, in spite of a great thirst, I had no taste for it. My mind chased up and down the alleyways of action, ruling out all possibilities of arresting a calamity if it had already happened. I longed to hear the familiar jangle of Pete's arrival which would make foolish all my worries, but I had been back over two hours by this time.

And then it came, the rattle of gear, the scrape of crampons on rock, no sudden rush of catastrophe but the slowness of control. My fears vanished but I could not find again the exultation with which I had wanted to greet him.

'Joe, can you see those lights?'

I looked out and saw nothing.

'Oh, they're gone. Can you hear voices?'

I could hear nothing, and wondered if he were delirious.

'You've been a long time. I thought you had an accident.'

'I did. A peg came out and I almost fell off. I ended up upside down, holding on by one hand.'

We were accustomed to recovering quickly from shocks; together again we lingered over eating and making hot drinks, without the discipline of another day of upward progress hanging over us. We indulged ourselves a little early in self-congratulations. Even if we died now we had proved that it was not impossible to climb such a route as the West Face of Changabang.

I was unquestionably pleased to be passing down the mountain for the last time. It was true that we had mastered it but all the time I had felt on edge, at every moment the forbidding nature of this colossal wall made itself felt. We were late leaving Camp 2 and it was night once more when we were still five hundred feet from the tent of Camp 1.

I stared and strained with my eyes into the darkness, trying to pick out details below. We were on the mixed ground of snow and rock, groping about from memory to find the rocks in which we had left pitons and marker ribbons. If we were only fifty feet off course in the dark we could miss the tent completely.

It became another bitter ordeal of cold, wind and fatigue, with my body screaming 'no more'. It was hard to think clearly. We could not find one marker and piton and we had differing memories about which direction we should aim. Pete had better vision in the dark and went down on a rope which I paid out, hoping to take his weight if he fell. After 150 feet he had found nothing. I tied on another rope and paid that out. We had to find the final marker point through the last stretch of icy rock otherwise we would never find the tent. He had gone 300 feet down into the blackness when his muffled shouts drifted up with the welcome news that he was on course. My feet were frozen and my legs shook with cold.

I descended, climbing down the snow slope, with the rope hanging loosely from my waist. I kept shouting to Pete for directions. I was thoroughly scared, able to see nothing and relying on my feet to tell of the changes in the texture of snow and ice.

The whole descent had become a fiasco, but I marvelled at Pete's psychic powers in finding the anchor points and markers and bringing us within striking distance of the tent. I slid down the rope, recognising the contours of the slope; my legs folded beneath me as the angle eased. A few steps more and I was home, collapsing on the platform we had levelled out and feeling a suffused elation welling up as I realised we were safe. We had been three hours groping down in the dark.

The urgency had gone from our actions. We did not reach the tent of Advance Camp till late in the afternoon of the next day. There was barely anything to eat there but we stayed overnight in order to retrieve from the glacier the bundles of equipment we had been unable to carry and had thrown down from Camp 1. It was 18 October, we had seats booked on a plane for this day and, with no hope of meeting this deadline, we had no more cause to hurry. We went about everything now in the leisurely manner that our weary bodies and spirits demanded.

Later that day we trudged with heavy loads back towards Base Camp. There were only the ties from home to hurry us on but they could influence little our pace. Base Camp itself held little attraction; the Americans had said they would be leaving around 10 or 12 October, so there was no welcome congratulation or celebration to look forward to. We stopped often, relaxed with each other as never before, resting our sacks on convenient boulders to save the effort of taking them off. I thought I heard voices but Pete heard nothing. When I heard them again I was not alarmed that hunger and exhaustion might be inducing more hallucinations on this same track that I had walked in delirium the year before from Dunagiri.

We paused at the vantage point from which we had a last view of Changabang before dropping down into the little valley leading to Base Camp. Streamers of cloud drifted past the mountain, revealing periodically the summit cone glowing red in the rays of the setting sun.

We photographed the sight until the colour left it and we stumbled in the rapid dark down the narrow valley, slipping in the dust and tripping over stones.

There was a smell of woodsmoke, and voices, this time we both agreed. We saw lights, a campfire. We hurried then, delighted to know there were people to meet. We shouted but had no reply; we approached our tent cautiously; it was dark, undisturbed, and the note unmoved. We dropped our sacks and hurried uncertainly and awkwardly in the dark across to the fire. A large tent loomed up, voices chattered away inside in a strange tongue oblivious of our presence outside.

We poked our heads inside. It was a huge tent full of people, warmth, colour, food, noise. They seemed to know who we were and to be half expecting us.

'Changabang West Face? Boardman, Tasker?'

'Yes.'

Mugs of lemon tea were pressed into our hands and chunks of parmesan cheese; we were made welcome and indulged ourselves in the glory of their admiration; the inevitable pride we felt in our accomplishment, drinking thirstily of their praise.

They were a group of Italians who had come to climb Kalanka, but having followed mistaken directions had arrived in the wrong valley for tackling that mountain. It did not seem to affect their joyous spirits; they had climbed a small peak, had even gone onto the lower slopes of Changabang, though one had broken his fingers in some stone fall. It was cosy in the tent, there were too many things and too many faces to absorb at first; it did not matter, we were accepted into the comradeship of fellow climbers and swept along in a lively exchange of experiences and climbs.

Pete was closer in to the main group than I, speaking for both of us, and he knew many people in Italy through his work at the British Mountaineering Council. I was light-headed from elation, fatigue and the return to safety. The warmth of the tent induced a drowsiness. I was content to let Pete do the talking.

I became aware that I was sitting next to the only woman of the group, a tired, drawn-looking woman who, I realised with surprise, spoke English very well. Without having to make the effort of conversing in pidgin English, I started to talk with her.

She told me she was a member of the American expedition and I wondered at the reasons for her staying on alone when the rest of the expedition had arranged porters for their departure several days ago. Then she told me that there had been an accident and I presumed this had caused a delay, imagining someone with a broken arm being helped slowly down the mountain, and that she would be leaving soon with the rest of the equipment.

I grew conscious of the selfish indulgence of Pete and myself revelling in our own success when others had not been so lucky. I tried to show some consideration for an event which had thwarted their ambitions.

'I'm sorry. Was anyone hurt?'

'Yes. Four were killed.'

And there it was, a stark non sequitur to my train of thought. A reply as outlandish and different to that anticipated as one would experience in a conversation with someone who was crazy. And it was over to me to adapt to this terrible fact, to assimilate and comprehend. Killed? How could she say killed? Why wasn't such an awful fact apparent on everyone's face, apparent in everything around me? Why wasn't it the topic of all our talk? How could something so awful be said so quietly, so casually? I looked to her for rescue from thoughts I could not contain.

'Was anyone related to you?'

'Yes, my husband.'

She said it so unobtrusively, in such a matter-of-fact way, her drawn face registered no change of emotion. For over a month Pete and I had run the gauntlet with death and escaped, to return shouting our triumph. But now I was meeting another side of such encounters. This woman was telling me that her husband had played the same game and lost, as had his three friends. My words, coming from someone who continually played such a game, seemed facile. I fled out of the tent, away from the warmth and chatter, to look at the stars and feel the cool night air.

She had told me that Yasu, my friend from Joshimath, was in a tent outside. I went to find him and he embraced me warmly.

He explained in shocked, subdued tones that Ruth, the woman, had been on the mountain when the accident had happened. Five of the members of the team had already gone home, the remaining five had gone onto the mountain. Ruth went as far as a tent on a shoulder of the mountain and waited there for her husband and the three other men while they made an attempt to reach the summit. The four had reached the crest of the ridge and spent a night out. Next day she had seen them coming down. She did not know if they had reached the summit or not. She was observing them from the tent doorway when she saw two of them fall and plunge three thousand feet to the foot of the mountain. When next she brought herself to look out, the second pair had fallen too and were lying near the two bodies a long way below her. She had tried to descend herself but had been too shaken to get down on her own. She spent a night in the tent watching the Advance Camp for any sign of Yasu, who had been asked to come up to help with clearing the camp on a certain date. When she saw his tiny figure approaching the lower camp she had shouted and waved. He had realised immediately what had happened, being able to see the shapes of the bodies at the foot of the mountain. By that time the Italian Kalanka expedition had arrived at Base Camp and he went back to obtain their help in rescuing the woman. Ruth did not know about the Italians and presumed that Yasu had understood her to be indicating that he should not clear the camp and had gone back to Base to wait until he was summoned. The next day, which was only this morning, Yasu had returned with some of the Italians and brought the woman down from the camp where she was stranded. Theirs had been the voices I had heard as Pete and I walked down the glacier from another direction. Yasu was going back to the mountain next day with his companion, Balu, to examine the bodies.

Pete and I had left gear up at our Advance Camp which we intended to retrieve next day, and I offered to Yasu that we would come over to Dunagiri on our way back. The whole story was shocking and incomprehensible, my reactions were those of someone stunned; this drama had come upon us totally unexpectedly and I was unprepared for the role I should play. The darkness hid any need to worry about what my facial expressions showed or failed to show.

I was starving with hunger; Pete and I had eaten virtually nothing all day. Yasu prepared a huge meal over his fire and Pete came stumbling out into the dark, rightly suspecting that I would have discovered some food.

Pete had learnt of the tragedy and that night in our tent we discussed the matter. It was not at all clear whether our help was needed; unquestionably the four would be dead after such a long fall, so it was not a matter of rescue. It did not seem right that the bodies should be left exposed on the mountainside. On the other hand, the Italians were probably fitter than we were for going up to the bodies, but they were not making any plans to do so. Pete and I both knew of the complications caused through deaths in the mountains, the endless problems for relatives when no evidence of death is produced, the long wrangles with insurance companies and government offices. We resolved to go up there ourselves next day with Yasu and Balu if the Italians made no move.

We both woke before dawn, restless from weeks of conditioning to hyperactivity, still highly charged from the weeks of tension. As Pete went off in the dawn twilight to find water, I went over to Ruth's tent.

She emerged, a tear revealing the pain of her night alone, and was quietly grateful as I explained our intentions. We were going to identify the bodies, and I felt clinically callous as I asked for any means of identifying them. I had to tell her that it was possible after having fallen so far that the bones which gave shape to a person's face would be damaged and the faces unrecognisable. Identification from their passport photographs might not be possible. She said her husband had a gold ring and that so far as she was concerned it was more appropriate that his body be left to rest on the mountain.

We left with empty sacks and long ice axes borrowed from the Italians. Pete and I trailed far behind Yasu and Balu, pushing on limbs which protested their need for rest.

Yasu indicated details of the Americans' route on the way to their camp on the glacier and when we reached it he pointed out the dots which were the bodies high up on a shelf above an ice cliff. We inspected them through binoculars and hoped that the many objects scattered round them were not their dismembered limbs.

We climbed up a steepening slope of the glacier. I could see the ridge, not very far away, on which Dick and I had spent so long the year before. It was impossible now for me to conceive of what had gone on. Now I felt strong and capable, with enough in reserve to go to the assistance of people less fortunate.

The bodies lay on an ice shelf, in a direct line 3,000 feet below the ice slope from which they had fallen. From what I could judge at a distance, that ice slope was very similar to the one on which Dick and I had both fallen the year before and, though the two places were thousands of feet apart, I suspected that both incidents were due to the same cause – fatigue and hard ice.

As we climbed up, Yasu and Balu, who had been so fit at the start, dropped back, Balu complaining that he was feeling ill. They were out of sight when we arrived on the sloping shelf at 20,000 feet close to the foot of the mountain. Fortunately the bodies were intact, the objects scattered around being items from their burst rucksacks. Some objects clung to a rock buttress above us, showing where they must have struck in their headlong fall.

We examined all four. They were joined together by ropes in two pairs. A fractured ice axe near to one body indicated a possible reason why they had not been able to stop each other from falling. We cut open their frozen pockets and searched inside, looking for a means of positive identification. But no one carries his passport or wallet on a mountain. We looked for cameras to retrieve the film so that we would know if they had reached the summit, but found none. We found Ruth's husband with his gold ring. I forced myself to photograph each body, aware of the morbid misinterpretation that this action was open to. To obtain a death certificate a body needs to be identified by a relative and certified as dead by a doctor. We were neither, but there was no way we could take the bodies back for identification, and our only sort of 'proof' that they were indeed dead, apart from our word, was a photograph.

Pete told me he felt sick. I was as if anaesthetised, I let myself feel nothing in order to cope with the job in hand. Pete was uncertain about burying the bodies, concerned that we were acting beyond our responsibilities. I had no time for the bureaucratic formalities which would leave the bodies exposed as food for the crows for weeks before anyone could return here if anyone ever should. I insisted that we bury them and we took a rope each, drawing the bodies in pairs to the edge of a crevasse. They were frozen and awkward in shape. I sensed Pete's wordless sorrow and saw the tears in his eyes. I slid two of the bodies into the depths, resting them on a bridge some distance below the surface. I took over from Pete, who seemed in a daze.

'Watch out, Joe, on the edge of that crevasse.'

I slid the second pair in to join the others and scrambled away from the brink to sink down beside Pete.

'Do you believe in God?'

'I don't know, do you?'

'If the prayers are for anyone, they're for those left behind.'

'Prayers don't need words. Let's just stay here silent for a while.'

In a few days the winter snows would start and cover the bodies completely. In time the crevasse would close and the bodies would become part of the mountain glacier forever.

We gathered up all the equipment we could squash into our rucksacks, responding to an unformulated notion of tidying up any loose ends. Descending, we could see the summit of Changabang poking over a small peak in the foreground – that dome we had been privileged to walk on and return from.

Back at the camp on the glacier we found Yasu and Balu warming water over a stove and we drank gratefully. They were visibly relieved to see us back and we understood now that they had been terrified of going any further and glimpsed something of the awe with which they regarded us now for having gone up to have dealings with the dead.

They loaded themselves up with all that they could carry – Yasu wickedly asked if we had found any watches or cameras – and we plodded down together.

It was night as we reached Base Camp, noisy hordes of people making movements round a campfire. Porters for the Italians had arrived and a sing-song was taking place. Ruth was in the circle and Pete and I pushed in to give her a report, feeling the unwanted bearers of bad tidings in the midst of a happy throng.

We both felt too estranged from such merriment to partake in it and we left to find our own tent and make a meal. I borrowed a large tin can from the Italians and went off to fetch water. It was much colder now than it had been all those weeks ago when we had first arrived. The stream near our tent was dried up. I went off up the hillside in the dark, tracking down the sound of trickling water. It was a long way before I found a flow substantial enough to scoop up into my bucket. I tripped and staggered all the way back, spilling water down my legs, longing for the rest I felt we so much deserved. Implicitly I imagined Pete getting the stove going and waiting impatiently for my return.

I heard no sound as I regained the tent. Pete was inside warmly clad and settling down into his sleeping bag. I presumed he had had trouble starting the stove.

'What's the matter with the stove?'

'Nothing. I've just been getting myself settled in.'

'Settled in? And I've been running about in the dark for the last half hour to find water!'

I was really angry that I had postponed relaxing until all was ready, assuming that Pete would be similarly motivated without need to discuss what we each should do. It was a jolt to realise that my impression of us complementing each other and working as a unity was an illusion. The paring away over the last few weeks of all superfluous niceties made me blunt and forthright in my indignation.

'I suppose you were waiting for me to cook you a meal as well?'

He grabbed the stove and worked furiously at it. In a while he had some water heating in a pan and the evening meal was in progress.

Yasu and Balu had come over and sat in front of our tent round a small fire. I sat with them. It was a simple life. Time passed; a little warmth was thrown up by the flames and we were three shadowy figures sharing it.

Yasu looked up: 'You know the monkey god, Hanuman? They say he has servants who are also monkeys and who rush about doing everything for him.'

He looked over at our tent.

'Just like Pete does for you,' and his eyes twinkled.

There were not porters enough for Pete and myself, so we agreed between us that I would leave with the Italian party and Ruth in order to send back five porters. Meanwhile Pete would go back up to our Advance Camp and bring down the rest of our gear. I was glad to be the one to leave. I had spent too long the year before on my own waiting for porters to want to go through that experience again. Pete for his part was glad to stay on because his feet were sore and he could have a couple of days' rest before having to do anything.

I packed a few essentials into a rucksack for my journey and raced after the main party who had left an hour before. The day was beautiful, I felt fit and strong, confident and satisfied. I crossed a plateau of grass browning with the arrival of autumn, and delighted in my effortless progress. I wanted the sensation of strength and capability to go on and on. I crested a hill and came upon Yasu and Balu, waiting for me. The spell was broken, I was amongst men again.

I fell into step with Ruth, the Italians chattered in their own little groups and I sensed that they felt inadequate at communicating in their imperfect English with someone whose sorrow was so deep. She was unsteady on some awkward steps where the track led over precipitous ridges. I slowed my pace and stayed with her. She never asked for help but I felt I needed to stay with her and I talked about anything to bring her away from that solitary vigil she had endured for two days and nights looking down on her husband's body and not knowing whether she herself would die too. I could not keep repeating how sorry I was at her loss, I just talked about anything, to give her a person, out of a crowd of strangers, to whom she could relate. I talked about my past and my ambitions, I told her about my training to be a priest and what a different life I now had. She told me something of how she had passed the time alone in the tent, reading a book until help should come and how she had despaired when she saw Yasu turn back. She told me of the things she had done with her husband and the plans they had had to travel round India after the trip, how she needed to return before it was in all the papers and burglars would raid their home because they would know she was absent. I wondered at her calm and control and told her how important it was to inform immediately the relatives of the other three dead before the merciless press should seize the news and broadcast it without thought for the hurt it might cause.

We stumbled together late at night through the woods into the clearing at Dibrugheta and I climbed with her next day up to Dharansi Pass and across the plateau. I told her the story of Dick and myself on Dunagiri the year before but felt guilty at the end of my tale as I realised that we had survived where her husband and friends had not.

I left her when we reached a broad path and it was all downhill. I met Jim Duff from the expedition to the south side of Changabang and his girlfriend, Sue. They had stayed on after the expedition to trek around the hills. His team had reached the top of the mountain a week before we had, by a route which had taken them two days, and clearly the snow had covered all trace of them before we had arrived on the summit. I asked Jim and Sue to take care of Ruth and rushed down to reach the road for the bus which I knew went past at 4.00 p.m.

I saw the bus, the only one of the day, when I was still some minutes from the road. I did not reach Joshimath until the next day and sent the telegrams which I hoped would appease the anxieties of all at home. 'Changabang West Face climbed. Both of us safe and well. Joe.'

I sent one to each of our parents. I knew that Pete's parents would wonder why my name was at the end of the telegram, but I decided against making it seem as if Pete had sent it. He still had to reach here from Base Camp and until he did I could not bring myself to pretend that he had.

Two days later the first snows of winter whitened the tops of the hills and my anxieties grew with the knowledge of the stuggle I had had to escape from Base Camp at the same time twelve months before in deep snow. I was thankful that I had not telegrammed any pretence. But Pete was safe and came striding into the rest-house late in the afternoon some days later, still carrying with him the wildness of mountain life and the aura of one newly returned amongst people.

We had by this time run out of money. Anticipating this possibility we had cabled home for more but it had not arrived. Bhupal Singh, proprietor of the Motel, loaned us Rs 1,000 on the promise that we would send it to him as soon as we reached Delhi. But his trust in us was so great that he said it could wait till we reached England. Rs 1,000 was approximately £50 but in that small hill town it was the equivalent of £1,000 and he lent on trust alone. In my two encounters with him I had come to regard him as a close friend whom I admired and respected.

We used the money to purchase bus tickets back to Delhi and returned there in a twenty-four-hour cramped and bone-jarring journey which was made unpleasant by the onset of the usual stomach pains and diarrhoea on coming out of the sterile hills.

In Delhi we made statements about burying the bodies and saw the stress on Ruth's face as round after round of questions from officials and press and acquaintances wore down the control and calmness she had managed to achieve for herself.

We made our goodbyes and boarded a plane. Pete, forgiven his long absence, to return to his office and myself, with no other ambition to fulfil, to look for employment. The adventure was over.

For nearly two years I had been totally absorbed with climbing three mountains. Each one had represented something different, each one had been at that moment, in its own way, the greatest test I could conceive of. Each test had been passed and I was left bewildered. I was alarmed to have succeeded; in a way it would have been more reassuring to have failed. Instead success left me with an uneasy, unsettling questioning about where to go next; something harder, something bigger? Where would it all lead? What had I gained from the last two years if all that was left to me was an indefinable dissatisfaction? Was I destined to be forever striving, questing, unable to find peace of mind and contentment?

We had met death and lent a hand in coping with the accident practically, as if it were an everyday occurrence in our sport, and I blocked out the questions those bodies had raised. As I had shut off all emotion in order to complete the task of burying them, I shut out all the doubts and uncertainties about my own involvement in a game which courted death in order to continue playing that game. I was certain that I did not want to die but I knew that the risk in climbing gave it its value. The sensation of being stretched to the limit mentally and physically was what gave me satisfaction and if there was danger it was another problem to solve, it made me more careful, made me perform at my best, and added a special uniqueness to the experience. If there was courage needed it was only the same courage required to meet all the everyday problems of life, to go for an interview, to bring children into the world, to propose to a girl, to take any new step. If we had shown courage in going up to bury four fellow climbers, the only difference was that our everyday problems were located on the side of a mountain and we were on the spot and suited to the task.

If I had died, I would have wanted no sorrow, I would have been achieving my ambitions, would have been exercising the drive and vitality which made me friends or enemies in ordinary life. If I did not do something to the limit, if I had not channelled my energies into climbing, I would not be a person liked or disliked, but someone mediocre. When a friend was killed in the mountains I could only regret that he had not fulfilled his dreams; when a friend was killed drunk and driving as usual too fast, my sorrow was selfish, I wished I had seen more of him. He lived fast, he lived at the limit, and his absence made the world a little less fun for those who knew him, but he died in the way he lived and in a way which he had escaped from only by a hair's breadth many times.

Four people had died and we knew how painful this loss would be for their relatives and friends. For them we had buried the dead and to them we wrote to let them know it was not all loss, that they had our sympathy, that they had contact with us who had last seen their loved ones.

Pete and I were united as one person, if need be one spoke for both; we had emerged from the trial of six weeks of confinement together with a friendship which needed no words. The animosities and estrangements of that period sank into insignificance, seen for what they were, products of particularly trying circumstances. Through it all the unity had prevailed, and the cooperation which had been needed to succeed had always outweighed any differences.

No longer strangers, there was now no need for the 'small talk' which Pete had felt at first; we knew each other so well there was also less need for more serious discussion. I could guess Pete's views and reactions so closely I was sometimes unsure whether we had actually talked about a matter or whether I had mentally resolved what would be his opinion. A girl complained to me once resentfully about Pete: 'The thing about you two is you don't need to talk to each other.'

He offered me a place in his house until I found a new direction in life, and I set about looking for a job.

FIVE

'Let's Draw Matchsticks'

K2

I

The invitation to join an expedition to K2, the second highest mountain in the world, marked the end of a naive attitude to climbing mountains. It was an introduction to an expedition, monolithic by contrast with anything I had known before, and to the massive organisational capabilities of Chris Bonington. It entailed the search for sponsorship on a scale undreamt of on the expeditions to Dunagiri and Changabang, and a courting of publicity in order to establish the importance and prestige of the venture.

Suddenly the business of climbing a mountain had become very much more complicated, surrounded with responsibilities to more than ourselves and subject to pressures from the attention of so many people.

It was autumn of 1977, a year since the sojourn on Changabang. I had more money and a more comfortable life-style than I had known before. I worked for a company which manufactured mountain boots, hoping to link my interests with my job. I went to the Alps and returned to get back to work. I felt empty and unfulfilled. The mountains of the Alps, which had absorbed me totally at one time, now seemed too civilised, too accessible. They were as difficult and dangerous as ever, but the adventure was lessened when it came home to me that no mountain there was more than a few hours away from a cable car or railway line. I did some climbs, had some narrow escapes and returned to work. Back in England, driving my car, meeting and making small talk with people, it was as if I had never been away. Six weeks in the European Alps and it had been almost a package-tour climbing holiday. There was none of the catharsis of total involvement with a foreign culture, of responsibility for the basic decisions and organisation of everyday existence, of planning survival in a barren land and of being removed by many days and much effort from any outside help.

There had been no compelling objective in my mind when we returned from Changabang. Pete had his job to go back to and a place on a team to attempt K2. I had drifted into finding work without any clearly defined intentions. I started discussions with friends about mountains to climb in the Himalayas and had already decided on one scheme when I was asked to join the team planning to climb K2 in 1978. I felt responsibilities to my earlier plans but was overwhelmed by the prospect of an attempt on one of the highest, most beautiful mountains in the world.

At 28,253 feet, K2 is second only in height to Mount Everest, but is considered to be a more difficult mountain. It has a history of tragedies associated with the attempts to climb it and by 1977 had been successfully climbed only twice. So far is the mountain from any habitation that no local name could be found for it and when this peak, denoted by the code K2 (K standing for Karakoram), was measured to be the second highest mountain in the world, the code stuck as a name and has become accepted worldwide.

The Karakoram range stretches across the north of Pakistan, forming a border with China, and K2 straddles that border. The mountains are more rugged, more barren, more remote than most other areas of the Himalayas, the approach to K2 taking fourteen days on foot from the nearest jeep track. The cost of mounting an expedition to any of the mountains in the Karakoram is much higher than an equivalent expedition in India or Nepal. Rates for the porters are higher, more porters are needed as the distances are greater and more supplies have to be carried. For the British expedition of 1978, Chris was working on a budget somewhere between £50,000 and £60,000.

The team was to have eight members, one of whom, Jim Duff, was specifically asked due to his experience as a doctor on expeditions and one, Tony Riley, for his expertise in film-making. The other six members were on the team solely on the strength of their climbing experience, with Chris having acknowledged supremacy in organising and raising money for expeditions.

I attended a meeting at Nick Estcourt's house with the whole team present. After the two previous trips, when any matter could be resolved by a phone call or quick chat with the other person, it took some adjusting to the need for organised meetings coordinating the whereabouts of eight people, to the steady stream of expedition circulars which poured through the letter box, the minuting of discussions and decisions in the meetings, and the endless talk of the money needed and the means of obtaining it.

I knew Pete, of course, more than I did any of the others. There were six new people to relate to, six people some of whom were already well-established figures in the climbing world when I was only starting. Chris was more organised and mechanised than I would ever have believed. His office was a den packed with typewriter, slide copier, ansaphone, intercom, computer, memory typewriter, racks of meticulously documented slides, bookshelves spilling out their contents and seats for himself and his secretary Louise, without whom he admitted he would be lost. He is a self-confessed addict of gadgets and with the enthusiasm of a kid with a new toy he used to encourage us all to visit him and try to work out for ourselves the logistics of climbing K2 and to estimate our chances of success on the computer he had borrowed from IBM for the purpose.

Chris's role in the past few years had been seen to be that of an expedition leader who organised and coordinated the younger members of a team. His more than any had become a household name associated with climbing. It was true he was older than all of us, being in his early forties, and if he had been climbing longer than any of us his record of achievement was also longer. If he himself had not reached the summit himself of the two biggest mountains to which he had led expeditions – Annapurna and Everest – it was not from lack of experience or drive, but more from the need to coordinate the movements of everyone else and make sure that the expedition machine was functioning successfully before allowing himself up to the front line.

He lived in the north of the Lake District with his wife Wendy and two children. More than anyone I knew who had moved to live in the mountains, he had maintained a boundless enthusiasm for climbing at its simplest. When I called in to go over some more details of the expedition, he insisted that we find time to fit in a climb in order to keep a freshness and perspective for the mass of paperwork and calculations that filled the rest of his time.

There was a separateness about him, living as he did out of the way of the main group of us, out of the main circles of social interaction which promotes an easy familiarity. He was self-contained in his family unit, his wife Wendy complementing his bursts of feverish activity. But there was also a remoteness which was noticeably accentuated if someone asked for his autograph and he was made to realise that he was no longer private but public and observed. His voice would become firmer and lose any uncertainty, and he would speak as if pronouncing to an audience.

As leader of the expedition he was the one who bore most responsibility, was the focal point for sponsors and media, and somehow had to relate to the disparate group of ambitious individualists whom he had selected as offering the best chance of climbing K2.

Nick Estcourt was the closest to Chris, having climbed with him in Britain for many years and provided unselfish and reliable support for the interests of expeditions as a whole on many occasions. Nick was unlikely as a climber. The wildness of his enthusiasms and vehemence of his expression were the opposite of what one would expect in a sport where calmness and control are essential. He was noisy and forthright in his opinions, but if he erred himself he was equally forceful in his own self-criticism. His appearance was unruly, a shaggy black mop of hair and an expressive face with piercing eyes would not help one to guess at his occupation as a computer analyst. Nick was a pillar for Chris, and, as a lively participant in the climbing scene, a contact for him with a world he lived away from.

Nick lived in Altrincham with his wife Carolyn, and their house as a halfway point was the usual place for us all to congregate for the periodic meetings.

Doug Scott I only knew very slightly as a powerful and determined individual. His relaxed manner belied the strength of his personality and weight of his opinions. Physically he dominated us all; he was built like a boxer. The drive which had taken him to the top of Everest and enabled him to crawl down another mountain, the Ogre, with two broken legs carried with it a charisma which it was difficult to ignore.

Paul Braithwaite, or 'Tut' as he was universally known, was a firm friend of Doug's. They had been on several expeditions together and seemed to have developed a cooperative rapport. Tut had become known for his superlative skill in climbing rock and ice in Britain and in recent years had turned his attention to mountains further afield. He lived to the north of Manchester and had a down-to-earth attitude to the extravagance of such a big expedition and the pomposity of some of Chris's pronouncements. In the course of the preparations for the expedition he became engaged to a girl who occupied his thoughts more than he cared to admit to us. Tut was given the task of organising all the equipment for the expedition and I was asked to help.

Tony Riley had taken part in making a couple of mountaineering films and was invited along as climbing cameraman. Making a film and sending back news reports was one of the means we had for raising money. I had climbed with him in Wales and found him agreeable company, perhaps feeling he was a kindred spirit amongst all the other well-known people on the expedition. He had a tendency to look on the worst side of life; his songs of preference were some by the band Dr Hook and the Medicine Show, expressing a morbid disenchantment with life. He would turn up the volume on the cassette player when they came to the words in a song, 'a coldness like something dying' or 'This is the last time I'll stay in this dirty, rat-infested apartment', and he would let out a harsh, cackling laugh, as if he knew well the sentiments the songs expressed. He was generous and cooperative but presented himself with such an air of disillusionment that this was easy to miss. In Wales we did a route in very cold weather and he excused himself for not getting his camera out by saying it was too cold. I wondered if he would find it warmer on K2. Next day we both stood shivering together on another climb, both wishing we were at home in front of a warm fire, reading the Sunday papers. When I learnt to take less seriously his moroseness I found him fun to be with.

Jimmy Duff, climber and doctor, I had known over a number of years. His leisured manner of talking and air of deep consideration gave him a reassuring bedside manner, much as his suave good looks and gracious politeness endeared him to all women. He had taken part in the expedition to Mount Everest in 1975 and reached the top of Changabang from the opposite side of the mountain to Pete and myself in 1976. Of any climber I knew, Jim carried such an aura of hedonistic indulgence that I could not comprehend him choosing to subject himself to the trials and discomforts that he had undergone in his mountain climbs.

I had never thought of having a doctor on a trip before but in Pakistan the rules stipulate that a party larger than four has to have a doctor along. With a doctor on the team there was a tendency to anticipate and worry about every possible contingency and add more and more suggestions to Jim's list of medicines, pills and medicaments.

With Pete, the rapport established during the long trial of Changabang persisted. He had abandoned his job at the British Mountaineering Council in the meantime to take up a role in Switzerland running courses in mountaineering. This suited him well as it enabled him to be near his girlfriend, who was also working in Switzerland not far from him. Currently he was at work writing an account of our exploits on Changabang and he volunteered to take on the work of estimating and accumulating all the food we would need for the three months of the expedition.

There were mixed views about the likelihood of our success. We had decided to make an attempt on the unclimbed West Ridge of the mountain. This looked to be a much more difficult route than the way K2 had been climbed previously. The first ascent, by an Italian expedition in 1954, had been conducted like a military campaign. The second, in 1976 by a Japanese team, had been the first million-dollar expedition. Both of these expeditions had been on the South-East Spur, or Abruzzi Ridge as it was called. Both expeditions had had many climbers and had used much oxygen.

The difficulties on our chosen route seemed to be high up on the mountain and we only planned to take sixteen bottles of oxygen for the whole expedition. There was beginning to be strong debate in climbing circles about the need for the use of supplementary oxygen on even the biggest mountains. The discussion rested on whether man was capable of functioning in any way at very high altitude and whether, if he did, he would receive permanent brain damage. There were reports of a Chinese expedition which had climbed Everest without the use of oxygen, but practically no information was available about this and the event tended to be ignored. Certainly no one had tackled difficulties as great as those high up on the West Ridge of K2 without oxygen and it seemed likely that anyone trying to do so would be moving so slowly that he would be physically deteriorating too rapidly to make any useful progress.

These were the doubts that assailed us and which fed the scepticism of the critics. We decided to take a limited amount of oxygen to give ourselves some margin for success without making the expedition so unwieldy that we would be hampered by the problems of the greater numbers of people needed to ferry vast quantities of oxygen cylinders up the mountain.

The editor of *Mountain* magazine, Ken Wilson, had, as always, his own strongly held opinion. He thought that we did not stand any chance of getting to more than two-thirds height, and felt that we should not be going given that we could not possibly climb the mountain. He maintained that no one succeeds unless he is totally convinced that a thing is possible. This viewpoint was radically opposed to my own, which was one of going to see how far we could climb. There was too much likelihood with the whole game of climbing that if one sat down rationally and analysed what one was doing or planned to do it could be proved to be not only beyond the bounds of possibility but pointless as well.

I could remember Ken's damning condemnations of some very big expeditions, so I was puzzled now to hear him criticising us because our expedition was too small to have a chance of success. As an authoritative spokesman on the sport, he surprised me in not seeming to understand the basic attraction of leaving an element of uncertainty in a project.

Chris had obtained sponsorship from a large firm, London Rubber Company. The money which they put up, together with the sale of the rights to news reports, a contract for a book subsequent to the expedition, a payment by the burgeoning film company Chameleon for film rights and a contribution of £800 by each member of the team, meant that all the money for the expedition had been found.

It was more important than ever to cooperate with the publicising of the expedition. Having accepted all the financial commitments from these various parties, it was no longer possible to engage in a private struggle with the mountain as we had done on Dunagiri and Changabang. Now, whatever reservations and anxieties I felt, I found myself making statements about hopes I would rather have hidden, presenting rationalisations for an activity which at root I believed to be irrational.

Having to justify ourselves in this way was uncomfortable but it seemed to affect Doug worse than the rest of us. He struck me as being in a dilemma in that publicity had made it possible for him to go on the expeditions and subsequently to earn a living lecturing and writing, yet he fought shy of the media, suspicious of the seductive lure of fame. He was ever dubious of the motives of anyone from the media, fearing lest they twist some statement round to mean something different from what was intended.

I had had less cause for such suspicions, and felt that if we chose to do something which put us in the public eye we stood the best chance of controlling the interpretations which people might put upon actions and statements. What I feared was that I might begin to believe the oft-repeated superlatives which reporters like to use, and begin to be taken in by their hyperbole. So long as I could keep a check on my real values, so long as I knew that we were not the best, we were only some out of many, and lucky at that, so long as I knew we were not invincible, so long as I knew how transient all this attention was anyway, it did not seem to matter what other people might mistakenly think. For better or worse, it would all matter little tomorrow.

In contrast with the other arrangements for the other expeditions I had been on, I discovered an element of alienation in my attitude to any problems which loomed up in the course of getting everything ready. Various people were doing different jobs and it was as if any shortcomings related only to the individual. If the oxygen sets did not turn up, that was Jim's problem; if cases of food did not arrive, that was up to Pete to sort out; if there seemed likely to be difficulties taking walkie-talkies overland, Chris would solve it; when the two van loads of gear had gone and were in Afghanistan at the moment of a military coup, what did it matter if the vans were hi-jacked, Chris would get things straightened out.

Many people had assumed that the expedition to Everest in 1975 would be Chris's last big expedition but now that he was in the full swing of organising this trip everyone was saying that he obviously wanted to make a success of it because this would be his swan-song. Chris undoubtedly had authority, his leadership of the expedition had attracted the sponsorship, and he himself aroused the interest of the public and media. Chris was the opposite to Doug; he knew how to use publicity to its maximum advantage and it was this calculating element, this ever-present ingredient of control which made him seem less relaxed, less of a 'giggle' than some of the others. I felt the sting in his comments and force of his authority when he rang to ask why I had not sent him the expedition contract with my signature. I had no experience of contracts and had wanted to read through it to see what was implied by abrogating the rights to use diary notes for one's own writing until after publication of the expedition book, of agreeing not to give lectures on one's own behalf until the official expedition lectures had taken place and all the other stipulations in the contract. With countless other things to do I had not looked again at the contract and when I brought out my questions to Chris he reacted angrily as if I was questioning his leadership or style of leadership. He seemed so hurt by my questions that I signed the contract without looking at it again and sent it off.

So much of the time associated with expeditioning is taken up with not being on expedition. Time spent preparing, meeting, discussing, anticipating. At another meeting there were still many loose ends to tie up. Tut was pressing for us to take some lighter 7 mm rope for high on the mountain; Pete, after the anxieties about ropes on Changabang and his ingrained concern for safety, was worried that the slightest abrasion would seriously weaken the rope.

On Changabang we had spent days at a time trusting to rope only 8 mm thick. In itself it would hold a ton, but we had had to rely on that rope when it had been fixed in place on the mountain, exposed to storms, rock-fall and the wearing action of the wind rubbing it against coarse granite. We had been so uneasy about the risk of the rope snapping or coming loose that we had taken it in turns to go first up the fixed ropes each day.

Chris resolved this argument with his comment: 'We'll be taking so many risks on that upper part of the wall that abrasion of the ropes will be the least of our worries.' And the meeting evolved into random discussions. Chris would be incommunicado for a month as he was booked up every day with lectures. Pete aired his problems about making a prior commitment to a publisher over a book. Tony was feeling left out because now that most of the money for the expedition was assured he saw his role of film cameraman as being less important. It was all far removed from what was going to be an inconceivably big test of every bit of our abilities. Tut's job with the gear was complete, Pete was going back to Switzerland, Doug was going off to Canada climbing. As 'new boy' on the big expedition I had the job of finishing off all the tasks which were minor in themselves but time-consuming when amassed together. I asked Chris what he did to keep fit. Did he go running? 'Yes, well my secretary is very good at that.' I was baffled at how he managed to deputise even his physical exercise.

I read the book about the 1975 expedition to the South-West Face of Everest. All of the rest of our K2 team except for Tony had been on that expedition. It was a relief to read of all the 'ups and downs' of the climbers in a physical and psychological sense. Even being as close to them as I was, I still tended to think they were superhumanly different. I was concerned at how I would perform alongside these others, whether the expedition would dissolve into a competitive scramble to grab what oxygen we had to go for the summit. I always doubted my own ability, tending to withdraw from competitive situations and being more confident, when unobserved, with total responsibility on my shoulders.

I seemed to be less physically active than the rest. Pete was ski-touring in Switzerland, Tut was packing in lots of ice climbs in Scotland, Doug was away climbing, Nick was 'being a good boy' as he put it, working hard and trying to establish a good impression of himself with his company. He was planning to become freelance after the expedition and he wanted good recommendations. I had grave doubts about how I could hope to perform alongside them when all that I was doing was driving up and down the country as a salesman and attending sales conferences. Before we left in the May of 1978 I had resolved to embark on a new venture, opening a shop selling equipment for camping, climbing and the outdoors generally. Being my own boss would, I hoped, give me more freedom to be absent for the frequent spells I needed.

Though the months of preparation for the expedition were not ideal as a way of passing the time, if the expedition was going to take place they were necessary. I had started going out with a girl, Louise, whom I presumed as a matter of course would be interested in the expedition. She helped with the packing of gear, spending many hours of her spare time loading boxes with the equipment and food. So sure was I that I wanted to go on this expedition that it did not occur to me to question what would be her attitude to it. Neither did she put any objections in the way. The single-mindedness and sense of purpose was what attracted her at the start, but the exclusiveness of my interests was hardly fair. A question I was beginning to ask was to what extent I could expect a girl to wait for me for perhaps three long, anxious months whilst I took part in such a dangerous pursuit. Chris had managed to maintain a happy marriage in spite of years of frequent absences but many other marriages had foundered under the strain. Had roles been reversed, had it been the women who were absent, the men may not have been so tolerant. I was interested to hear Maggie Boysen, married to a well-known climber, telling of how worried the men had been when Pete, whom they knew well, and myself were overdue from Changabang, of the days of fretting and phone calls to the Foreign Office to see if any accident had been reported. She had been amazed at how these other climbers reacted under circumstances she had known only too well many times over.

When we finally left for K2, my parents came down to Heathrow to see us off and my mother pressed on me a religious medal for each member of the team, a symbol of the concern she implicitly felt at such absences, whatever reward she received from seeing her son fulfilling himself.

II

We were met off the plane in the sweltering heat of pre-monsoon Islamabad by one of our vans. Most of the gear and food had been driven overland in two Sherpa vans, by Tony Riley of the expedition and Allen Jewhurst and Chris Lister from Chameleon Films. Allen was to accompany us for the early part of the long approach to K2 in order to get the feel of the film which Chameleon would put together from Tony's camera-work.

Being in the entourage of a Bonington expedition brought with it certain advantages. We were welcomed at the British Embassy and obliging members of the staff put their air-conditioned homes at our disposal. We no longer seemed in control of events: sumptuous banquets were laid on for us by the Ministry of Tourism in Pakistan, at the embassy we had available the open-air swimming pool and a liberal supply of drinks. Having left Britain, it was as if we had surrendered individual volition. Only Chris seemed in total control, coordinating events and channelling arrangements towards getting all of us and our equipment flown to Skardu, a town an hour away by plane, unreachable then by road, from where a jeep would take us to the start of the fourteen-day march-in to our mountain.

The white-painted buildings of the embassy residential enclosure were a haven for us from the debilitating heat. As mountaineers we were favoured guests, and the trust that our hosts had in our ability to climb K2 was touching. The embassy is the largest of the British embassies abroad, in order to service the close ties of the two countries. There was something of the old colonial air about the attitudes in the place, though the buildings were modern. Attendants sat in the shade of trees at the entrances to the enclosure, keeping out unwelcome intruders. Drinks from the embassy club were handed to us in the swimming pool by ever-present servants. Our only justification in being there was that we were a welcome distraction and breath from home for these exiles serving out their assignments in this posting.

Pete went off with the army captain, Shafiq ur Rahman, our Liaison Officer, to purchase the requisite local produce in the bazaar; Nick and I escorted each other to the banks where we changed £15,000 into local currency in notes of small denomination for paying our porters. The quantity of notes was voluminous and filled a small trunk which we carted around with us in the boot of a taxi. Nick, with a meticulous mind for figures, was treasurer of the expedition. We both fantasised on the vistas open to us by this quantity of money, formulating in fun a scheme for abandoning the expedition and running off to South America. Our progress through Islamabad, counting out the wads of money under the watchful eye of an armed guard, scouting up and down the street before rushing to a waiting taxi, flinging the trunk into the boot and ordering the driver to move, encouraged such gangsterish daydreams. Nick was ideal as a treasurer. If anything would stop him running off to South America with money it would be his fanatical desire for exactitude and the discomfort he would feel at not being able to balance the books by such an untidy method of disbursing the funds.

My memories of our departure are coloured by my feelings of being extremely ill with dysentery, lying on the floor of the lounge, rising periodically to vomit into a nearby receptacle. Chris, attending to last-minute arrangements, was at work on his typewriter, oblivious of anything around him, changing plans, rearranging ideas. Somehow a decision had been made to retain ten porters to ferry loads up to Camp 1, three or four to carry loads to Camps 2 and 3. The number of porters needed overall was creeping up astonishingly and at present count we looked to need three hundred all told.

Chris noticed my presence as I rose to be sick once again. 'Joe, could you tidy this place up? Could you start loading the van? Could you find out what the others are doing?' It was typical of his total concentration that he could be quite insensitive to anything peripheral.

The flight to Skardu is only an hour in length, but reputed to be amongst the most dangerous in the world. The planes are small and the mountains high. The wing-tips sometimes seem to be only a few feet away from jagged hillsides. It is not unusual to be held up in Islamabad or stranded for days in Skardu if the weather is not clear enough for flights. For me the flight passed in torment, as each jerk in the progress of the plane brought waves of nausea.

Skardu was an earthenware-coloured town, littered with oasis greenery where irrigation channels made fertile patches in the desert. Here we selected the majorty of our porters, trying to impose some sort of order on an unruly mob of eager, insistent Baltis. They had trekked in from miles around, some walking for two days, at news of the work on the expedition.

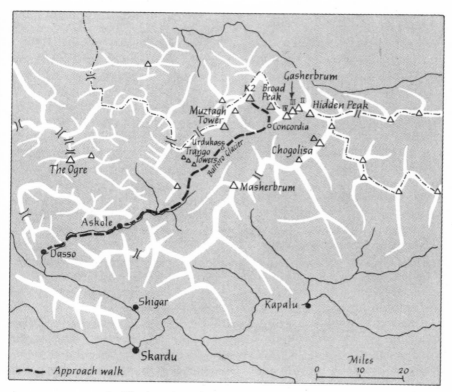

6. The location of, and walk-in route to, K2.

In the daytime the arid land burned under a powerful sun, but they congregated, all wearing their layers of homespun wool, the same colour as the earth. Our expedition meant good employment, and money for the local economy, so the local police were on hand to lend authority to the proceedings.

Doug took charge of selecting the porters. He had been to the area twice before and could remember some faces. In theory he inspected each one for any obvious signs of illness; in practice he selected the ones whom he thought looked interesting characters. And they were interesting. Though dressed in the same drab, camouflage attire, each face had an expressive distinctiveness, and most of them could brandish letters from previous expeditions testifying to their efficiency and worth. The police were liberal in their use of the sticks they carried, beating back the crowds as they pressed forward in their keenness to be hired. Doug was appalled; such violence offended against his philosophy of gentleness and peace. He remonstrated with a policeman who understood not a word and looked bewildered as Doug made gestures of using his own stick on him. The beatings did little to curb the enthusiasms of the villagers. They dodged out of the way till the blows had stopped, laughed at their comrades who had not escaped and returned to press forward again at the first opportunity. Jim Duff, also checking for illness, waxed eloquent about 'these beautiful people'.

The Karakoram region is much more arid than the mountain areas of India and Nepal, and the scenery is harsh and rugged. For several days we walked as if through a desert, with only infrequent oases where huts clustered round a stream. Here villagers eked out an existence, enduring the extremes of climate to live in the mountain valleys, separated from the next village by huge gorges with walls of mud which are dangerous to pass under in the rains.

We had with us Tony Robinson, a director of London Rubber Company, who had chosen to spend his holidays coming part of the way to Base Camp, and Allen Jewhurst of Chameleon Films. The approach to K2 is as hard as anything I have come across which is not actually climbing. Each day we had obstacles to face, rivers to cross, steep-sided gorges to negotiate, hills to climb, and all under the blazing heat of the sun with no streams of water to rely on. The Braldu river, a mighty torrent of water fed by the meltwater from glaciers high in the mountains, was a frequent companion. But its waters were dark with mud and silt carried along under its frantic momentum. The rumbling of boulders could be heard as they too were swept along the bed of the river. It contained the effluent of all the villages along its banks and thus, though water was near us for much of the time in our thirsty trek, it was as little desirable as sea water.

Tony Robinson and Allen Jewhurst were the least at home in this environment, but they coped well with the brutal contrast to their accustomed ways of life in boardroom and TV centre. Tony put his administrative skills to work in assisting with payment of the porters and Allen jumped to help with the worst chore of the day, doling out the vast quantities of rations to our porters. In city life Allen had been a flamboyant, quick-witted playboy whose company I greatly enjoyed. As one day gave way to yet another of toil and sweat with never enough to drink during the most exhausting part of the day, his chirpy conversation came to a complete halt. The further we drew from civilisation, the more withdrawn he became. In spite of knowing him well I found I preferred the company of the members of the expedition. I felt uneasy about what we had before us and was more at home with those who shared the burden. Inevitably it was as though our discussions and behaviour were being observed by these two who could not share the hopes, anxieties and uncertainties of the rest of us.

We travelled on through that ochre-brown land of dust and over the hills of mud with our ragged army of porters. They were a cheerful bunch but, without language, we had little interaction with them. At dawn we would wake to see them emerging from the ground as silent shadows, facing Mecca in prayer; then they would leave, governed by an indiscernible order, each with his numbered load tied to his shoulders by the rope of his trade.

We made our own pace, carrying little, guarding our energies for our big undertaking. It varied from day to day, from hour to hour just who one walked with. The track was long enough and the number of people large enough to spend time with someone, then to slip off to walk with another as if going to call in at someone else's house for a chat. I walked with Tut and listened to his unsettled and uncertain dreams. I chanced upon Jim and Nick, overcome by the heat, sheltering under a solitary tree and risking a drink of the murky Braldu water. Nick, with his adamant views and forthright opinions, was always good for a laugh. We congregated at the hot springs, lounging in the warm pools in view of snowy peaks, listening to the stories of those who had been there before on other trips. Until we had walked for a week we would always have to live the places we were in through the eyes of those who would reveal what was round the next corner before we reached it, or predict the length of time to the next camp-site and describe the mountains that would be in view.

On the way to Paiju camp we caught our first glimpse of K2, a hazy pyramid poking above the intervening mountains. It was only for a moment, as our course altered and it disappeared from view.

That night the camp-site was on the lower slopes of the beautiful peak of Paiju, in a small wood, out of place in so barren a land. From here

we were to go onto the Baltoro glacier, the great untidy serpent of ice
snaking down from the mountains many miles distant, carrying with it and
pushing before it mounds of rubble scoured from the sides of the hills it
passed. At Paiju camp we paid off twenty of our porters. Between ourselves
and our three hundred porters we ate so much each day that we now had
twenty fewer loads. With the porters, Tony Robinson and Allen Jewhurst
were to return too. We had had to cross a wide, deep river two days
previously and if they were to continue any further with us they ran the risk
of finding it had become too deep to cross as the meltwater increased with
the heat of the summer. We had a rest day at that camp. Some tensions
came to a head in a violent confrontation between Captain Shafiq and a
porter. Tut, who had organised and packed most of the gear, was seriously
alarmed that a strike by the porters might make all his work useless if the
gear never reached Base Camp. He castigated my theorising about the
amount of bluff and counter-bluff in the behaviour of the two sides as being
unreal and irresponsible. Chris pushed himself to the centre of the row and
through the barriers of a four-stage translation of statements and proposals
managed to exert some of the authority he presumed would have influence
even with these Baltis.

That night, tensions defused, no trace of resentment was left, the darkness was noisy with singing and bright with fires. Allen took an active part
in the dancing instigated by the porters, winning approving applause and
gaining much popularity with the audience. I was sad to have him leave
next day but the dangers for him and Tony on their own, with little
experience of the mountains, were too real to ignore.

Chris produced a new plan for two people to go ahead of the main party
to break trail up to Base Camp. The weather had deteriorated and we
envisaged deep snow for the last few days before reaching the mountain.
It would avoid delay and forestall any objections from the porters if a trail
was already made through the snow. Doug and I were the only ones who
did not have a specific task which would prevent us going ahead. Jim, as
doctor, had to stay with the main party; Tut, as the one who knew most
intimately all the different loads, of necessity had to be with the bulk of the
baggage; Nick as treasurer, had to make regular payments as a few more
porters were paid off each day according to the diminution of the loads of
food. Everyone apart from Doug and myself had an indispensable role. The
prospect of going ahead was exciting but the thought of breaking trail
through deep snow was unwelcome. Tut seemed to fret at being tied to the
main party. I did not know if he was keen to get ahead himself or felt that
I was encroaching on his friendship with Doug. Most people work well in
the mountains as partnerships and it was inevitable that we should all be
getting to know each other with this in mind. On this trip, with Chris in

overall command, there was a tendency to analyse his every statement or action, to sift out his train of thought and underlying intentions. On other expeditions he had engineered the pairing of people and subsequently the ordering of the movements on the mountain which would dictate the role of anyone in an attempt on the summit.

Chris was changeable in his opinion and his great failing or strength was that he usually thought aloud. This gave the impression of uncertainty but was simply a process which most people conduct within themselves and then produce a considered, final decision. An interpretation of Chris's overt mental process as uncertainty, and any subsequent attempts to impose a decision on him, was a mistake. No one succeeded in changing Chris's mind by any outright statement and each of us guarded the conceit that we had worked out the way to get Chris to adopt our own point of view, whatever premise he had started from, as if it were his own.

In the camp-site at Urdukass, the night before Doug and I were to leave to go ahead, we all conspired to see whether we could each manage to win Chris over to doing what we wanted him to do given that we knew that his initial reaction had been negative. Tut set out to overcome Chris's inexplicable objection to us sending off the mail runners before reaching Base Camp. It was going to be nearly six weeks after leaving Britain before we got any mail at this rate, but Chris felt it preserved the value of news reports if they were not diluted by the leaking out of titbits beforehand. Doug and I set out to convince Chris that Quamajan, our Hunza high-altitude porter, would be better off coming with us than staying with the main party. Quamajan was excellent company, intelligent, good-humoured and capable. He was to assist us on the mountain but before we reached there part of his duties were to assist Shere Khan, our cook. Quamajan was proving to be much more effective and reliable than Shere Khan, always ready to help and resourceful at sorting out problems. Doug and I thought he would be very useful coming ahead with us, but the rest of the team were equally keen that he should stay with them.

In the night it snowed. Our tents sagged under the weight, but by morning the sky was clear. The camp at Urdukass was on a grassy promontory above the glacier. Here the porters insisted on another day of rest in order to prepare their chupattis and dahl for the next few days when each night the halt would be in the middle of the ice. Doug and I left with a handful of porters and Quamajan, who had been assigned to us as our only means of communicating with other porters.

It was a relief to escape from the chores of the main group and head off towards the massive snowy peaks at the head of the valley. I was glad of the opportunity of getting to know Doug better. As a powerful personality it was not easy to pick out the real person in him from the role imposed by the dynamics of the group we were in. Alone together, the very business of basic interaction with each other would reveal much more of our real persons to each other. On either side we were enclosed by great mountain walls of untamed rock. The Trango Towers, the Baltoro Cathedrals, the shapely summits of Masherbrum and the Muztagh Tower. They were all names to conjure with; names I had only read of for years were now taking form. For three days we travelled towards Concordia, junction point of three glaciers, dominated by the stupendous wedge of Gasherbrum IV with Broad Peak as a neighbour, gentle-shaped but huge.

On the first day the sun was bright on the new snow, so we issued sunglasses to all the porters. They regarded them as ornaments or charms and try as we could to keep check they wore them anywhere but over their eyes. That night they complained of headaches and came for medication for their eyes which had become inflamed from the rays of the sun, unweakened by its passage through the rarified air. At 13,000 feet the atmosphere absorbs much less of the damaging ultraviolet light than it does at sea level. By morning three of the eight were completely snow-blind and all but two were in extreme pain.

We were late starting anyway as when we made camp for the night I opened the box which I had selected as containing fourteen days' worth of food to discover it was box 14E, not box 14, and contained only gas cartridges. Without food we were helpless and despatched the two still-healthy porters back to Urdukass to bring, in double-quick time for extra pay, the box we needed.

They arrived back with the box by 10.00 a.m. next day but our group made a sorry sight as the snow-blinded porters held onto those who could see in order to make a halting progress. Doug took the load from one and carried it himself to hasten movement, but it was a waste of effort. We went less than a mile before having to halt completely with the sick and woeful porters.

Our camp on the rubble covering the ice was at 14,500 feet. When the sun left the sky the cold immediately made itself felt. Doug and I stayed up on a mound in the ice photographing the sunset till we were thoroughly chilled and rushed back to our tent, sleeping bags and down jackets. The porters settled themselves down inside a circular wall of stones which they had rapidly constructed. They had little as insulation against the cold rocks they lay on and for covering had only a blanket each. For warmth some of them doubled up, sharing body heat and blankets with a partner. How they slept in that cold I could not imagine.

By morning their eyes had recovered and we hurried on to keep ahead of the main party, but there was no deep snow, and no trail to make. At Concordia we caught the first full view of our mountain, K2. It was colossal, a symmetrical pyramid, so vast that we could only gaze on it with faith that somewhere in all that mass were the lines of weakness which would enable us to reach the top. Clouds came in and saved us from looking at it more until we were too close beneath it and the upper reaches were obscured by the lower buttresses.

We were half a day behind schedule when we reached a camp-site at the foot of the South-West Ridge of K2, a site overlooked by the snowy pinnacle of Angel Peak, a 20,000-foot adjunct to the main mountain. Our objective, the West Ridge, lay out of sight up the Savoia glacier, which curved down round the flanks of Angel Peak. Doug and I planned to survey the route up the Savoia glacier to where we wanted our main Base Camp. The weather was unsettled and we planned to wait but we were made to look foolish as the 'spearhead' of the team by the arrival of the main party only an hour or two after ourselves. There were complaints from them at Chris's insistence on doing a double stage to Concordia which had irritated the porters at the extra-long day and annoyed the team since it was dark before the baggage arrived and they were chilled and hungry in a spot exposed to wind from every direction.

Pete told me of how he had felt enthralled at the sight of the glacial valleys radiating from Concordia, and the breathtaking mountains which enclosed them. He said that he wanted to play some Bach or Beethoven on the tape deck and had been horrified when Nick, with characteristic irreverence, had played 'Bat out of Hell' by a modern band called Meatloaf, at full blast.

The presence of more than two hundred porters introduced an urgency which Doug and I had escaped from for a few days. With a large wage bill for every extra day the porters were with us, there was no longer any option about waiting till the weather cleared to find the way up to Base Camp. We left in deteriorating weather with a couple of porters from our advance group and skirted the flanks of Angel Peak to gain the upper plateau of the glacier.

Visibility was poor and we had to return after three hours, sure we had found the approximate region for the camp but unable to see more than a few yards in the thick mist.

There was old avalanche debris where we came onto the glacier but the mist hid the area of mountain it had come from. Doug was insistent that the trail we should take ought to be much further out on the glacier, but there were many crevasses and the deep snow concealing them made me favour risking the quicker route close to the mountain. Doug stressed his point of view in an opinionated way which seemed to have a self-importance I had not suspected in him. I offered the view that it might be more dangerous to take two hundred porters across an area riddled with innumerable hidden and deep crevasses when the alternative was an exposure of short duration to risk of avalanche. Neither option was ideal and neither of us conceded the point. The porters with us indicated that their preference was to stay close to the mountain, on firm ground for as long as possible.

Back with the rest of the team our efforts seemed futile anyway as another of those decisions had been made which reinforced the sense of being detached from the ordering of events. All except twenty-five of the porters were being paid off, and Base Camp was not going to be established in one day with one carry of all the equipment. Instead, the twenty-five porters selected would be issued with extra clothing and paid extra money to ferry the loads up over the next week.

When eventually Base Camp was habitable and we occupied it as our duties lower down permitted, Pete was overdue in arriving one afternoon and the fears about the dangers of the route along the flanks of Angel Peak were revived. He had stayed down at what we came to call the 'dump camp', to supervise the despatch upwards of the food loads, as Tut was doing with the gear. We knew he was due to arrive but by mid-afternoon there was no sign. Nick and Quamajan went back, keeping contact by radio, to ascertain the reasons for the non-appearance. They reappeared not long after with Pete, who was looking shaken and was coughing fitfully.

He had been later leaving the dump camp than he had intended. Tut was staying down there longer to continue his supervision of the movement of the loads but had opened a bottle of Pernod to celebrate his birthday. Pete was drunk by the time he left and had just stepped onto the glacier, an hour above the dump camp, when an avalanche broke loose from the mountainside above him. He dropped his sack and ran back, collapsing in exhaustion when he reached the safety of the rocks he had not long left as the outlying flurries of powder snow from the avalanche dusted over him and entered his lungs. He had had to lie there for an hour before he felt recovered enough to retrieve his sack and carry on upwards.

Early on in my climbing career, before I had experienced their force, I had not understood how powerful and deadly an avalanche could be. I could not understand why people were killed and whole villages swept away by snow which I only knew as soft and insubstantial. But I had come to know how snow, even only a few inches deep, can slide down a slope gathering more snow on its way to form a colossal falling mass weighing thousands of tons which will obliterate or sweep away all in its path. In the mountains we had to be wary of every open expanse of snow. Firm, consolidated snow is the safest, and usually only moves if the warmth of the sun increases the moisture content and alters the equilibrium of the mass. Fresh snow on a firm base is the worst, as the firm base provides a smooth, frozen surface to which the new snow will not adhere and that new snow has no cohesion when it first falls. Ideally, one should avoid all potential avalanche zones, but it is not always possible.

13a. K2

13b. Nick Estcourt counting our money in the bank at Islamabad.

14a. Hiring porters at Skardu. Captain Shafiq, our Liaison Officer, is conducting the negotiations, with Chris Bonington standing on the right.

14c. Quamajan, our Hunza high-altitude porter, who was holding the rope attached to Nick when he was swept away in the avalanche.

14b. Porters crossing the Punmah river, waist-deep in icy, fast-flowing water.

15a. The porters with Doug and Joe at the glacier camp where they discovered that they had brought the wrong box and that the porters were snow-blind.

15b. The porters in the middle of the Savoia glacier coming up to Base Camp below the West Ridge. Jimmy Duff is in reflective foil as protection against the sun.

16a. Nick, with Tony Riley in the background, on the way up to Camp 1 at sunrise.

16b. Joe looking out of the tent, buried in snow, at Camp 2 during a lull in the three-day storm.

I felt responsible for having urged this route in the first place; and of course my reasoning that a once-and-only passage across it would be safer than an intricate course through the crevasses had been lost in the process of altering the manner of establishing Base Camp.

III

Gradually we came together as a group and the chaos was channelled upwards into an agreed route through another frightening zone of crevasses and narrow clefts between ice and rock. We fixed ropes when we started up the mountainside as a hand-line for the ten porters who were ferrying loads up to Camp 1 for us. With eight of us expecting to be on the mountain at the same time, and the need to establish the six camps we were calculating on, much had to be carried up. Using the porters to carry the loads up the easier lower slopes liberated us to get on with making the route higher up.

We sat long and often staring at the mountain, trying to make sense of its features, trying to visualise whether a shadow indicated a gully, whether the rock step between two slopes of snow could be climbed, whether there were ledges high up wide enough for a tent. We discussed the possible lines we could take, discussed the likelihood of succeeding; we were all ambitious and without jostling for place we all wanted to reach the top. Nick stood out in one discussion, and I saw why he was so valuable when a group effort is needed. We were all agonising about whether individually we could make it to the top when Nick outclassed us all by saying, 'I don't care if I don't get to the top, so long as someone else does. It'll be bloody marvellous if any of us get up this,' and the vain soul-searching of the rest of us was made to look selfish.

Camp 1 was made beneath a buttress of rock, at the top of a smooth slope of snow. Always we liked the security of solid rock near which to camp, and, tucked in as we were on a platform dug by ourselves, we could sleep without fear of being overwhelmed in the night.

We occupied the camp on the mountain as we were liberated from the tasks below. Pete had completed his work with the food, Doug and I had been 'assistants' with no main responsibility for anything, so the three of us were first to take up residence in the camp.

It was snowing steadily as we erected the tents. I was slower arriving than the other two, any load seeming inordinately heavy, and I realised I was not yet sufficiently acclimatised. I did not feel ill, my mind was alive and willing, my body just would not move any faster. Doug was pouring abuse on the tent he had unpacked as I arrived. It was a model he had used before and found needlessly complicated to erect and, once erected, too confined for comfort. The wily old hand used this as a basis for suggesting, without waiting for demur, that Pete and I should have that tent whilst he chose another which he preferred for himself and in which, as compensation, he offered to do the cooking for all three of us.

We had radio contact with Base and thus had a chance to rectify omissions which had occurred through being out of practice with the business of making ourselves totally self-sufficient. At 4.00 p.m. there was no response but at the fall-back time half an hour later we were able to ask for mugs, spoons and plates, for my toothbrush and pens for Doug to keep his diary, and some down boots for use inside our sleeping bags. We wrote letters and cards to be taken down next day ready for despatch with the mail runners who were finally being sent off.

We led out more rope and fixed it in place up steeper snow. Camp 1 was at 19,500 feet and though we were slow from the altitude it was pleasing to be free of the tasks below to concentrate on the climbing.

It was a paradox of the expedition that those of us who had had least responsibility in organising the essentials should be first to be in the prime position, lead-climbing, breaking new ground and savouring the excitement of discovery – the very reason we had come.

Pete was going well. He had made an effort to stay fit by running as often as he could on the hills near the village where he lived in Switzerland. It seemed to be paying dividends; he and Doug were resolute in pressing on up in snow I thought too soft. I carried ropes in support and left them to finish the day when there was no more I could do. Doug had energy to spare for philosophical discussion, analysis of the people around him and of the progress of the trip. I talked with him a while before descending to Camp 1 as Pete was leading above. He told me how he did not find me easy company and wondered if there was any antagonism; he canvassed strongly his interest in trying to climb the mountain without using the oxygen equipment at all, since we had heard shortly before leaving about the ascent of Everest without oxygen by Messner and Habeler. He was always the same, always pushing forward plans to do more, go further that I had the confidence to promise.

Chris closed down on his administrative calculations and came up to join us at Camp 1. Tut still had work to do sorting out the gear into a logical sequence for sending it up the mountain, but he welcomed the stay below since he was feeling weak from a chill and a harsh cough contracted during the cold hours at Concordia waiting for the tents to arrive. Tony was filming some news reports but he too was not well. Jim stayed below to be on hand with the sick and to tend the ailments of the porters. Nick still had duties as a paymaster to the porters bringing gear up to Base from the dump camp.

Chris and I shared the lead next day from the high point Doug and Pete had reached. Chris was becoming a different person now that he was on the mountain. He seemed to relax from his assertive role once free of his paperwork, calculations and the onerous duty of presenting reports on progress for TV news, radio and newspaper. It was only the second time I had climbed with him, and he was eager to do as much as anyone. He took pleasure in the progress so far and enthused simply and directly about how well everything was going.

We climbed up a narrow, snowy gully and onto a rock rib leading directly up to the ridge. Above us the ridge, in profile, was horizontal running into the main mass of the mountain. I had favoured going onto the ridge but the profile was broken by towers of rock and it was impossible to tell from this distance whether our progress would be frustrated if not halted altogether by the many fruitless ups and downs on those towers. From the rib of rock we dropped down onto a steep slope of snow and gained a niche below a bulge of ice fifty feet away. From there the angle of the slope was much more gentle. We no longer fixed ropes in place because we were

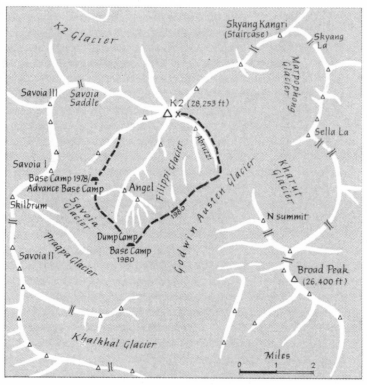

7. K2, showing the attempted lines of ascent for 1978 and 1980 and the second attempt in 1980 up the Abruzzi Ridge.

moving horizontally – it was little more than walking – and a rope would not have speeded up or made any easier passage across this section.

Chris went first for a while, breaking the trail. That was the hard work, tramping down the soft snow to make it easier for everyone else. He stopped frequently, as anyone would, tired by the effort, but pushed himself on and on, as if proving that he was not only good as an organiser. Every one of us had a similar struggle through the pain barrier of acclimatisation, every one of us had that struggle on his own, with only private reasons to drive him on. And everyone assumed, in the absence of complaint, that everyone else was better suited to the struggle. Chris stopped and asked if I wanted to go ahead in a tone which told me he had been waiting for me to offer. So I went further than he had, stung by the implication that I was not pulling my weight, and in six hundred feet we reached a cleft in the slope, twenty feet below some rock, which we thought would be safe for a camp. Doug and Pete arrived and dumped their loads of rope and tents. It was agreed to make this Camp 2. From here the ground steepened; it would be more difficult, take longer and offer less chance of a site for a camp. At 21,400 feet it was high enough.

No one was to occupy the camp that night, tomorrow we would bring more gear up from Camp 1 and two of us would then install ourselves, taking the first place in a rota of people climbing and fixing rope up the ground above.

We expected to place six camps on the route. Camp 1 would have to be able to accommodate us all, but thereafter the number of tents and supplies at each camp would diminish according to the number of climbers it was thought useful to occupy a particular camp. Ultimately the final camp needed to be only one tent for the summit pair. Even if we did all reach the summit, it was highly unlikely that it would be on the same day, and one tent would suffice, since anyone who had reached the summit would immediately be trying to descend lower than the top camp.

Nick had arrived at Camp 1 while we were away, bringing a liveliness and no-nonsense good humour to the company. We had to decide who would take up the choice position occupying and pushing on with the route from Camp 2. The lead pair would have all the excitement whilst the rest ferried supplies up to keep them moving. On the mountain, in a situation where we were all on an equal footing in terms of ability, Chris was reluctant to impose the authority he had exerted when there had been organisational and logistical problems earlier on in the expedition. It was Nick who resolved the question. 'Let's draw matchsticks,' he said, and the contrast could not have been more acute with the computerised print-outs of logistics for the mountain in Chris's office.

'Changabang rules,' said Nick, as the shortest matchsticks were drawn by Pete and myself. Out of five people it was not wildly unlikely that Pete and I should be selected by chance, but I did feel that it was something more than coincidental that we, who had grown to complement each other so well, should be thrown together again.

On 8 June, barely a week after reaching Base Camp, Pete and I moved up to occupy Camp 2. The other three carried loads up and scurried off down as we dug a platform out of the snow on the lip of the crevasse below the rock buttress we were relying on to prevent any slides of snow coming onto the tent. Clouds had moved in and squalls of snow forestalled any plans to do more than make ourselves comfortable in the tent. By the afternoon only radio contact at 3.30 p.m. kept us from feeling totally isolated in the swirling maelstrom of wind and snow that raged outside. I appreciated now Doug's fury over the tent below. Pete and I were again in a similar model only worse weather forced us to keep the entrances zipped tightly closed. We had no other tent to cook in and we had to choose between suffering constant flurries of snow if we ventilated the tent or suffocating in the fumes from the stove. Thickly falling snow weighed heavily against the tent and constricted the space inside. Lying full length we could feel with head and feet and side the walls pressing in under the weight.

I woke with a headache and when Pete tried to look outside we realised that the tent was almost buried under new snow. We cleared the air hole and resigned ourselves to another long wait. The storm was still strong and we could not move from the tent.

We were quite relaxed and passed the time eating, sleeping and reading. Pete had not lost his assiduous habit of keeping copious diary notes. I read Evelyn Waugh's *Scoop*, finding it light relief, but it was soon over and I too resorted to scribbling to pass the time. Pete persevered with a book called *Meetings With Remarkable Men* by Gurdjieff, exclaiming in amazement every so often.

On the second morning we were all but suffocated again by the depth of snow over the tent. Only a corner poked clear. Pete spent a long time braving the furious wind to dig free the tent. Most of the time we did not need to stir outside. Doctor Jim had even issued us with hospital 'pee-bottles'. I contributed to the communal well-being by erecting a makeshift canopy over one entrance in an attempt to create a ventilated but wind-free area for cooking. Time had begun to drag. With the lack of exercise and poor ventilation I seemed to have a headache most of the time. On the radio we learnt that the others at Camp 1 were only better off in that they had more tent space and more people. News from Base Camp was discouraging. Pete and I had no cause to speak to Base but we listened in at the separate time arranged for communication between Camp 1 and Base. This was another break in the monotony, another milestone round which the time could hinge. Tut was very disillusioned by the jobs which had kept him below, by sickness and now by the relentless storm which imbued the expedition with an air of hopelessness. Tony too was still unwell. Certainly the quantities of snow which had fallen would not help us once the storm did abate. A radio call full of such pessimism was worse than the isolation we had known on Changabang. Here we were with other people, but from them, whom we imagined walking about freely, we felt not a morsel of optimism or encouragement.

By the third morning we accepted the continued howling of the wind and swirling snow with the resignation of lethargy. Then Pete went outside at 10.00 a.m. to relieve himself and shouted in that he could see figures leaving Camp 1 and moving upwards. Snow had stopped falling and only the wind blowing snow from the surface gave the impression of a storm. We hastened to depart, fearing their wrath should they arrive to find us in bed.

We need not have worried. Pete and I led out and fixed six hundred feet of rope, watching the ant-like progress of the three figures from below. We could not distinguish who was who, tiny specks as they were from our height. They were slower than any of us had been on the stretch above Camp 1. We could not say why, whether they too were feeling the effects of two days of inactivity, whether the snow was too deep and soft or their loads were very heavy. There was no deep snow on the slope Pete and I climbed. It was steep ice, too steep to hold new snow, and then we reached stretches of rock also steep. From there we turned back – it was well on in the afternoon – and as we did we noticed that the three from below had not reached our tent but were turning back, having dumped their loads.

On the radio Chris said the snow was terribly deep and they had had to dig clear all the ropes fixed in place. Tomorrow they would start earlier and really try to reach Camp 2 because we were almost out of gear and food.

At Camp 2 we had grown accustomed to the discomfort of our cramped quarters and had agreed on the routine from Changabang days of Pete cooking breakfast and me the evening meal. Pete read his book, announcing his growing conviction that *Meetings With Remarkable Men* was not the light sort of reading he would choose in future for the mountain. I unwrapped the evening ration packed all those months ago in a Salford warehouse and wrapped for fun in a centre-spread from *Playboy* or *Mayfair*. The pictures, contrived at the best of times, now were as meaningless as arcane hieroglyphs. It had been a secret joke to amuse the other members, not ourselves.

We lay content after breakfast till the sun warmed us and eased the start to the day. At last the weather was fine. The night had been a cold, inky blue. At dawn it changed to pale and still it was fine. We left the tent, pulling ourselves along the ropes from yesterday. The headaches and lethargy of days of confinement in the tent evaporated with the clear air and satisfaction of movement.

High point 1980 23,000 ft

High point 1978 22,500 ft

1980

C2 1978

C1 1980 21,000 ft

C1 1978

*Site of avalanche, 1978

Base Camp 1978
Advance Base Camp 1980

4. The route up K2, showing the high points reached in 1978 and the first attempt in 1980.

It was Pete's turn in the lead. I stood paying out the ropes, watching the three little dots leaving Camp 1 at the start of their long haul upwards, bringing supplies so that we could keep going without any break in progress. The three anonymous specks were still moving slowly as on their previous sortie, but there would be plenty of time for them to reach our camp with their loads.

It was wonderful to be out in front. I looked forward to the time when I would take over from Pete, even though that would be harder work. Meanwhile I stood gazing at countless mountains that had come into view now that we were so high. The day was completely calm, I was content to be there. There was something unreal about the situation, something of the atmosphere of a bank holiday in sunny weather, a day quite different from an ordinary work day. I had to bring myself back to reality, remind myself that this was just another day in the life of the Karakoram, that on just such a day Herman Buhl had died on Chogolisa, Bride Peak, which I could see in the distance.

Two of the matchstick men from below had started across the slope to our camp when it was time for me to follow up the ropes and take over the leading. I carried coils of more rope, adjusted the zig-zag course that Pete had laid as he sought the best way up. This was the toil without interest. Mechanical actions one after the other and a pause for breath. Always we subjected ourselves to this mindless effort; there was no inadequacy, one could only do so much at a time.

I heard vaguely the roar of an avalanche. There were so many in this cirque of mountains that one hardly glanced up any more. We could often hear the roar echoing from mountains miles away. I heard Pete shout and caught the note of awe in his voice as if this avalanche was particularly spectacular. I glanced round and looked at the distant peaks. Seeing nothing, I turned to move upwards again.

'No, look!' It was urgency, not awe, and below me I saw the slope beyond our tent sliding away in a billowing column of cloud. Where I had last seen two figures there was now only one.

The foreground hid the tent itself from view and I prayed that the impossible had happened and that the missing figure was also concealed there.

I shouted. There was no response. Pete was not certain if anyone had been on that part of the slope. I dumped my load and slid off down towards the tent a thousand feet away. I could see nothing for a time as a rise in the slope still hid the tent and figure. Tears of anticipation sparked my eyes as I rose over the hump seconds away from knowing. Only one figure was there. It was Doug, drinking from a water bottle. I was relieved that he was safe. I could see another figure six hundred feet away across the other side of the avalanche-swept slope. Still I hoped.

'Was anyone in that avalanche?'

'Nick.'

I sank down and cried.

Pete arrived and Doug told us how he had escaped. He had been crossing the slope first. It was deep in snow and he was taking a thin line across to fix as a hand-rail lest the surface of the slope should slide away and someone lose their footing. Nick had set off after him, following in his tracks, with a karabiner clipped to his waist, running freely along the rope. Doug said he felt a tremor in the snow and then another. Looking back, he saw the slope above Nick breaking away and then Nick was engulfed in huge blocks and carried off down towards the glacier thousands of feet below. Doug himself, though clear of the avalanching area, was dragged down too because tied to his waist was the rope to which Nick was clipped. He had tumbled in the air helplessly, landed heavily in the deep snow and stopped. The rope had snapped. He was still clear of the avalanche but Nick had been taken with it. He showed us the frayed, uneven end of the thin line where it had parted and threw it down in disgust. A friend was dead.

We could not say if anyone else knew. Across the slope was Quamajan, our Hunza helper. Chris had felt unwell and stayed behind. Doug suggested trying to make radio contact. Pete made a few attempts at raising Camp 1 or Base but there was no response. We left the radio open as we talked over what to do. We had to go down, go and meet the others, and then . . . ? A friend, a husband, a father, a son was dead and it had happened so quickly. I could not take it in. I had always associated death with a struggle, the inevitable end to suffering or deprivation. But this did not seem right. Nick had gone so unexpectedly, with so little fuss, that I half-imagined we were enacting a scenario, that we would go down and find he was at Camp 1, chortling mischievously at our foolish fancies.

The radio crackled with a voice.

'Camp 1 to Camp 2, anyone listening? Over.'

Doug, big hands, capable and in control, took it up and spoke.

'Hello, Camp 1, Doug here. Nick has been killed in an avalanche. Repeat Nick has been killed in an avalanche. Over.'

There was no response for a while. Then we heard words and sobbing and Doug told them we were coming down.

We had not decided to end the expedition at that but we took down with us anything of personal value lest we did not return. The slope from which Nick had been lost was now swept clear of snow. Firm ice was the foundation left. There was no danger as we made our way across it. Doug went first, running out a rope from the tent back across to where Quamajan was waiting and trembling. I saw the hollow in the snow where Doug had landed in his somersault downwards and the tracks he had made to climb back to the tent. Inexplicably the snow he had been on had not moved, though there had been nothing visible to distinguish it from where Nick had been. The frayed end of the other half of the line was still lying in the area where Nick had last been seen.

At Camp 1 Chris was waiting, unashamed tears streaking his face, as if he too was hoping desperately that there had been some error, that his best friend was not really dead, that somehow we could discuss it, go over it and solve the problem and that all would not be as hopeless as it now seemed. Quamajan's face too showed sadness, regret and dismay. He opened his hands for me to see the burn marks where he had tried to hold the rope as Nick was being dragged down until the snapping of the rope had eased the strain. He had shared a cigarette with Nick and had got up to carry on but Nick had stopped him and said he would go next.

Jim Duff was at Camp 1. It was he who had been apprehensive when he saw the avalanche. Chris had thought it was well away from where any of us would be and had been taking photographs of the monstrous column of snow as it fell. Jim's uneasiness prevailed and he had switched on the radio on the chance that anyone from Camp 2 might be listening or trying to call and that was when we had picked up his reply.

We were lost and aimless. The day was too late for us to descend to Base Camp, and we settled into the tents to pass a bleak night. Quamajan shared a tent with Shere Khan, who had also come up to Camp 1. As cook, Shere Khan had been leisurely and uninspired. On the mountain now he looked quite out of place, staring about, weakly smiling for reassurance. Pete appeared composed, seeming to have come to terms already with the accident with the resigned fatalism of a doctor on a casualty ward. He pushed himself into the tent with Chris, seeming to sense that he needed someone near to share his grief. Doug and Jim shared a tent and I lay alone as darkness came and tried not to think of Nick in the frozen chaos of those thousands of tons of ice and snow below.

I could hear Doug voicing aloud his heart-searching questions about the point of what we were doing, the point of coming to the mountains, the damage it does to ourselves, our friends, our families. For those moments when he too was being dragged down by the rope he had thought the end had come for him. He had not been afraid, he said, just interested to see what there was on the other side of that thing called death.

I felt the need for some company and I edged precariously over to the tent where Chris and Pete were also talking. Chris welcomed me with an unnecessary look of apology for his obvious display of emotion. He was heartbroken. We shared memories of Nick and talked of what to do. I had no intuitive feeling about it. Whatever we decided I knew Nick would not mind. He had always been eminently practical and in a similar situation I believed he would have come up with a rational rather than emotive decision.

At first light we went down. Doug was away first to scour the avalanche debris on the glacier below. There was no trace. The mountain was heavy with cloud, the tents of Base Camp were hardly visible until we were on them. Thick snow had started to fall.

As soon as he was back, Chris initiated the discussion about the future of the expedition. We all sat in the huge box tent, a leftover from the 1975 Everest expedition. There was an awkwardness about the gathering, an attempt to talk about other things, talk heartily about any petty detail rather than the real issue. Experience did not help to decide how to behave after a death.

This expedition, the product of two years of preparation, the hopes of many of us, the object in which other people had invested money and their aspirations, an entity in itself fashioned by press and television, had been in the end the means by which someone was killed.

We had each to decide what we wanted to do; in this no order could be issued, only personal volition carried each individual upwards. There were always a multitude of reasons on a big mountain for not going on, and every reason a valid one, but the most powerful, the one which decides above all others, is the lack of will. Without the will to go on, no amount of authority could force anyone upwards.

Chris's mind was made up. In the long, restless night he had come to the conclusion that we would achieve nothing by abandoning the expedition, that we had put too much into the preparations for this climb to call a halt now. If we could find a safer route up the mountain there was every justification in having another attempt.

Doug was adamant against going on. He had experienced Nick's death in a way none of us had, and was deeply affected. It threw into question the reasons for climbing at all, it showed how dangerous our route was and he felt our progress had been slow anyway, showing our route to be impractical. His heart was no longer in it and he would not be able to settle down to spending more weeks on the mountain when his wife, Jan, and his family and all our families and friends would be living through agonies for the next weeks when they heard the news, unless we all returned at once.

Jim Duff was of the same mind. The prospect of climbing K2 had ceased to promise any enjoyment.

Pete was as strong as Chris for continuing with the climb. To him it was illogical to abandon the climb when that was the reason he had come. He said he felt more at home in the mountains and that to come to them, with all that they had to offer, was a decision he had made long ago.

Tut had given up hope of achieving much himself on the mountain; the illness which had bedevilled him for the last two weeks was still with him. He thought we should give up the climb, but if it was decided to carry on he would go along with that and do what he could in a supporting role.

Tony wanted to continue but he felt ambivalent about voting for that because he too had not acclimatised well and felt that he had not contributed much to the climbing so far.

I tried to sort out in my own mind, as everyone else was talking, what I wanted to do. Chris had said on his arrival back that there was no point in delaying the discussion about the future of the trip and I thought I must be alone in not knowing my own mind. Either decision would be justified, I thought. There was no shame in abandoning the climb because a colleague had been killed; it emphasised the risks of this route, risks which had been with us since the dump camp, up through the narrows, across the crevassed areas, up and across avalanche-strewn slopes. It was understandable to call a halt and draw back for breath. Returning now would be a demonstration to Nick's wife, Carolyn, of the sincerity of our sympathy and regrets. On the other hand, nothing we could do would bring him back, and only that would be a satisfactory solution to the awful catastrophe. We had all climbed for years, we all knew and accepted the risks. We had come to climb K2 because implicitly we had decided the risk was worthwhile, to attempt to climb something so difficult and improbable. We had taken on commitments, accepted sponsorship, had responsibilities to more than ourselves, because we had chosen to sell our project to make it possible. If we returned now we would be £20,000 in debt.

The team was now substantially weakened. Of the seven of us remaining, two were not confident of recovering sufficiently to make any positive contribution. It did not seem at all fair to expect assistance from our two Hunzas or any of the ten high-altitude porters who were still with us. We were here because we chose to be; if it was dangerous, we had made up our minds to court that danger against the chance of obtaining the satisfaction of climbing a mountain. Our porters were with us because the pay was good and they would go further and run risks if we asked them because they needed the money for their families, but it was wrong for us to rely upon such pressures purely for our own gratification.

Chris, with his mind made up, argued forcefully and Pete gave him strong support. But Doug and Jim were at a polar extreme in their attitudes. The debate was concluded with a decision to call off the expedition. Enthusiasm is not something that can be engendered by a majority vote; it had to be all of us or nothing. No one would make any progress if only half-hearted about continuing.

Once the basic question was resolved, events had to move fast. We had to decide how best to get the news back to Carolyn and avoid any leak before she had been personally told. We did not dare risk using the radio transmitter, for once on the air we would have no control over the distribution of the information. Someone would have to go back immediately and only break the news publicly once Carolyn had been informed. Chris, whose influence would gain him a seat on a plane and access to communication which we would not have, was the best person and Doug was to accompany him.

In the afternoon, having mulled over the decision and obviously dissatisfied with it, Chris brought everything up again. He was anxious that we were being too hasty in the decision. Even now it was barely twenty-four hours since the accident and there was still time to reconsider. But the decision of the morning had crystallised everyone's views and if there had been little chance of convincing anyone by argument then, there was less chance now that the decision had banished one possibility and directed thoughts along a separate path.

We began the heart-rending process of dismembering the expedition, jettisoning the unnecessary food and equipment to rationalise the amount of gear we would take back, once Chris and Doug had sent back sufficient porters. They left; Pete and I returned to Camp 1 to clear that of all valuable gear and all of us ferried loads down to the dump camp ready for the arrival of the porters some two weeks hence.

We waited in a limbo, reluctant sharers of a knowledge which would shatter some lives still continuing their daily routine. We learnt to live with the knowledge, came to terms with it in our own ways, though I still had the feeling that it was all a mistake, and that Nick was still there, lying in the tent next door, listening to some music. As the days went on and I accepted the fact that he was no longer with us, I grew apprehensive of the arrival of the porters and the return to another life where we would meet people, Nick's family and friends, and where the horror would revive, kindled by their reactions.

I saw more clearly now the reasons for some of the reluctance I had sensed in Ruth, the American woman, when I had accompanied her back from Dunagiri – a reluctance to face a reawakening of grief which she had begun to bring under control.

Shafiq spent his time hammering out a memorial plaque to Nick from a large disc of aluminium, one of the covers from a big cooking pot. Pete and I took the plaque up to our Camp 1 when we returned to retrieve sleeping bags and clothing.

The walk-out was joyless exertion. Long, hard days trying to cover as much ground as possible, but even so it still took eight days of walking from Base Camp before we arrived at the pick-up point for the jeep. The rivers were much more swollen and we spent the latter days alternately sweltering under the heat of the sun and being numbed by the cold of the rushing torrents across which we had to wade.

We arrived in Skardu on 29 June and a week later we were still there. There were supposed to be one or more flights per day to Islamabad but none came. We were only an hour away by plane but the planes used on that sector are not strong enough to outfly the bad weather which builds up over the intervening mountains. The planes would set off from Islamabad each day but turn back from halfway, and each day we would journey down to the airstrip to sit in the dust and wait with new hope and eventual disappointment. When the first plane did arrive, Tut and Jim talked their way on board, but officially we were down for the third plane and it was another three days before the rest of us reached Islamabad. After all the forced marching to reach Skardu, we had had to wait a frustrating ten days, able to do nothing because a substantial part of each day was taken up with the waiting for the possible arrival of another plane.

During this period of waiting Pete and I began to discuss returning to K2, returning to climb it by any route, as Pete had never wanted to abandon the attempt and I was coming to feel a growing resolve to complete our unfinished business with the mountain.

SIX

In the Treasure House of the Great Snow

KANGCHENJUNGA

I

Shortly before we had all left for K2, Doug had asked me if I wanted to join him and his American friend, Mike Covington, on an expedition to Nepal, to a mountain called Nuptse in the Everest region. Nuptse, 25,850 feet high, is one of the three peaks of the horseshoe of mountains which includes Everest and Lhotse. Doug had planned to go there the year before but had been prevented by the accident on the Ogre in which both his legs were broken. His interest in Nuptse was undiminished and, having booked the mountain, he wanted a third member for his team.

Without a thought I agreed, although the climb was planned for the autumn of 1978 and that would leave me only three months in England between the two expeditions.

We were not at all successful on the mountain. Hampered by frequent storms and constant heavy falls of snow we gave up before long. This second failure in a matter of months left me disillusioned and dissatisfied. I wondered if we did not have sufficient motivation after being so recently away, wondered if we had really tried hard enough and whether other things were drawing us back. After K2 I had regretted agreeing to embark so soon on another expedition, though, after a week back in England, I was yearning to be away again. I had not thought to consult my girlfriend, Louise, taking it for granted that the decision to go concerned me alone, but when the time came I was sorry to leave. Doug was to be a father again around the time of the expedition and I did not know what strains this might impose.

During the expedition, Mike Covington became critically ill and never recovered enough to come onto the mountain, which left just Doug and myself. We spent days in the Western Cwm encircled by the horseshoe of mountains – Everest, Lhotse and Nuptse – as the snow piled deeper and deeper over the tents. When we did get onto the mountain we floundered to a halt, having taken many hours to climb up only a few hundred feet of normally easy ground. Conditions on the mountain seemed unanswerable and we turned back, but afterwards I could never be sure if I had pushed hard enough. Afterwards there was always the niggling doubt that I was not strong enough in resolve for when the going was rough, and the doubts undermined my intentions for the future.

The expedition to Kangchenjunga was planned for the spring of 1979, a few months hence, but that held no consolation. I was beginning to see that my whole way of life was dependent upon the pursuit of a most difficult and unlikely goal – the climbing of mountains by their hardest routes. All my hopes and aspirations seemed to have become linked with that objective, and I no longer knew if I wanted that sort of life.

Nepal had been fun; after the rigorous atmosphere of Islam, there was a relaxed good humour about this little country imbued with Hindu and Buddhist tradition. As a trio we had worked together well, Doug showing an energetic commitment that had not seemed to be there when he was swamped by the size of the K2 expedition. I only met Mike Covington for the first time the evening before we left for Nepal. He was easy to get along with and seemed to look with wry amusement on Doug's philosophising and soul-searching which I found wearing. In the end it was Mike who surprised us all by announcing he was not coming back with us but was staying on in the mountains for a while to marry the Sherpa girl who had nursed him while he was sick. Later she joined him in America, leaving her village which had neither water nor electricity, more than a week on foot from a road, for a future in Colorado.

The winter of 1978/79 back in England was one of deep snow and frustration. Louise had had enough of a boyfriend who was away for half the year and when not away was preoccupied with preparing to go. The Kangchenjunga departure date in March drew near and every spare moment was taken up with the arrangements to go away. The snowfalls which kept the country disrupted and the village where I lived frequently cut off emphasised the illogicality of this chosen way of life, preparing in the depths of winter for an expedition into more cold and snow, and setting off at the approach of spring.

Doug and Pete had been talking about this expedition to Kangchenjunga for some time. They had first asked me to go in the autumn of 1977, making up a team of four. Doug, with his typical presumption, put the question:

'Do you want to come to Kanch in 1979?'

'Yes, of course.'

'Good. We've already got you on the notepaper.'

Tut Braithwaite had also been coming but he had not sufficiently

17a. Pete leading up mixed ground above Camp 2 on the day of the avalanche.

17b. Doug re-crossing the slope now swept clear down to the firm surface beneath by the avalanche. Marks in the snow, lower left, are where Doug landed and stopped when the rope snapped.

18a. The team for Kangchenjunga. Left to right: Doug Scott, Joe, Georges Bettembourg, Pete Boardman. (Photo: Doug Scott)

18b. The village on the crest of the ridge between the Arun and Tamur river valleys, at 8,000 feet. Near this village two Europeans had been found murdered a few years before. In the sky in the distance, what appears to be a cloud is Kangchenjunga itself.

recovered from the chest infection he contracted on the K2 expedition. We needed a fourth. In the autumn of 1978 I suggested that Doug ring Georges Bettembourg, a French climber living in America. I had met him for ten minutes in a bank in Islamabad and Doug had met him on a couple of other occasions. None of us could say we knew him, but we had all been impressed at the very rapid ascent he had made of Broad Peak in the Karakoram with Yannick Seigneur. Only nine days after establishing their Base Camp they had climbed this mountain of over 26,000 feet. Subsequently he had been phoning Doug, dropping very large hints that he was available for an expedition if the opportunity should occur. Oddly enough there were few people who did have the experience for a mountain as big as Kangchenjunga who were available.

Doug phoned Georges and he accepted immediately.

For long thought to be the highest mountain in the world, Kangchenjunga was finally recognised during the precise tabulation of heights undertaken by the survey of India in the nineteenth century as ranking third in height. The two higher peaks, Everest and K2, lurk scarcely visible from places of habitation. Kangchenjunga, on the other hand, lying at the eastern end of the Himalayan chain, is readily visible from Darjeeling. To the colonials, escaping to that hill station from the heat of the plains of India, the ethereal mass of Kangchenjunga, sprawling above the clouds, came to represent the Himalayas.

The mountain sits astride the border between Nepal and Sikkim, and is regarded by the people of Sikkim as the home of a deity, and therefore sacred. The name Kangchenjunga means 'The Five Treasure Houses of the Great Snow'. The 'Great Snow' refers to the eternal snow which rests on the mountain, contrasting sharply with the heat of pre-monsoon India. The 'Five Treasure Houses' refers to the five distinct summits which stand up from the main mass of the mountain.

By the time we were coming to climb the mountain the main summit of 28,208 feet had been reached by only six people – four British, one Indian and one Sherpa. All had promised not to set foot on the summit itself out of deference to the belief of the Sikkim. They feared that if anyone did set foot in the home of the gods then avalanches, floods, landslides and pestilence would be unleashed in retribution.

Attempts on the mountain had been made as early as 1905 when a motley assortment of individuals under the leadership of Alistair Crowley arrived in Nepal. They set up camp at the head of the Yalung glacier and reached an estimated 21,325 feet when tragedy struck. Three European members of the expedition and three porters were on their way up to Camp 7, situated at 20,500 feet, when one of the porters fell and pulled the others off balance one by one. Their efforts to arrest their fall came to nought when the snow broke away beneath their feet and they were swept down in an avalanche. One of the Europeans, Pache, and the three porters were buried deeply in the snow. The two survivors, Guillarmod and de Righi, extracted themselves but had an impossible task trying to dig free their buried companions with their bare hands. On hearing of the accident, Crowley refused to descend to help. He stayed in his tent drinking tea and declaimed: 'A mountain accident of this sort is one of the things for which I have no sympathy whatever ... Tomorrow I hope to go down and find out how things stand ... the doctor is old enough to rescue himself, and nobody would want to rescue de Righi.' The four buried in the snow died and their bodies were not recovered till three days later.

The sentiments expressed by Crowley during that incident indicate an attitude to events quite different from the ethos which normally governs behaviour on a mountain.

Kangchenjunga is a massive mountain, with long ridges and subsidiary peaks sprawling over many miles on axes north-south, east-west. To go from one part of the mountain to another – from the south-west to the north-west or south-west to south-east – requires an arduous journey of several days or a difficult ascent over one of the ridges. These practical difficulties prevented ready exploration of all the possible ways of climbing the mountain but they were political reasons which usually dictated the way the mountain was tackled.

A German expedition under Paul Bauer made two attempts in 1929 and 1931 on the North-East Ridge, starting from Sikkim. They were driven back by storms on both occasions but their efforts met with the highest praise and Kangchenjunga came to be regarded as a 'German' mountain, much as Everest was long considered a 'British' mountain as most of the attempts to climb it originated from Britain.

The only expedition to make an attempt from the north-west, which was where our intentions lay, was an international expedition in 1930 led by George Dyhrenfurth. He had managed to obtain permission to enter through Nepalese territory to reach the mountain, but called off the expedition when an avalanche from the route killed one of the Sherpas.

The mountain was not climbed until 1955 when a British team led by Charles Evans put four people on top – Joe Brown, George Band, Norman Hardie and Tony Streather. They found a way up the South-West Face, using oxygen equipment from their top camp.

The only other expedition which was successful in climbing the mountain was from India in 1977 led by Colonel N. Kumar. Major Prem Chand and Naik Nima Dorje Sherpa reached the top, thus completing the route attempted by the German expeditions. They also used oxygen, and described the route from the north-east as being particularly long and difficult.

In recent years no expeditions have been allowed to attempt Kang-chenjunga from Sikkim, apart from the one from India. In Nepal the mountain is in an area not easily accessible to foreigners and relatively few expeditions are allowed there either. We regarded it as a great coup when, in October of 1977, we learnt from our expedition agent Mike Cheney, in Kathmandu, that permission to attempt the mountain from the north-west had been granted to us.

II

For Kangchenjunga we worked on a budget of £9,000. We each paid in £1,700 and the rest was found in the grants from the Mount Everest Foundation and British Mountaineering Council. This expedition swallowed up the rest of the money I had saved over the last couple of years, but it was more important to me and to the other members of the team to go on the expedition than relish the security of money in the bank or anything it could buy. Georges had an extensive collection of rare crystals, some of which he sold to find his share of the money.

Returning to Nepal in March of 1979 was like coming home; it was as if I had just slipped away briefly for a holiday and had returned to a mountain country where I most belonged. I emerged from the storerooms of Sherpa Cooperative, our expedition agency, after a day spent packing gear, sorting supplies and making arrangements for insurance and mail despatch. Kathmandu was busy with movement, the sky above was blue and the youthful Nepalese flowed past the gates. I realised that all day I had not given a thought to where I was, to the different culture we had come into, to the wonder of arriving in a place which excited the imagination of my brothers and sisters and all my friends. That evening, having a meal in one of the convivial restaurants of the city, I found I was looking about expectantly as if I was in a pub at home and people I knew might drop in at any time.

Georges impressed us all with his dynamism. He bubbled with energy and darted about forever active with the preparations for departure. Beside him, we three who had been together several times on expeditions appeared to be leisured old-timers who had learnt the tricks of the trade and had absorbed some of the unhurried pace of life in the East.

Pete flew out two days later than Georges, Doug and myself. He had had some commitments in England which had prevented him leaving with us. We chastised him for the delay, since it threw more work onto us, but it enabled him to bring out my cameras, which I had forgotten, and some new plastic boots we wanted to test on the mountain. Always feet and hands are most at risk from the cold and we had heard that these plastic boots were much more effective than conventional leather boots, so we intended to try them. When we opened the boxes we were disappointed to discover that they looked little different from normal ski-mountaineering boots.

Doug too was quite at home in Kathmandu, having visited it so many times that he now had a small cache of equipment there and friends among the Sherpas who had come to settle in the city in order the more easily to be on hand for work with expeditions.

Because we were uncertain of the scale of our objective, and because we wanted a replacement on hand lest any of us became sick, we asked the agency for the services of two Sherpas who were known to be competent climbers. Doug knew Ang Phurba from Khumjung to be an excellent Sherpa, having climbed with him on Everest in 1975, and subsequently regarded him with high esteem. Ang Phurba selected Nima Tensing from Pangboche as a partner and though Nima seemed to be older than someone we would have chosen, we were intrigued to learn that, as a youngster, he had been a Sherpa on the first successful expedition to Kangchenjunga in 1955.

We believed four to be the best number to tackle the mountain but were aware of the risk of illness weakening the team. The alternative would have been to have more climbers from Britain, but the expedition would have been much bigger and more unwieldy, and any climber would expect to have more than a secondary role if he was in fact capable of climbing the mountain.

Since we were planning to climb the mountain, if possible, without oxygen equipment, there was no need for the logistical build-up necessary when many weighty oxygen bottles have to be carried up a mountain to a position in which they will be useful for a summit assault. Once the lower part of the route was assessed and climbed, our intention was to go for the summit, carrying all that was necessary on our backs, in one go. At this time, however, we knew of no mountain as big as Kangchenjunga that had been climbed by a new and difficult route for the first time without oxygen and by a team as small as four. There were many unknowns and, unlike the detailed planning that had gone into the K2 expedition, there were many things we could not plan for until we were confronted by the mountain itself.

Ang Phurba was quiet and reflective. He listened to a question with his head tilted to one side, his cheeks sucked in, as he considered all the implications and then he would answer in a serious and assured manner. He knew the mountains, he knew the people and he was totally reliable. We entrusted him with money and he made the necessary purchases of food, hired and paid off porters as was needed and when he came to the end of the money he presented us with meticulously detailed accounts on scraps of paper of how it had been spent. Nima was ever present as his dependable colleague. His English was not fluent, so he transmitted his good-will and readiness to do anything with a huge smile and alacrity of response.

The first time I went to the Himalayas I was worried about everything; I stayed with the porters to keep check on the loads, I could not discern any order in their behaviour and felt that the success of the expedition was subject to their whims. Kangchenjunga was the fifth expedition I had been on and now I had learnt to relax, to leave the ordering of events to our trusted men of the hills. They arranged more efficiently than we could the porters to hire, the food to buy, the places to stop each night.

It suited us to be relieved of these everyday duties and when we started walking we could use the time to relax after the frantic months preceding the expedition and begin to re-focus on the mountain ahead.

From the previous autumn I carried a memory of the approach to the mountains in Nepal as being one long, leech-filled tunnel through jungle greenery and I dreaded the walk-in to Kangchenjunga. The route starts in the plains of the Terai region and passes for days through humid, leech-infested terrain, up along forested hillsides and down into sweltering valleys. We had been told that this region was worse than most but we were lucky that it was March, for we learnt that the leeches do not appear till the monsoon rains of the summer.

We started from a Gurkha camp in Dharan Bazaar in a long toil upwards. It was a punishing climb in the heat of the day, dripping with sweat, the aches from a sedentary life making themselves felt as our bodies were introduced to the new regimen. It was unclear for how long we would have to walk before reaching Base Camp; so few expeditions had been this way that there was no defined routine of stopping places, length of a day's march, nor exact route that we could ascertain. The closest estimate was that it would take us between two and three weeks of walking to reach the northern side of the mountain.

Doug tended to make his own pace, shouldering his sack soon after breakfast and disappearing along the track, preferring to walk alone with his own thoughts, reading and writing at every stop, as if not a moment was to be wasted in his search for insights into the mystery of life. Sometimes we would come upon him having already soaked up all he wanted to see and photograph of an interesting village or temple, proffering for us to sample some delicious oranges, another of his discoveries.

Georges, Pete and I often walked together. It was fun to have someone as boisterous and volatile as Georges to discover as a person. Perhaps because we knew so little of him or perhaps because, being French, there was a cultural difference in his attitude, Georges had a viewpoint on many topics quite different from any I had known. He spoke English very well but he still retained the directness of language of someone speaking a foreign tongue and was not inhibited in his words and expression. He had not learnt to cloak his meaning with nuance and metaphor.

Georges fulfilled in many ways the stereotype of the eligible Frenchman. He was married and talked often of his wife, so we felt that we knew her, but he could not resist playing the Gallic charmer. He was dark-haired, bronzed and wore a neat head-band which gave him a cavalier attractiveness. On the flight from London we had touched down in Moscow and, seeing two Russian air stewardesses sitting alone, Georges sat himself beside them. He embarked on a rapid chat, of which they understood not a word, looking at him in confusion until an armed guard inspired them to move off.

Georges talked freely of many things. He spoke of his love life and his attitude to relations with his wife and other women with a frankness which Pete, with all his reserve and delicacy of expression, found astonishing. Pete talked more frequently than I had noticed before of sex and marriage, questioning Georges, as if he were an expert, about the whole business. Georges was glad to expand on his ideas about 'chicks' or 'birds', as he put it, using the words consciously, proud of their acquisition into his vocabulary as marking a step forward in his grasp of the language. He believed in open relationships and felt that if two people were living together or married this need not preclude relationship of a temporary nature with other people, given that one understood who one really loved. If two people were separated for a long spell, such as we ourselves going off on this expedition would be separated from wife or girlfriend, he thought it perfectly acceptable that either partner should form a relationships with someone if the need was felt during the separation. Pete would listen in open-mouthed amazement to these opinions which were radically opposed to his own concepts of love and marriage. But he was fascinated by Georges's openness and quizzed him again and again about subjects he himself was normally too reticent to discuss except in most general terms.

We were all aware that we were imposing a strange mode of living on ourselves by cutting ourselves off for many weeks from our loved ones. Doug believed that having any female company on a trip would exercise a civilising influence on behaviour and introduce a more balanced element into the little, isolated society of the expedition. For some reason Pete thought I was opposed to the idea, giving me a glimpse of the impression he had formed of me as a single-minded fanatic, who wanted no distraction from the chosen objective. In principle everyone agreed that a mixed expedition or female company on an expedition would be desirable, but we suspected that many people held an idealised view of expedition life and did not see it for the hard work and deprivation it was.

We were some days along the way before I really turned my attention to the mountain we had come to climb. For two days I was ill with severe stomach cramps, nausea and diarrhoea, wanting to do nothing but rest and forcing myself along the track oblivious of the surroundings. Doug was all solicitous and caring, seeking out medicines and preparing herbal teas which he thought would cure me. He gave me a bottle of Kaolo Morphine and I walked with it in my hand, taking swigs to quell the nausea and hoping the morphine would drug me enough to blank out the physical distress.

Pete voiced his concern that we were being too casual in our approach to the mountain, that we would all have to be at the peak of form to have a hope of reaching the top and that we were perhaps taking too much for granted. He had taken to following Doug's example in taking milk drinks in Kathmandu instead of beer; he followed Georges in what he ate and the exercise he took. Georges had climbed a very high mountain without oxygen in a rapid time and Pete wanted to find and use the formula for success which he believed Georges must have had. Lest the secret lay in his diet or training schedule, he imitated Georges's every move. If Georges went for a run, so did Pete; in the evening when the restless Georges scrambled about on boulders, practising climbing moves, so did Pete.

When I thought about it seriously I knew he was right, I knew I too should be pursuing a rigorous training programme, and wondered if I had left it too late to achieve the fitness necessary to climb this mountain. Always I intended to join them but always the next chapter of the book I was reading drew me on and they would be back from their exercise before I was ready to go.

For two days we walked along the crest of the rounded ridge dividing the Arun and Tamur valleys. We passed through the villages of well-built houses and forests of rhododendrons. The track was the main highway for the villages of the region and streams of porters dwarfed by their colossal loads passed in both directions, carrying vegetables and fruit one way, returning days later with boxes of footwear and products bought in the bazaar. The climate was ideal for those two days, for we had climbed out of the sticky heat to 8,000 feet and a cooling breeze made life pleasant.

We reached a village at the end of the ridge and from there we had to descend to the valley, to the jungle and heat once again. Above the village, in the sky hovering white and unobtrusive in the distance so I thought it was a cloud, was the mountain. We were not yet halfway there and it stood up big and massive. From the warmth of the track amidst this greenery I could not imagine how cold it would be twenty thousand feet higher, amongst those snows, and I could not imagine how we four could climb a mountain so big. Suddenly I was aware of how small we were.

We passed above a cluster of huts from where the metallic reverberation of transistorised music made itself heard. It seemed grotesquely out of place in these surroundings, many miles from the roads and pylons which symbolise modern life, to hear the strains of an English song, the words and music distorted by too much volume, but just discernible as 'Goodbye my friends it's hard to die . . .'. We had to laugh at the irony of the coincidence of our passing at that moment. Georges was full of equally macabre comments about what might happen to us on the mountain and preyed on Pete's nerves in his artless manner.

There were none of the tensions which might have been expected under the pressure of the difficulties and prolonged effort ahead. Most of the everyday chores were attended to by our cook, Kami, and the cook boy whom we had not asked for but had known better than to object to when Kami brought him along. There was some dispute with the porters when we reached a halfway point in the approach about a week after starting. Ang Phurba and Nima sorted out the problem while we lay in the sunshine and swam in a clear, pleasantly warm river. The Liaison Officer, Mohan Bahadur Thapa, who had been assigned to us, turned out to be a comic character. He always wore a little woollen hat, shy of revealing the bald patch on his head, and blaming that for his failure to marry. He spoke English well, with the quaintness of tongue of someone reared on Dickens and Shakespeare, using words which were appropriate but had long passed out of common usage. He liked to talk with us, gaining practice in the use of English and recounting tales from his life in the police force. Some of his anecdotes were very amusing and he recited them, rolling words round with his tongue and repeating a word if he liked its sound, so that it was as much a pleasure to listen to his manner of speech as to his story of some narrow escape. In theory he was with us to make sure that we did not contravene any of his country's laws; in practice he knew that we had no intention of doing this and he was settling into the expedition to enjoy a break from his routine duties, to enjoy the company of visitors from abroad and the prospect of valuable clothing and equipment at the end of the expedition.

On the ninth day of the walk-in we had reached the camp-site for the night by early afternoon. I lay in the shade of a rock reading *The Seven Pillars of Wisdom* by T. E. Lawrence, intending to finish a chapter before joining the other three who were a short distance away, scrambling up and down steep walls on the huge boulders littering the clearing in the forest. Pete appeared from behind the rock in whose shade I was lying and I saw that he was limping.

'What have you done?'

'I don't know. Georges bloody well pushed me. I heard something crack. He was really stupid. It might be broken.'

Georges had climbed a smooth slab of rock, tilted at an angle of 70°, relying upon the friction of his footwear on the rough rock to inch his way up the fifteen feet to the top. It was a game, Pete, Georges and Doug each trying to find something to climb which the other two could not follow. Pete did follow up this problem and Georges, boisterous as ever, had played

'King of the Castle', pushing playfully at Pete as he made to stand on the top. Knocked out of balance, Pete had nothing positive to grasp for, and he fell to the ground, landing awkwardly on a tuft of grass. His foot twisted under him and he both felt and heard a crack somewhere in his left ankle.

At first he had thought it was a bad wrench, but the pain was so intense that he could hardly stand on his foot. Georges, looking very contrite and crestfallen, hovered about, regretting the outcome of his restless energy. Doug took Pete's foot in his large hands, squeezing gently but firmly, searching for the source of pain and trying to decide whether a bone was broken or some ligaments sprained.

The full implications of the situation only gradually emerged as Pete's ankle became more and more swollen, the pain grew no less and any attempt to walk on it was unbearable.

We were nine days along the trail. Three days away in another direction was an airstrip with one flight each week. For us all to go back could mean the end of the expedition and for Pete to go back for treatment in a hospital would mean he would have a difficult task, if his foot did recover in time, to get back into sequence with us and reach the level of acclimatisation which we would have achieved after a couple of weeks on the mountain. Whatever he was to do there was the problem of how to do it in this mountainous country, where narrow paths wound up and down precipitous hillsides and the only means of movement was by foot. Suddenly Pete's chances of climbing Kangchenjunga were thrown into doubt, a heavy depression emanated from him and influenced the whole camp.

He controlled his appearance of anger, but let fly occasional biting comments which revealed his inner turmoil. Georges flinched at every word, mortified now, like a child who had meant no harm, at the consequences of a thoughtless action.

I tried to reassure Pete that he would be all right, that break or sprain there was still a week before we would even reach the mountain; a break would have time to knit together by then, a sprain would linger on but, supported in a boot, should be better.

We ordered bowls of hot water from the cook and bathed his foot to ease the pain, then someone said cold water was better for sprains so we ordered cold water and he bathed his foot in that. If the worst happened and he could not walk by morning we toyed with the idea of hiring a yak, though whether he would be able to ride such a beast of uncertain temper along these narrow tracks we did not know.

The spirit had left the boisterous Georges, he took on a lack-lustre appearance and his innocent spontaneity seemed to be gone forever. From that one incident he had become wise. Nothing would revive his former playfulness and sense of fun; he tried to apologise with that anguish of regret for a thing done that cannot be undone, and lay sombre and silent in a black mood of guilt and paranoia. Pete shuffled restlessly, unable to settle comfortably. In whatever position he lay or sat he seemed to feel the stones from the ground, the rock behind dug into his back. He did not know what to do with himself. Everything depended on his being able to walk again in time to climb the mountain. I could only guess at the disappointment he was feeling, because he appeared so normal. I thought back to the time when I too had faced the prospect of failing even to reach a mountain through a simple toothache. I told him that story as a parable of hopes shattered and then restored to show him how all might not be lost however bad things looked for the moment. He stopped making notes in his diary – there seemed little point in keeping a diary of a non-expedition.

At evening a cluster of hill people formed round the cook's fire. Among them was a young girl, the prettiest we had seen among the mountain people. To distract Pete from his woes I asked the cook to persuade the girl to carry the evening meal over to him, but even her good looks failed to lighten the misery which had settled on him.

At daybreak it was clear that Pete's foot had not improved. He had resolved to carry on with the expedition in the hope that the injury would heal and give him back the chance of climbing the mountain, but even on makeshift crutches he could not get more than a few yards on the rough ground.

Ang Phurba, resourceful as ever, produced the answer. A yak would be too unpredictable on the mountain paths but he had found a porter who was prepared to carry Pete on his back for the same price as we had intended paying for the hire of the yak. The porter stood behind Ang Phurba, barely five foot in height. He had on short cotton trousers and a well-used jacket. He wore nothing on his feet and his bare legs were thin, all sinew and muscle, with no surplus flesh. Tucked under his arm was the hemp rope, blackened from much use, the symbol of his trade. He could hardly have weighed eight stone and he was proposing to carry Pete, who weighed thirteen stone.

A conical basket, normally used to carry fruit or vegetables to market, was cut into and fashioned to make a seat. Pete was helped into it and the porter cradled the basket in his loop of rope, settling the other end of the loop over his forehead. Carefully he eased himself upright, taking the strain on his forehead, and a slow, halting progress was achieved, with Pete facing back along the track, swaying uncertainly as he accustomed himself to this odd means of transportation.

The porter could only walk for a few minutes before having to stop, resting his heavy burden on the T-shaped stick he carried for this purpose, to avoid the laborious procedure of having the basket lifted down and back up. Pete would sit, helpless and immobile, as the rest of the porters plodded by, as if symbolising the expedition drawing away from its wounded member. There was an invisible and unmentioned barrier between the injured Pete and us who were fit. We hovered near his litter, reining in on our natural pace to keep him company so that he would not feel an outcast. But walking more slowly than usual, and halting more frequently than needed, was fatiguing. There was also hesitation in that Pete might feel we were pitying him, so gradually but inevitably he was left behind, and we would see him after hours apart when we halted for a tea break.

After two days of extremely slow progress two porters were hired to carry Pete in relays. The narrow track wound up ever-steeper hillsides, zig-zagging upwards above dizzying heights. Looking back at the tiny figures on the track which was barely two feet wide, I wondered at the likelihood of the porter stumbling and sending Pete flying over the edge, down the thousands of feet to the torrent whose noise was faint by the time it reached us.

The porters who shared the enormous burden seemed resigned; when they hoisted the load upwards, their faces set into the grim expression of someone under the utmost strain, sinews on neck and legs stood out like cords and they strode purposefully, unable to linger long under the load. The task represented a way of earning more money. They showed neither pleasure nor displeasure, as if resigned to an existence which was always hard work.

For the first two days Pete had a problem with sunburn, since he had to sit motionless in the fierce heat of the sun, but the weather changed to days of mist and rain. What had been at the start alarming and extraordinary became everyday and matter of fact. A routine was established in which Nima took charge of the attendants who carried Pete and it seemed that they could carry him almost anywhere. It was certain now that he would physically reach Base Camp but his morale was low.

The pretty girl whom we first saw on the day of Pete's accident had joined our convoy. She was with her mother, a sister and a brother. They too were going in the same direction, making for their summer home in the village of Ghunza. We learnt that the pretty girl's name was Dawa and when the mother saw us photographing the girl and enquiring of Ang Phurba about her marital status she replied that the girl was married to a very big man who had an equally big gun and was very jealous. But it was all light-hearted. They shared our campfires at night and when it rained we lent them tents. The mother sought help from Doug for her hard cough and fractured ribs. I felt that we belonged more to the country travelling as we were. Only the four of us were foreigners. Our fifty porters were all from the region, Ang Phurba and Nima knew the area and spoke the language, though it was a different dialect from their own. We were not so big a foreign group that we swamped the villages we entered. We needed local produce and the local people came to us for medicine. Walking was the normal mode of travel and it seemed a sign that we were accepted when the family tagged on to our party and later policemen and their wives, on the way to the police post at Ghunza, joined us too.

I dreamt one night that one of us was killed in an avalanche on the mountain, but in the dream there were five in the team. There was panic because the news had leaked out before we had time to inform all concerned; then I woke with a restless sense of disquiet. I did not like to admit to any superstition in myself which would give credence to the content of a dream and I did not tell the others for fear of arousing thoughts which might undermine confidence. Later in the day I wrote down the dream, wanting to face up squarely to the thoughts and fears in my subconscious and hoping thus to exorcise any morbidity from my mind.

On another night I dreamt that Pete and I were going for the summit. I did not think that this was prophetic either but I told Pete about the dream to let him see that I was not simply encouraging his hopes out of charity but even subconsciously I still saw him as capable of getting up the mountain. He was visibly cheered as if I had passed him a compliment.

At Ghunza we had to wait for a while. The village was at 11,480 feet and here we paid off the lowland porters and arranged to hire yaks for the remaining days up to Base Camp. After four days of being carried, Pete began to make his first faltering steps. We waited an extra day as we all felt breathless from the altitude and Pete's mobility was increasing daily.

Georges, who had been subdued ever since the accident, was further adversely affected by a heavy cold which made him fret and sample every sort of tablet and medicine he could find.

We had each brought a selection of cassette tapes, but Georges, as with books, showed least interest in listening to music and he found punk rock completely intolerable. Doug played mostly Bob Dylan on a small cassette deck which he never let far from himself, as if he could not bear to be without the solace of music. Pete and I played mostly rock music, though in more reflective moments Pete liked to listen to something classical or some jazz. We had only one other cassette deck so Pete and I usually camped close to each other so that we could each hear the music no matter who actually had the machine. One night I had the tape deck on low close to my ear and had fallen asleep to the sound of Pink Floyd, wondering if it was loud enough for Pete nearby to hear. I was startled awake by Georges shouting to me to turn the volume down as he couldn't sleep, and by the time the message had got through to my sleepy brain I was aware by the sounds from the other tents that everyone else had been woken up too.

Next morning the camp was woken again by Georges announcing that he was feeling much better, and his cold seemed to be gone. A few minutes later he announced that it was snowing heavily outside and that we should go back to sleep for a while till the sun should be up. Georges's extrovert spontaneity was quite different from the more silent and deliberated behaviour I sought myself. I did not like being woken needlessly but in many other ways Georges's manner contributed a freshness and vitality to the reserve and restraint which had come to be the mode of interaction between Pete, Doug and myself.

When we left the village Pete was able to make the distance to the hamlet of Kangbachen, our next stopping place, in good time. He limped along, leaning heavily on ski-sticks, to ease the pressure on his foot. In the determination which he showed in overcoming the seemingly hopeless restrictions imposed by a broken foot, and not to let himself be beaten in his resolve to climb Kangchenjunga, it was possible to glimpse something of the relentless sense of purpose which drove the man. Beneath an exterior which sometimes seemed helpless and awkward there was an iron-hard will which was only applied when the need arose. With the improvement in Pete's performance, some of the old restlessness returned to Georges. He shot off up the hillside as soon as we made camp and finished the afternoon scrambling about on another boulder.

The distance to Base Camp was nothing like as far as the wily villagers of Ghunza had described it to be. It was three days, not five, and each day we were only walking for three or four hours. The camp was on a level grassy shelf, half a mile long, a quarter of a mile wide. It appeared suspended part way up the slopes of the mountain. Above were rock-strewn slopes rising to snow and below a steeper slope of crumbling mud and boulders dropped clear for five hundred feet to the glacier. Base Camp was at 16,000 feet, rather low for such a high mountain, but this was the last stretch of grass before we had to start onto the icy wastes of the glacier. As a place to rest and recuperate when not on the mountain a camp on grass was more preferable to a bleak existence in tents on the ice. Certainly our Sherpas, cook and Liaison Officer preferred to stay on the grassy camp-site. The shelf of Pang Perma was also the site of the camp of the 1930 expedition which made an attempt from the north, and the remains of the rough wall they had constructed as a windbreak were still evident. Our Sherpas made a large cooking-cum-dining shelter using the existing wall of stones and a light tarpaulin for a roof. We paid off the porters and yak herders and settled in for the long siege on the mountain which dominated the valley opposite the camp.

III

We spent a week exploring the approaches to the north ridge, carrying tents and supplies onto the glaciers and making Camps 1 and 2. Camp 1 was quite low, only 17,500 feet, but the site of Camp 2 at 19,000 feet was too long a day for us from Base Camp at first; we were not sufficiently fit nor acclimatised for such a long day's walk.

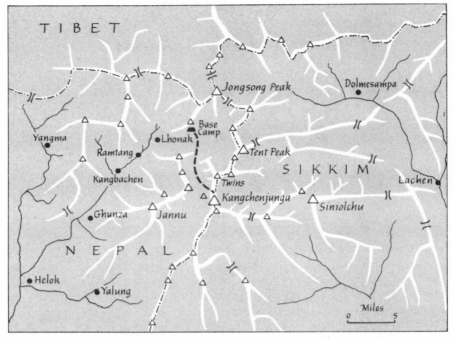

8. The location of Kangchenjunga, showing the route from Base Camp to the mountain.

The week was useful to help us all adjust mentally and physically to our surroundings. It allowed time, before we were committed to the mountain, for Pete to gain confidence and strength in his foot for the work ahead, and it allowed time for bouts of sickness and dysentery to pass which affected Georges and Pete in turn.

By all accounts Kangchenjunga had a fearsome reputation for danger. Being the highest mountain mass at the eastern extremity of the Himalayas, it is subject to ferocious winds and heavy deposits of snow. All the earlier expeditions had warned of the constant avalanches from its slopes and during the days when we placed and stocked the lower camps our ears and responses grew accustomed to the roar of yet another ice cliff breaking away and crashing thousands of feet down, or another mass of snow breaking loose and falling to drum with menacing force against the slopes below. Georges had only been on the one expedition to the Himalayas and that had been so quick that he had not witnessed many avalanches. The frequent thunderous roars which ruptured the silence of the days were new and worrying for him. They worried us all but we tried to find a way across the glacier least threatened by slopes above, and to place the tents far enough away from danger zones so that we could sleep in peace.

The first night at Base Camp was disturbed by the noise of a wind which seemed likely to ruin our tents and confirmed us in our fear for what lay in store high on the mountain.

Camp 1 was below Twins Peak, a small neighbour to Kangchenjunga, on whose flanks was perched a huge cliff of ice. We were wary of its threat but thought that the crevasses and ridges of the glacier between our tents and the side of the mountain would swallow up anything breaking loose from the cliff. The night we occupied Camp 1 Pete started up at the sound of an avalanche, but it was far away, and he settled back into his sleeping bag, confessing that he believed himself more timid than the rest of us, and rationalising out loud that he would have to accept that we would hear those roars every day, and even every hour, for the whole northern face of our mountain seemed to send down avalanches at any time of the day or night. Our chosen route was designed to avoid these dangers, climbing up to reach a ridge which stood clear above any avalanche slopes. I was sharing the tent with Pete and felt nervous too, without the reassurance that we had got the feel or the measure of the opponent we had come to face. I expressed my fears less readily than Pete, knowing how easily he could be influenced and made more nervous. I preferred to face my fears alone first, to come to terms with them in the process of making a decision before voicing my thoughts aloud. I could look at our situation in a way which let me laugh at our anxieties if there was nothing we could do or nothing we were going to do to resolve it or make it more safe. Pete told me that I was heartless and lacked imagination and we both drifted off to sleep listening to the ice of the glacier creaking and groaning beneath us.

On Friday 13 April, the Good Friday of Easter, all four of us were at Camp 1, Doug and Georges in one tent, Pete and I in another. Ang Phurba and Nima were with us too, occupying a third tent, ready to help us with the move up to Camp 2 the next day. Not long after dark the sound of an avalanche, louder than usual, grew outside. I could hear Georges's muffled, frantic exclamations and Pete leapt to the tent door.

'Oh, my God, look at this!'

Reluctantly I left the warmth of my sleeping bag to peer through the door of the tent. Out of the darkness of the night a white wall of billowing snow was advancing towards us, colossal and implacable. We could not tell how substantial it was, whether it was a dust-cloud of snow which would pass over with little damage or a solid mass which would bury us or sweep us for a mile across the glacier.

'Zip your tent closed,' I yelled to the others, and seconds before it reached us we zipped ours closed too, to keep out the choking powder of the snow. There was nowhere to run to, the advancing wall would reach us and toss us out of the way, or pass harmlessly over, far more quickly than we could move. We held onto the tent as the first winds of the avalanche tugged at its fabric. In that moment it was impossible to know if we would be there when the avalanche stopped, but I felt no fear for there was nothing I could do, as if my emotions were frozen until I knew that there was a future for them.

The wind grew stronger and shook the tent furiously; snow battered at the outside and forced its way in through tiny openings; then the commotion subsided, all of a sudden, and all we could hear was the murmur of Nima chanting his prayers and Georges swearing in disbelief.

The main force of the avalanche had been broken and swallowed by the small valley along the edge of the glacier and by the mounds and ridges in between. We had been hit by the wind of the displaced air and settling debris from the ice which had disintegrated in the fall. Minutes later the same thing was repeated and we resolved to move the camp to a different place at daybreak. I felt uneasy for the rest of the night but Pete was visibly shaken by the occurrence and complained bitterly about the folly of siting the camp in such a place.

Camp 2 was notably quieter than Camp 1 had been, in a snowy basin encircled on three sides by the wall of Kangchenjunga's North Face, the wall up to the North Ridge and another facet of Twins Peak. We pitched the tents to one side of a chute on Twins Peak which seemed to present the only danger, and were able to observe with more equanimity the puffs of white cloud on the mountainsides which marked the distant falls of ice before the sound reached us.

We worked in pairs on the steep wall up to the lowest point on the ridge between Kangchenjunga and Twins Peak. The wall was almost 3,000 feet high, and it was the most difficult part of the route we had chosen. None of the photographs we had seen before we arrived showed this wall, and we had come in faith that there would be a way. The way was hard, up steep ice and ice-covered rock which took us days to climb. The only alternative was the line chosen by the expedition in 1930, further to our right, but there a Sherpa had been killed by a fall of ice, and though we saw no avalanche from that area, blocks littering the glacier pointed to the need for continued caution.

The wall was two hours from the camp, across a gentle slope of snow-covered ice. A few crevasses made us worry and we marked the way with bamboo sticks so that we could always retrace our steps in mist or after new snow. Georges and I were standing together so we started the rota. Pete and Doug dumped their loads and went back to camp. Only one could climb at a time, so rather than waste time awaiting a turn in the lead, it was a more efficient arrangement for two of us to climb and fix rope for a day, then to let the other pair take over the lead for another day. The days could thus be alternated between resting and working, the resting pair being able to have food cooking ready for the return of the workers.

At the end of the first day Georges and I returned, weary after our efforts, to a lavish meal inspired by Doug's vegetarian preferences: cabbage, red beans, tofu and a tin of lamb slices for those who liked meat. It was delicious, and we all congratulated Doug. But in the night we all woke with sickness and diarrhoea, and the next day no one was well enough to move. Ang Phurba chortled with amusement when he arrived with a load of rope from Camp 1 and nodded with understanding when he saw the red beans in the snow.

'Ha ha, beans not properly cooked.'

The rest was welcome. The day slipped by in the lazy completion of the many little tasks outstanding; the heat of the sun was trapped and concentrated in the windless basin of glaring snow. Until the sun sank below the horizon we crept about listlessly, all energy sapped by the heat, and nibbled cautiously at food lest we be struck down again.

Doug and Pete spent a day fixing rope on the wall, and we could see that that section was hard by the way they moved so slowly. They returned towards evening, Doug shambling along weakly, ill from over-exertion and pausing intermittently to retch green bile onto the snow.

One day as Georges and I were high on the wall a thundering crash caused us to look around and see leaping down from Twins Peak and hurtling across our tracks far below the column of a colossal avalanche. We were safe above its path and Camp 2 was far enough away on the other side, but the avalanche covered our tracks for a quarter of a mile and travelled for two miles before subsiding. Returning that evening, we crossed the solid mound of ice debris and blocks which had fallen from the mountain, thankful that we had been safe above. We heard the rumble of another avalanche far away and Georges told me, with pride in his voice, that he had not even looked up to see where it was.

In four days of climbing between 15 and 20 April, we had overcome most of the difficulties on the wall. On what had been a huge, uncharted obstacle we had mapped out a route and fixed in place the ropes which would facilitate more rapid movement upwards and retreat when the time came.

On the 21 April all four of us left together, carrying sleeping bags, tents, stoves and food, intending to reach the top of the wall and make a camp at the North Col on the crest of the ridge. At the foot of the wall we stood in a group, adjusting harness and making ready prusik clamps with which to haul ourselves up on the ropes. Doug was apprehensive about the possibility of one of us dislodging loose rock onto those below.

'Have you got your crash helmet, youth?' he asked Pete.

'Yes.'

'Well you can go at the back. I've forgotten mine.'

'Hold on. Why didn't you bring yours?'

'I don't like climbing with it on. Gets in the way.'

And Doug's persuasiveness won the day.

With heavy sacks we toiled upwards for hours, but a blizzard was blowing by mid-afternoon when we reached the high point, there was no

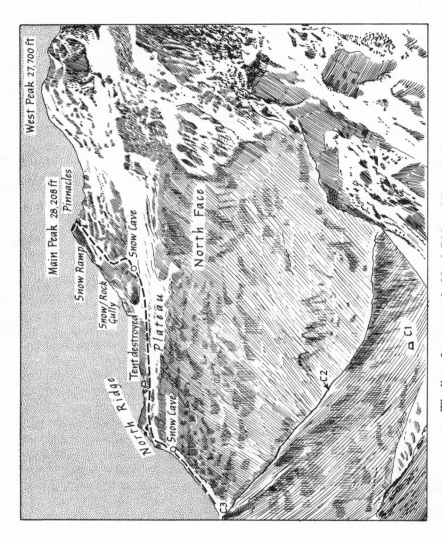

West Peak 27,700 ft

Main Peak 28,208 ft
Pinnacles

Snow Ramp

Snow/Rock
Gully

Snow Cave

Tent destroyed

North Ridge

Snow Cave

Plateau

North Face

C3

C2

C1

5. The line of ascent up the North Ridge of Kangchenjunga.

time left to climb the remaining unprepared sections and we slid off down, first dumping our loads, and went back down to Base Camp next day when we woke to a sky heavy with snow.

We had worked hard for a week and the sudden return to grass and the comfort of a fire made me realise how weary I was. Kami, the cook, prepared chips, eggs and tinned fish for us, and we let ourselves be spoilt by his constant concern that we had enough to eat and drink. Mohan, the Liaison Officer, beamed his pleasure at our return, proud of what we were doing but happy to have our company again.

We stayed down for four days. Heavy snowfalls covered the grass but it was still more reassuring than snow-covered ice with all the hidden pitfalls and inherent inhospitality. Ang Phurba went off for us with a message to a Czechoslovak expedition, camped three days away for an attempt on Jannu. They had sent up their good wishes with our mail runner whom they had met on the trail. The wall up to the North Col had taken up most of our ropes and in the note we asked if they had any rope to spare.

When not on the mountain I liked to relax completely. I could not find the energy to go off and explore the valleys and smaller peaks nearby, preferring to read and linger over meals. I felt a great sense of freedom from the threat and fear; any rumblings I knew were no sort of danger to us. Our grassy plateau was safe from any avalanche and no crevasses lay hidden to catch us unawares. Only now did I realise the strain we had been living under up on the glacier, menaced constantly by the avalanches, whose sound waged a campaign of fear even if most of them fell safely far away.

But I was keen to return. The lack of fitness and reluctance to face physical effort had gone; the subconscious, panicky fear of the unknown had disappeared; we knew the mountain now for what it was. The dangers were still there but we had had a chance to take their measure, we had tested ourselves on the difficulties and found we could master them. I was still anxious about the altitude, about how I would feel higher up when, without oxygen, we would try to reach the summit. We knew that there were difficulties close to the summit, we knew that we would have long distances to travel from our last bivouac, but whether it would be possible without the support from oxygen equipment we knew not at all. We had read of the dangers of damage to the brain from going high into rarefied air, we had read Messner's account of his double vision and distorted perception on the summit of Everest when he reached it without oxygen support. We knew from the descriptions of others who had tried to go high how slowly they moved and how difficult the simplest task was when the oxygen content of the air was less than half that of normal. Kangchenjunga is a bare 800 feet lower than Everest and on its summit there is only a quarter of the amount of oxygen in the air that there is at sea level. Apart from the difficulty of performing any action with such a low oxygen intake, there is also an unquantifiable risk of contracting pulmonary or cerebral oedema, the sickness of high altitude which fills the lungs or brain with fluids. This, at best, is incapacitating and at worst is fatal. The slow acclimatisation of climbing gradually higher over days and weeks is the best way to avoid this illness, and optimum acclimatisation is only reached after a month or six weeks of such preparation, in which time the blood alters in composition to absorb more oxygen from the thin air. We had spent nearly three weeks walking in to our Base Camp and another three weeks since then working on the mountain and felt that we should be fit enough and well enough adjusted, but there was no guarantee that any one or all of us would not be adversely affected by this altitude.

The only cure for severe high-altitude sickness is descent to a lower altitude or an increase in the supply of oxygen by artificial means. We had brought with us one bottle of oxygen and one set of breathing apparatus in case any of us became critically ill. It was not enough to climb the mountain – the bottle would last perhaps eight hours – and if anyone was to carry it to near the top he would not be able to carry anything else. It did, however, offer the chance of saving a life, for cerebral oedema can be fatal in a matter of hours, and we discussed frequently the merits of taking the bottle up to the North Col at 22,500 feet where it would be most needed to help someone down who might have contracted high-altitude sickness.

Doug and Pete had climbed Everest using oxygen equipment, and Doug had survived a bivouac on the descent at 28,700 feet without oxygen. Georges had climbed Broad Peak, a mountain 26,402 feet high, without oxygen. All three had more experience at high altitude than I had and I presumed that they shared a confidence in their ability to perform high up which I did not have. To make the first ascent of Kangchenjunga without oxygen and to do so by a new and difficult route would be a major achievement for us all but, with the insecurity of one who always expects the worst, I felt as if it was more of a step into the unknown in terms of whether my body would function high up in the way that the others had already proved theirs would. We all had the greatest respect for the handful of people who had forced themselves to the top of the highest mountains without oxygen equipment and we discussed often what it was that made them different from us. We could not believe they were supermen but somehow they seemed to possess a confidence which we did not have when we looked at the mountain we had come to climb. Everest and K2, the two highest mountains in the world, had been climbed without oxygen equipment. Kangchenjunga, the third highest, had not. Now that we were close to the mountain, the final 2,000 feet appeared more difficult than the final part of the other two, and our team was certainly very much smaller than usual for so high a mountain. Those who had reached the top of Everest and K2 had done so as members of large teams, many of whom had contributed to the effort of ferrying loads up the mountain and fixing ropes, and most of whom had used oxygen equipment. It puzzled me sometimes how we had presumed to come here at all, and why there were so few of us.

The snow-storm which had chased us off the mountain deposited a layer of snow at Base Camp too. Six inches of snow fell but it soon cleared in the heat of the sun. I lay outside my tent on the grass in view of the mountain, feeling in a state of suspended mental animation. I had grown accustomed to Doug spending his time on expeditions in abstract reflection, often absorbed in books of a philosophical nature, the *Tibetan Book of the Dead*, the *I Ching*, the Carlos Castaneda series on the teachings of Don Juan, or any of many others which he kept by him for constant reference. I preferred the escapist reading of racy novels but these were soon finished so I borrowed a Carlos Castaneda book and devoured that rapidly, which Doug thought did not do justice to the content.

I did not like to spend too much time in reflection since on expedition we were cut off from contact with the real world and could have no influence over events there. In the years in the seminary I used to spend the weeks of term-time planning all the wonderful things I would do in the holidays which I visualised as being the ideal. The reality was always less wonderful than the dream and I grew wary of the habit of living in the mind. Our situation here was similar and I hesitated to try to resolve problems with relationships, and make plans for when I returned, or resolutions for a mode of living, when I knew that so many things would interfere and alter the most careful plans.

I did think in general terms about why we were here, why I was here. I had once nurtured the thought that you could not be a climber if you were a 'bad person', a thought springing from the religious conviction that 'sin' brings its own retribution and that in climbing there are too many situations of risk, of which the 'almighty powers that be' could take advantage, to discourage any climber from 'bad behaviour'. I could no longer separate my thoughts from the religion instilled from early on and I could not answer my own questions of whether I was here because I really wanted to be or whether I felt I had to drive myself on no matter the suffering involved. Certainly climbing Kangchenjunga was a long way from the fun of climbing a small rock cliff, vying with a school mate to see who could do the hardest things. I wondered if climbing one of the world's highest mountains made one a better person, if it would give courage and strength in other aspects of life. Only reaching the top would answer that and I no longer knew what the motivation was which would enable me to put one foot in front of the other when there was only pain, and shortage of air and no fun or enjoyment.

I was glad that on the return from this trip I had nothing planned for almost a year. Doug had asked me to go on a trip to Everest in the autumn but I had decided not to go. In the last eighteen months I had been away three times, so that I had had no time to do anything satisfactorily. I was either away or preparing to go away, and work and friendships suffered. After this trip I wanted time to pause and take stock of what I was doing and where I was going.

Ang Phurba returned with 500 feet of rope and a tin of Czechoslovak alcohol. He had made the round trip in only two days. We needed the rope to fasten in place on a buttress at 25,000 feet forming a step in the ridge. That buttress looked to be the last difficult section before the final 2,000 feet of the summit pyramid. We had not rope enough to fix a safety line all the way up that, but even if we had we could not have carried its weight. We could only trust that the difficulties would not be so great that we could not descend them quickly enough without a line in place.

We could see how well we had adjusted to the altitude and how fit we had become by the speed with which we returned to Camp 2. The distance we had covered in two days we could now do in a few hours, suffering more from the furnace heat of the sun concentrated on us by the snowy bowl than from the stress of altitude.

After a night at Camp 2 we returned to the wall. Georges and Doug went up first carrying lighter loads, to climb and make secure with rope the last few hundred feet from which we had retreated in the blizzard. Ang Phurba and Nima were with us too, carrying rucksacks of gear and food so that we would have a good stock in the camp on the ridge.

Such steep climbing, even with ropes in place, was new to the two Sherpas, so Pete took care that Nima was coping all right and I looked after Ang Phurba. They were competent enough once they started, but they needed some initiation in techniques where the rock was vertical and ice on the ledges prevented secure purchase. At half height Nima turned back, saying he was tired, to wait at the foot of the wall for Ang Phurba's return.

It took hours and hours of tedious effort, pushing the clamp upwards on the rope, stepping upwards in the nylon loop attached to the clamp, pushing up the other clamp which attached my chest to the rope. Slow and boring, with none of the satisfaction that Georges and Doug would have, knowing that they were going to solve the last problems of climbing this wall and be first to stand on the crest of the ridge on which all our attentions had been focused for two weeks now.

The ropes up which we were climbing were 150 feet long, anchored in place at each end of their lengths by a piton driven into rock or ice. We kept an anchor point between each of us so that none of them would have to take the weight of more than one person. Georges and Doug were far ahead, out of sight. Ang Phurba was above me and Pete below, each a hundred feet away. I had started up a rope which hung free for part of its length, coming over a bulge of rock which Georges had climbed most skilfully one day that I was with him. As I came over the bulge I looked upwards to see how Ang Phurba was progressing and at that moment saw a mass of black objects falling through the air towards me. I ducked under the bulge instinctively, the rocks crashing above, below and to one side of me, but I was safely sheltered, hearing the rising crescendo of noise as the rocks rushed past. When the murderous crashes quietened, I looked up to see Ang Phurba crouching in fear but unscathed. Below, Pete was doubled up and I realised he had been hit.

'Are you all right, Pete?'

'I've been hit on the wrist,' he shouted in pain and frustration.

I took off my sack and slid back towards him. He had taken off his mitt and showed me the rapidly swelling lump where the rock had struck him. Already the swelling seemed as large as an egg. He could not use his hand, could not grip or take any weight on it. He seemed close to tears at the injustice of it all, this new injury, after he had recovered from the injury to his foot, seeming as if it might rob him yet again of his chance of reaching the top of the mountain. This was a hurt greater than physical pain. The angry red swelling mocked any attempt I made at showing sympathy.

Pete said that he felt able enough to descend to the foot of the wall where Nima would be waiting and he set off down, fumbling awkwardly with his injured hand. I could not assist him, only one could descend at a time on the rope, and I continued upwards to let Georges and Doug know what had happened.

The afternoon was well advanced by this time and Ang Phurba turned to go back in order to return to Camp 2 before darkness came. I took from him the sleeping bag he was carrying for Georges and crossed the ice slope to the bottom of the dark cleft of a chimney. The chimney was eighty feet high, narrow and difficult. Doug's sack hung near the bottom, obviously left there to ease his passage upwards. He appeared some distance above me, lowering a rope with an empty sack for me to fill with his gear so that he could haul it up. I argued with him when he asked me to go back to his sack for his books and it was almost dark when I hauled myself up the chimney and over the ledges above covered in loose rock. Doug showed me the way into the shallow-angled gully of snow at the top of which was Georges busy making ready the tent.

A keen wind knifed through my clothes as I waited in the dark outside while Doug settled himself into the tent. It was a two-man tent with little room for a third person, but it was too dark for me to erect my own tent so I had to make do with the space that was left in the porch of the tent and along the side of a wall where the other two squeezed together to make some room.

The wind howled all night, buffeting the tent and spraying the taut fabric with hail and snow. Each of us shuffled and moved constantly through the night, trying to find more comfort in the cramped space. By morning I had slumped to the end of the tent in a ball, and woke feeling ill and listless. The wind was furious outside, cloud enveloped us and regular volleys of snow showered the tent.

The previous day had been long and hard for all three of us and the night barely tolerable. With the wind as fierce as it was and with such poor visibility we put off any thought of trying to get further up the ridge. Then Doug braved the elements to relieve himself and came back shouting some good news.

He had climbed over the crest of the ridge looking for a corner less exposed to the wind where he could open up his clothing without it filling with spindrift. He found the crest of the ridge to be a rounded hump and the slope only twenty or thirty feet down below the ridge on the other side was almost calm. The relentless wind coming from the west streamed across the ridge running north and south but the east side, looking down into Sikkim, was protected. We packed up and dragged the tent, which bucked like a kite in the wind, to the calmer slopes and dug a platform large enough to take a second tent.

At last we had space to stretch out in and peace to rest by. Georges and I shared a tent which linked up to the second tent, occupied by Doug, with a nylon sleeve through which we could communicate and pass drinks. The wind still hurled itself at the ridge above us, but was only a dull roar from where we were and the snow did not fly with such force in the lee of the slope. We made drinks and ate to make up for the nourishment we had missed when we had had hardly space to stand the stove upright, and looked forward to resting for the remainder of the day.

I needed the rest. A headache lingered on from the discomfort of the previous night and a nauseous feeling periodically brought me to my knees in fits of retching. The col on the ridge where we were camped was 22,500 feet high, high enough to make every step an effort. As I felt at the moment, I could not hope to climb any higher along the ridge and I dosed myself with pain-killers and sleeping tablets to rid myself of the headache. But headaches at altitude can be the warning signs of high-altitude sickness and they do not disappear easily.

Next day I was no better and the sleeping tablets had not helped me pass any better a night. I did not feel capable of joining Doug and Georges when they went down to retrieve the rest of the loads dumped below that difficult chimney.

I lay in the tent when they had gone, feeling sorry for myself, wondering if this was my limit, if after all I could only reach altitudes of 22,000 to 23,000 feet. Doug and Georges seemed unaffected by any headaches, able to put in the extra effort to descend the five hundred feet to the gear and ferry it back up.

I must have dozed off because they seemed to be back in no time at all with the news that Pete and the two Sherpas were on the way up. This was a complete surprise as the weather was still wild outside and we had not expected any movement at all from Camp 2. With this in mind, Georges and Doug had been clearing loose rock from the chimney area which had been the source of the rock-fall which had injured Pete. Their good intentions had been embarrassed by the sight of figures below, but they returned pleased with the sacks of gear they had retrieved.

Pete and Ang Phurba flopped down outside some time later. It was marvellous to see Pete again and to hear that he thought he could now use his hand sufficiently to carry on with the climb. He had strapped it up with bandages and, though swollen and painful in use, it was bearable. I could not help admiring his utter determination to let nothing stop him. Nima had gone back down from halfway again and was waiting at the foot of the wall for Ang Phurba. After a drink and an appraising examination of our camp-site, Ang Phurba set off down with instructions to wait for our return at Camp 2.

Pete settled in with Doug, chatting chirpily in his relief to be back in the front once again. He threw questions at me through the connecting sleeve but I could only respond feebly and apologetically that I was not on such good form as he seemed to be.

After a third wretched night I had to accept that I was not going to improve if I stayed up longer, I was extremely tired but unable to sleep and my head ached constantly. I told the other three I would have to descend if I was going to recover, and they made their sympathetic farewells.

I was dejected and lonely as I plodded the short distance over the ridge to the top of the line of ropes leading down the wall. I paused before starting down, wondering if I was making a great mistake. If I went down I would be completely out of sequence with the other three. They had enough food and equipment to reach the top from the col and if it were possible they would have to press on making use of whatever spells of fine weather there might be. We had reckoned that another two camps would be necessary, so there was a chance that it would be some days yet before they would be in a position to reach the summit, but if they were too far ahead I would never catch up with them. Today anyway there would be no movement, the weather was still too wild. I dithered, unresolved whilst there was still time to change my mind, but I knew it was hopeless; even if I stayed I would never be able to keep up with them.

With the greatest sense of regret I slid off down the ropes, seeing now, with a sense of resentment, our handiwork which had traced a masterly route up that huge wall only to find that I was almost certainly excluded from reaping the rewards of all that effort.

At Camp 2 Ang Phurba and Nima welcomed me with a touch of sympathy. There was little solace in plunging into the comparative luxury of the largest tent and letting them bring me meals and drinks. I fell into a deep sleep. Three thousand feet lower in altitude, with slightly more substantial air, was enough to banish the headaches and nausea. I slept more soundly than at any time on the expedition so far and woke feeling refreshed and restored. The damage of three sleepless nights had begun to be repaired. Another night's sleep and I believed I would be able to go back up onto the ridge.

Down at Camp 2 the weather was calm but the clouds still churned about the ridge and hung off the mountain in long streamers. In the middle of the morning Ang Phurba's acute eyesight picked out three figures moving upwards along the ridge and through the binoculars I could see them leaning against the wind but making rapid progress.

I felt sickened at the inadequacy that had let me down and jealous of the prowess which enabled the other three to move so steadily upwards. I envied them the success which seemed within their grasp. At the rate they were going they seemed certain to reach the summit in another day or two. My jealousy and envy were irrational. I knew well that they could not afford to delay if conditions were favourable, that the weather was all too unpredictable, and delay when it was fine might cost them the summit. Still I fretted and longed to get back up onto the mountain.

I asked Ang Phurba if he wanted to accompany me onto the mountain to make an attempt on the summit as my partner. He laughed in his non-committal way and said he would wait and see how the others found it. He told me that Nima was not well and needed to descend to Base Camp. For the first time I realised that Nima's usual smile and willingness to help had been lacking. I had been so wrapped up in my own woes that I had not been aware that Nima was injured and in pain.

He explained that a rock had hit him in the back and he showed me the bruise. I could not tell if a rib was broken and though there was little that could be done to treat it he would be better off at Base Camp. He appeared feverish and moved about in obvious discomfort.

My own ambitions seemed selfish beside the distress of one who had been injured whilst working so hard for us. I prepared to go down to Base Camp next morning with Nima when the snow was frozen hard, to safeguard him across the crevasses which had begun to open as the season advanced towards full summer, and to ensure that all possible was done to alleviate his pain.

I loved the greenery of Base Camp, the luxurious cushioning of grass underfoot, but the pleasure and comfort felt fraudulent and transitory, much as the pleasures of freedom seem to a prisoner who has briefly escaped. I was over-sensitive to the sympathy I suspected behind the warm welcome from Kami and Mohan, feeling diminished in their eyes by my failure.

The air was wholesome at Base Camp, richer in oxygen than higher up, and I felt strong and fit once more, capable of anything. As we walked down from Camp 2 I had scrutinised the mountain often through the binoculars and saw the distinctive shape of a tiny figure reaching the vast terrace which spanned the whole of the North Face. From there only one more camp would be needed before the summit. It seemed certain that they would be on their way there next day whilst I was stuck at Base Camp.

Mohan was overjoyed that I was there. He bubbled with enthusiasm and cheerfulness, telling me how he missed our company. He had sat in his tent most of the time we had been gone, bored and lonely; he described himself as behaving like a young bird in a nest, sitting there, mouth wide open to have food dropped into it, with no other thing in the day to look forward to but the arrival of more food. Mohan's main distraction was the radio which we had given him and to which he listened most of the time. In the evening there was a weather bulletin in English for the benefit of the foreign expeditions in Nepal and Mohan paid assiduous attention to it, fulfilling, as he saw it, a duty to the expedition. We were never punctual enough to remember to tune in on time. On the day that we came down with Nima, Mohan told me that for the past few days very strong winds had been forecast at high altitude. This confirmed the experience we had had on the North Ridge of the mountain. That evening the forecast predicted winds of 120 mph at 23,000 feet, and I feared for the safety of the three on the mountain.

I could not settle at Base Camp. Nima was visibly reassured to be back on solid ground and had regained something of his former spirit. The following day I returned with Ang Phurba to Camp 2, revelling in our ability to reach the camp in three and a half hours instead of the two days it had initially taken us. Ang Phurba was prepared to come back up onto the mountain but was not keen on committing himself to going for the summit. I was in a quandary. There had been no more sightings of the other three and I went over all the possible variations of their movements on the mountain. If they had gone across the great terrace we should have been able to see them; if they had found a better way on the east side of the ridge they would not be visible. There was a possibility that they had dug a snow hole and in the back of my mind there was the knowledge that they could have had an accident. We could have brought walkie-talkies but, as a small team, we had imagined ourselves being together all the time and had decided against them. If we had had radio contact, much of the uncertainty about movements and intentions would have been taken out of the occasions when we were separated.

It was like solving a complex puzzle with people, food and equipment as the variables. If there was no tent or stove left at the North Col, Ang Phurba and I would not be able to stay there; if there was no pan we would be equally frustrated. Whether there was any chance at all of my reaching the summit I no longer knew. I thought we would have to go up to the camp on the Col at the least with supplies of food and possibly the bottle of oxygen, about which we were still undecided. If they had reached the top and were retreating, or if they had had an accident or someone was ill, they might have been depending on the supplies I had said I would try to bring up with me.

We had reached Camp 2 before the sun had come onto the tents, and consequently had all day to wait. There was plenty of time but it would have been an exhausting day to go from Base Camp to 22,500 feet in one day. The long day only gave me time to worry and fret more. My enjoyment of the expedition was completely gone; I was heartily sick of the whole enterprise and wanted it over. The worst of it all was being totally out of touch with the other three, not knowing what was going on. I appreciated the agony of frustration which Pete must have felt first with the injury to his foot, then to his wrist, but he had come through all of that to be up at the front again.

Clouds filled the sky to the west and raced across the mountains, catching in trailing streamers on the ridges of Kangchenjunga which thrust up far above any other peak. The noise of the wind built up into a roar over the North Col and could be heard above the sound of the wind which was battering at the tents of Camp 2.

By late afternoon the volume of sound from the wind on the mountain was indescribable. It had that massive power which makes one duck instinctively outside airports as jets take off. I read Eric Newby's book, *Love and War in the Apennines,* to fill the time. His pastoral descriptions made me homesick for England as outside gusts of snow hurtled against the tents and reaffirmed my fears for the other three. I kept listening for footsteps and voices. If they were exposed on the mountains in this weather they could not hope to survive. Their only chance would be if they were in a snow cave, protected from the wind; no tent would stand up to such force.

I asked Ang Phurba to wake me at 4.00 a.m. so that we could start early for the Col, but we were both up all night with the noise of the wind, tying down and retying the tents which were being ripped and flattened. By morning the wind had eased off around Camp 2, though it was still roaring on the ridge above. I felt that we should be taking more food and gaz to the Col in case it was needed but we were both exhausted and fell deeply asleep.

My night had been troubled with thoughts about the fate of the other three. I tried to come up with something positive that we could do from Camp 2. If they had had an accident, would we be able to get up to help them in the present wind; could they all have perished; how could I tell their wives and families; how could I explain that I alone had survived; would there forever be doubts about whether I was being completely honest about the accident?

After a rest it was imperative that Ang Phurba and I returned to the mountain as soon as the wind eased off to go as far as we could in looking for any trace of Pete, Georges and Doug, but it would not be possible to search the whole mountain.

Then late in the morning Ang Phurba woke me, shouting to say that he could see three figures on the ridge, and the tension lifted away.

They were out of sight for a long time at the camp on the Col; so long that I began to doubt that they were coming down. But by mid-afternoon they appeared over the crest of the ridge one by one and made their way down the ropes on the wall and slowly back to camp. My earlier gloom had turned to joy at seeing them safe and the loathing with which I had come to regard the mountain reverted to respect. My hopes soared of joining with them once again for an attempt on the summit when I saw they carried nothing. Had they reached the top they would have been heavily laden, but now I knew everything had been left on the mountain for the return.

Doug arrived first, his movements giving off an aura of weariness. Snow goggles shielded his eyes, which he said were smarting from wind and sun. He held out fingers for me to see the cracked and inflamed tips, symbols of the ordeal he had survived, and he started to tell what had happened as Pete and Georges, similarly battle-scarred, trailed into camp. I noticed that for the first time since he had hurt his foot, Pete was no longer limping. The events he had just come through had been so traumatic that all other aches and pains had become insignificant.

On the days when I had observed them on the ridge they had dug out a snow cave at 24,500 feet and carried up to it supplies from the tents at the North Col. Unable to know that I had gone down to Base Camp with the ailing Nima, they had kept watch for any movements from Camp 2 which might indicate that I was coming back up to join them. The weather had seemed fine and all three were fit so, rather than delay, they left with a tent in an attempt to reach the summit.

The previous day they had climbed onto the plateau, five hundred feet above the snow cave, and reached the crest of the ridge at 26,000 feet by the afternoon. A fierce wind was blowing from the west so they had pitched their tent on the east side of the ridge, below the crest, where they were sheltered from the wind. All three of them were squashed in the tiny tent which began to be buffeted by gusts of wind in the middle of the night. The wind had seemed to change direction, and from being sheltered they began to receive the full force of that wind which was keeping Ang Phurba and me awake far below with its noise and the damage it was doing to the tents.

The wind they felt bludgeoning their tent was unbelievable in its force. Their situation, perched high on the ridge, was precarious and when they felt the tent begin to lurch free of its anchorage under the wind's onslaught they started to pack ready to leave. The fabric of the tent was ripped by the wind, the centre pole snapped and gradually their shelter disintegrated before their eyes. Doug held onto the poles, trying vainly to hold the tent together till sleeping bags and all other essentials were packed into rucksacks. They evacuated the tent and when all were clear they let it go. The wind snatched it away into the night.

Safety lay in descent. A gentle slope led to the ridge and down the other side onto the plateau. They could hardly move against the wind. Even downhill, to reach the plateau, they crawled on hands and knees, pulling themselves forward with their ice axes clawing into the snow ahead. Georges had lost his rucksack. Before he had time to put it on, the wind had whipped it away to follow the tent down into Sikkim.

Georges was as awestricken by the power of the wind as he had been by avalanches earlier in the expedition: 'You should 'ave seen them, the rocks, they were 'alf a metre across, and the wind it just picked them up and blew them off the mountain. It was terrible.' He pronounced the word as 'terreeble', lending colour with his French accent to what was a horrifying memory. Georges kept shaking his head and muttering exclamations as if he could not believe he had been through the events they were now recalling.

Paradoxically I envied their experience, though I knew it must have all been hell. They had gone through the worst that the mountain could offer and, having survived it, were all the stronger. They had the togetherness of having shared hardship and a weary expectation of rest well deserved.

Doug's fingertips had been damaged by the cold as he held the poles of the tent together, Pete's fingers and nose were frost-nipped too. Georges was quite shocked by the savage fury of the elements to which they had been subjected and he was slightly snow-blind.

They drank gratefully the liquid which we had ready for them but did not want to stay long at Camp 2. They had been on the mountain, above 20,000 feet, for nine days and they longed to see the greenery of Base Camp and rest for a while. Together we all hurried downwards before nightfall to meet Mohan and our Sherpas, who showed their happiness at seeing all safe and relief that their mountains had not claimed more victims.

Rather than being a deterrent or cause for further doubts about the feasibility of climbing the mountain, the ordeal at 26,000 feet gave renewed confidence and a finer appraisal of the objective. Doug reassured me that 'wandering' about at 26,000 feet without oxygen equipment had been all right, not the crippling effort we had feared it might be, and said how he had regretted the lack of radio communication so that they had had to set off for the summit in the absence of any information about whether I was feeling well enough to rejoin them. They were all encouraging that I should have no more trouble than they with the altitude. Most reassuring of all was their achievement in descending all the way from 26,000 feet back to Base Camp at 16,000 feet, covering many miles, in one day. They had done this in appalling weather conditions and that gave us cause to believe that we could survive such storms again should they arrive when we were high up.

We plotted the next moves, scouring the upper reaches of the mountain through binoculars. Another snow cave was needed rather than tents and we pinned our hopes on finding deep enough snow into which to burrow in a gully beside a crescent-shaped buttress of rock 2,000 feet below the summit. Georges propounded a different idea. He suggested that we should abandon thoughts of digging a cave at 26,000 feet and use all our energy in making a push for the summit from the existing cave at 24,500 feet.

'We should go for 'eet,' he would say forcefully, backing up his idea by reasoning that if we carried nothing we could move faster and if we left at midnight we would be in position on the difficult lower part of the summit pyramid by dawn, with all day to climb the final 2,000 feet.

The idea was a radical departure from the methodical approach of digging out another snow cave at the start of the difficulties, and going from there to the summit. Whether we could climb those 2,000 feet in one day was questionable, but Georges was suggesting we try to do nearly 4,000 feet, covering two or three miles horizontally, in one stretch. Whatever plan was decided upon, everything depended on being able to climb that gully through the rocks at the base of the summit pyramid.

The gully was in shadow and no matter how much we scrutinised it through binoculars we could not determine if there was a continuous line of snow forming a link with the snowy ramp above the rocks or whether a step of rock blocked the way. If the gully was passable, the way to the summit seemed assured. The ramp above, being snow, we expected to be at an easier angle than the rocks. Only on reaching the gully would we know for sure if we could climb it.

We stayed at Base Camp for a while. It took three days for the weariness to leave the limbs of Pete, Doug and Georges, and we waited an extra day because the mail runner was expected, and we thought it would be nice to receive letters before going off once more. Time seemed to drag once everyone was rested, there was no purpose to the day and, though many uncertainties remained, only returning to the mountain would restore a sense of purpose. It was early May and we had been at Base Camp for over a month, almost two months since we had left England. There was an air of tedium about the camp as if the expedition had gone on long enough. Mohan was dropping hints that he would have to be back in Kathmandu soon to attend training camp, the implication being that we too should be on our way back soon. Kami had discovered that a large part of our milk powder was unusable and we were running short of other supplies; the stream near the camp had all but dried up. It was as if a subtle conspiracy of hints was being made to us to end the expedition.

By evening the mail runner had still not arrived. It was the fifteenth day since he had left and he was well overdue. We congregated for the evening meal, disconsolate that we would have to leave for the mountain next day without the satisfaction afforded by letters from home. I had grown accustomed to many things since my first couple of times in the Himalayas and hiring a mail runner had come to be almost an essential expense. The seclusion of expedition life endows the receipt of letters with an importance beyond measure and the failure of the mail to arrive was a great disappointment. Home was prominent in all our minds, and the often-expressed, fervent wish was that one more attempt would see us on the summit.

Then, when we had given up hope, he appeared out of the night and was welcomed with a warmth inspired by the treasure he carried. The package was opened and we all waited expectant but anxious lest this time there be letters for all but oneself. There were letters for all but the light in the dining shelter was too dim and soon after eating we retired to our tents to read by candle-light.

I played the romantic hits of Motown on the cassette deck, angling the speaker so that Pete could hear the music too. It was 8.00 p.m. At 4.00 a.m. we planned to be up and on our way to Camp 2 before the heat of the sun made uncomfortable the walk up the glacier.

I heard Georges shouting: 'Hey, Pete, Pete,' but Pete could not hear him. I suspected that Georges thought Pete had the music machine and wanted it turning low, but I said nothing; it was very low anyway. If he failed to make Pete hear him I thought that Georges might give up shouting, but he called me the next time: 'Hey, Joe, can you ask Pete to turn the music down. I want to sleep.'

I turned the sound lower. Then Pete was shouting to ask why he could not hear the music any more.

IV

Back at Camp 2 we rested with the restrained enthusiasm of anyone who faces a major contest. We shared a confidence about reaching the summit this time, but ever-present doubts and anxieties kept the atmosphere highly charged. Georges snapped in response to the taunts about him, a mountain guide, losing his rucksack on the mountain. He was restless and erratic in

19a. Pete being carried in a basket by a porter after he had broken his foot. Kami, our cook, waits in attendance.

19b. Dawa, the lovely girl from Ghunza.

19c. The north side of Kangchenjunga. The main, highest, summit is the pyramid-shaped one to the left of the rounded dome of the west summit.

20a. Georges on the wall up to the North Col.

20b. Doug coming through the ice-fall on the way to Camp 2.

20c. Camp 2, below the North Ridge of Kangchenjunga, at 19,000 feet.

considering our chances and his own ability. At one moment he was advocating his plan for a daring rush to the summit, at another he was worrying over the slightest trace of a headache and searching out every sort of pill with which to treat himself. Pete and Doug had long since attained a mode of living on expeditions which enabled them to cope more readily with these spells of unsettling anticipation. They both read and made notes while I read and dozed.

Ang Phurba was going to carry a load up to the Col and we debated still the pros and cons of taking the oxygen cylinder and mask up in preference to extra food. Pete often showed more caution than the rest of us and he was firmly for taking it to the Col, where it would most be needed if any of us was taken ill. On the other hand, more food taken to the Col would be an asset if we should have to spend a long time on the mountain. A compromise was reached by which Ang Phurba would carry the oxygen halfway up the wall to where Nima had left a sack full of food. There he would leave the oxygen and carry on up with the food, thus bringing the food stocks up to a high level but also making the oxygen more accessible.

Nima was not going to attempt to come up the wall but he was to come to its foot in order to wait there for Ang Phurba's return, as a partner on the return journey across the glacier.

We started out early on the morning of 10 May, just two days before my birthday, and I could hardly remember whether I would be thirty or thirty-one years old. At the foot of the wall we learnt that Ang Phurba had not brought his prusik clamps with which to climb up the rope. As with much of the equipment issued to him, he was keeping these in good condition for the return to Kathmandu where he could sell them for a high price. We were angry at this acquisitiveness when the prusik clamps were essential for climbing the mountain. There was no question of returning to Base Camp for them and we had to divide up the eight clamps we did have between the five of us. Doug needed two as his fingers were very sore and he would make progress up the ropes more easily with two of the clamps. We gave Ang Phurba two because we felt obliged to ensure his safety, and for the four clamps that were left Pete, Georges and I drew lots. Georges won, leaving Pete and I to make the best we could of hauling ourselves up with one clamp and one bare hand.

Doug mentioned crash helmets, impenitent that he had left his yet again at Base Camp and insistent that he should go first lest he be hit on the head by a rock dislodged by any of us going first. He won his point but agreed to wait at the final chimney, where the rock was loosest, until all below were safely to one side. Then we started upwards one at a time.

For over five hours each of us was alone in that vertical journey. I found my mind going over problems, re-examining mentally what lay ahead. Climbing up ropes fixed in place is uninteresting and exhausting, but the mind is free to wander. With only one prusik clamp, the effort was twice as great. Instead of being able to move up, alternately supporting my weight on one clamp or the other, for half the time I had to grasp the rope in my hand and pull myself upwards. It consumed much more energy. Pete was having a similar struggle.

In the chimney, high up and not far from the camp, a sharp-edged block of rock came loose as I brushed past. Before it could fall I pressed my body against it, holding it in place lest it fall and hit Pete or Ang Phurba below. The block was two feet high, several inches thick and very heavy. It was all I could do to keep it from falling. I waited until they were clear from below me before trying to move, but still did not want to let the block fall for fear it should damage the ropes below. I took its weight in my hands and edged it up to a deep cleft in the chimney, fighting for balance and straining to lever it upwards before my arms gave out. I could feel its sharp edge cutting into my hands and when I finally heaved the block into the cleft, patting it to make sure it was stable, I saw blood oozing through my torn glove and could see a deep gash in the flesh of my fingers before I clenched my fist tight to staunch the flow. I was thankful that the main difficulties were almost over and the camp on the Col was only half an hour away.

Ang Phurba arrived last, bringing with him the oxygen bottle after all through some misunderstanding or perhaps, because in his own inscrutable reasoning, he thought we had more need for the oxygen than for the food. He slipped away down to join Nima and to return to Camp 2. We asked him to keep watch and to come to meet us at the foot of the wall if he saw that we had reached the summit and needed helping back with our heavy loads.

At last all four of us were together, unhampered by injury or illness, on our way upwards. Pete's wrist still hurt and Doug's fingertips were painful but both of them had achieved a working relationship with their disabilities. From the camp on the Col every step further was new to me. We left after a night's rest, Doug and myself paired off, Pete and Georges coming up behind. A steady wind streamed across the ridge, every upward step was tiring. I assumed that I felt the effort more because it was my first time higher than the Col, but Doug told me that he found it more taxing than the other times he had been up. Pete and Georges were weary too so, on reaching the cave, we decided to stay for a day. We had come up from Base Camp at 16,000 feet to 24,500 feet in three days, taking in some hard climbing on the way. No matter how fit we were, it was little wonder that we felt fatigued.

Doug woke me the morning after our arrival at the cave with a 'Happy birthday, youth,' and I realised it was 12 May. We idled away the day, savouring the view of the mountains of Sikkim bordering with Tibet and the sight of Everest and Makalu far away to the west. I tried to compose a speech I would have to make as best man at the wedding of Don and Jenny, the two friends who had put up with all the disruption of my earlier preparations for expeditions. In a way, having to give the speech gave me more cause for worry than the rest of the mountain ahead. The anxieties of climbing a mountain were the sort which were familiar, but standing up in public, making a speech, having to be witty, was a disquieting prospect. The other three all chipped in with their suggestions about what I could say.

The cave was palatial. I was told how it had taken hours of excavation to achieve a chamber large enough for four people to lie in side by side and to sit in without banging against the ceiling. They had started digging from opposite sides of a wide rib of snow. The snow rib was formed by the wind in a bay at the base of the rampart of rock, 'the castle' as we referred to it, barring access to the vast plateau above. It had been for this rampart that we had asked the Czechoslovaks for the rope. The plateau was 500 feet above the snow cave and the intervening barrier of rock and steep ice was difficult enough to warrant fixing with rope to assure safe progress up or down, whatever the weather. This had been done during the previous attempt by Pete, Doug and Georges. The way to the summit was now largely prepared.

Georges had persisted with his proposal that we should try to reach the summit in one long push from the snow cave and gradually we had come round to his way of thinking. Vertically we had almost 4,000 feet of ascent to reach the 28,200-foot summit, and we would have to cover nearly two miles to get there. It was a lot to do in one stretch, so high up, and we knew of no precedents. The attraction of this plan lay in not carrying much weight. A rucksack of twenty pounds is a wearisome burden at altitude, but with no necessity to carry more than a little chocolate and sweets, with no need for sleeping bags if we were not going to spend the night out, we hoped that the lightness of our loads would compensate for the distance we had to travel. Another factor influencing our decision was the brightness of the moon. The moon was almost full and not only would this light our way, but the deprivation of altitude made us impressionable and receptive to Doug's contention that we would all be at our greatest strength as the moon waxed larger.

All day too of 13 May we lay in the cave, or outside on a platform in the snow when the wind dropped. The waiting preyed on our minds and we began to regret the passage of fine weather whilst we were inactive. We had planned to leave at 1.00 a.m., using the hours of darkness to climb the 500 feet of rope above and to cross the plateau to the base of the final pyramid. However, the waiting aggravated our impatience and we knew we would not sleep if we were to leave at 1.00 a.m. so we prepared to leave earlier. Activity appeared more desirable than the constant checking of watches in anticipation of departure and without any firm suggestion it seemed logical to start before dark to have done with the roped section by nightfall. So we left in the afternoon, in spite of an approaching bank of cloud, climbed up the ropes through the rampart of rock and congregated in darkness on the edge of the plateau. The wind had freshened, so we huddled together for warmth and to make ourselves heard. Stinging flurries of snow were blown up from the ground, but the plateau was set at a gentle angle, the surface was mostly small stones, and progress was only a matter of walking, bowed against the wind.

We stayed roped together in pairs to keep in contact, for all we could see of each other was a head-torch beam, or a dark shape outlined by the light. The heavy cloud of the afternoon obscured the moon and, though roped together, we were each alone in this journey through the night. The wind increased in strength and the driving snow was more persistent; time crept by in hours.

Though we were moving steadily, the movement was monotonous and I felt drowsy. My thoughts floated freely and it was as if the landscape around me, glimpsed by torchlight, and the figures moving in it were not real. The hood of my down suit, drawn protectively round my face, became the frame of a television screen from inside which I was observing the outside world. Instead of watching images on the screen, I was an image, detached from the discoloured rocks, the moving shapes, the wind, the cold, the snow.

I would snap out of this delusion to realise that I had to keep control of my imagination, that tiredness combined with the altitude and hunger were inducing hallucinations, then I would be caught up in them again, an observer, not a participant, my mind roaming independently of the automaton movements of my limbs.

Anything positive pulled me back to reality. We all crouched down in the shelter of a large rock discussing which way to go, whether to go on, whether attempting to reach the summit now was too ambitious. We pressed on, hoping that the weather might improve by morning.

At midnight we were in the region of the crescent-shaped buttress beside which was the gully we had to climb. All our plans had depended on being able to see our way at this point either by the arrival of dawn or by the light of the moon. Dense cloud blocked the beams of our torches and vicious streams of snow kept our faces turned to the ground.

Doug and I favoured digging in to the snow where we were, and forming a cave in which to shelter until dawn, but Pete suggested going further to where the base of the buttress above could just be seen. There he believed the snow would be better for a cave. Georges set off to follow Pete; I untied and stayed with Doug to burrow into the snow where we stood.

The snow was hard, it was not such a good place to burrow into, but in a while we had a passable shelter. By this time we simply wanted to escape from the harrowing wind and snow. We tried to communicate with Pete and Georges but the words were lost in the wind. We saw a flash of torch as the cloud thinned momentarily and set off towards it. But we saw nothing more and lost our direction in the swirling whiteness. We retreated to the hollow we had dug in the snow only finding it with difficulty and erected a wall using lumps of snow against the wind. Without sleeping bags to hide in, we sat in our suits of down, plagued by the jets of wind which penetrated the gaps between the blocks of snow. Doug chopped away with his ice axe at the hard snow, enlarging the cave and keeping warm with the activity. I tried to fill the gaps in the outer wall to shut out the draughts and dozed spasmodically as fatigue overtook me.

I became convinced that we had so badly miscalculated our movements that we had spoilt our chances of reaching the summit on this occasion. The cold seemed to reach my bones, and alternately I shivered and was gripped with cramps. I admired Doug's strength which enabled him to keep chopping away at what was now ice, only marginally enlarging the cave but able to keep himself warm. I picked away sometimes with my axe at what snow I could reach but my arms wanted to drop with fatigue.

We talked about Pete and Georges, unable to believe that they had been able to go much further. Partly we felt embarrassed at losing touch with them and partly we felt that it had been much more sensible to stop when we did and that the storm had interfered with our efforts to communicate.

The cold sapped our strength too, and at the first glimmer of dawn we left the cave, glad of the movement, to climb up and look for the other two. We had hardly started when we saw them emerging, 300 feet above us, from a hole in the snow beside the buttress of rock.

We met for a hasty consultation and agreed to descend to the large cave below 'the castle' where we had food and sleeping bags and could recoup our strength. It was a crestfallen retreat in the hard light of dawn back across the plateau and down to the reassuring comfort of the cave we knew.

Pete and Georges had discovered a crevasse alongside the rock buttress which they had used to hide in from the wind. This was why Doug and I had not seen their lights or heard their voices. They had tried to climb further – Georges had thought that the summit was not far away – but they had lost their way in the darkness and cloud and had retired to shelter in the crevasse.

Georges seemed deflated as if he bore the full responsibility for the plan which had backfired. Now we were all so tired we needed a good rest before going up again. Pete and Georges had caught sight once of the pinnacles on the summit ridge which marked a point where the first people to climb the mountain had emerged from the South-West Face. We knew for certain that that point was only 300 feet below the summit. Georges believed that he and Pete had been level with that point but Pete was not so sure. It seemed hardly credible that they could have climbed so high in a relatively short time.

We began talking of a change of tactics, considering using the snow cave or the crevasse near the rock buttress as a proper bivouac stop on the way to the summit. With a good rest there, taking up food and sleeping bags, we stood a better chance of climbing the last 2,000 feet. The long push from this snow cave was too much.

Georges was not convinced; he felt sure that he had been very close to the summit, as close as one often went to the summit of a mountain in the Alps where the objective was to climb a difficult route and the last few hundred feet of easy ground to the top made no difference to the validity of the ascent. It was obvious one could do it and it served no purpose to go those last few hundred feet for the sake of appearances.

He spoke in generalities as if, as a mental exercise, we could consider ourselves to have done what we had set out to do. We had overcome the main difficulties and in that sense we had completed the climb and had no need to continue right to the top when we could see that no more obstacles blocked the way. I was surprised that he and Pete could have got so close to the top but that only gave me encouragement that we could after all make it to the summit and it might turn out to be easier than we had feared.

We were all dead beat. Georges withdrew into his sleeping bag, remaining mute and unresponsive all day. Pete lay next to the inert Georges, near the tunnel entrance where the air was fresh. He tended the stove, producing drinks and food in such quantities that he became resentful of the passive gratitude from the rest of us, who made excuses to avoid working the stove ourselves. In the back of the cave where Doug and I lay, the air was stalest. I felt a certain claustrophobia in this icy tomb of our own making. The walls and roof were firm, but the weight of snow outside caused the ceiling to sink imperceptibly lower. Each day a few more inches of snow had to be scoured from the ceiling to save us knocking our heads every time we sat upright. The stove would only function near the entrance in the fresher air. Inside the cave the air was too thin, too stale or too cold to enable even a candle to burn. I wanted to sleep but the claustrophobia, the subconscious registering of the fear of suffocation, made my sleeping shallow and my rest fitful.

Doug mentioned the impression he kept having that there were more than just the four of us on the mountain and awoke memories of similar impressions in us all. On returning to the cave I had been unthinkingly waiting for 'the others' to arrive. Not Pete, nor Georges, nor Doug but an indistinct group of people whom I imagined were also on the climb with us. They were, I fancied, other members of the team and this impression of being part of a larger group, part of something greater than the little band that we really were, created a sense of reassurance as if someone else more capable, more perspicacious, was directing events and bearing the responsibility. The illusion created too a sense of harmony with the mountain. Pete recalled the very firm belief, as he was bringing up the rear on the way back to the cave, that he was not the last person at all. It was not a thought that needed verification; he was simply aware of the presence of someone behind him, just as firmly as he knew we three were in front of him. Discussing these impressions openly banished the phantoms from my thoughts, but the sense of harmony remained.

After a day of mute inactivity, Georges sat up and announced that he had decided to go down. It should have been a startling announcement but one's responses at altitude are dampened down as if all mental as well as physical activity has adapted to the need to conserve energy. All necessary effort is to be avoided and when Georges told us, directly and emphatically: 'I 'ave not enough juice left. It would be too dangerous for me to go for the summit. If anything happened I would not be able to get myself out of difficulties. I will go now, back to Base Camp, while I 'ave strength,' he evoked little more reaction than if he had said he did not want anything to eat. Someone reassured him that he probably had as much strength as any of us but that was a reason, he felt, for all of us to go down now because we were so exhausted. If we were entitled to decide to carry on he was entitled to decide to go down.

Georges often voiced aloud his thoughts; it was not unusual for him to come out with an idea radically different from any that had otherwise been suggested, but it was only his spontaneity which caused him to speak his mind immediately an idea occurred to him. In practice he was much more likely to have drawn closer to the majority view by the time any action took place. By morning I suspected he would have changed his mind. All of us had experienced such moments of doubt and the longing to end the toil by simply turning round and going back. Often I relied upon other people being at a different level of enthusiasm to sustain me when my spirits were low, just as I knew that at other times I was more confident and buoyant than others around me.

Doug, however, began to voice his own doubts, aroused by Georges's openly expressed decision. He wondered aloud at the purpose in what we were doing and whether, like the long-distance runner in Alan Sillitoe's novel, we would show more mastery over the game we had chosen to play if we were to turn back now that the goal was in sight. Doug had been on expeditions to big mountains more times than anyone I knew, but he was forever asking himself why he felt such a compulsion to climb them, and on the mountains he was forever questioning how he came to be away again, what it all meant to him and whether it would matter if he gave it all up.

Pete felt the impetus of the expedition threatened by the verbalisation of such self-analysis and appealed to me to discover where my resolve lay. The points at issue had all become very clear to him many weeks before when the injuries to his foot and then to his hand had made the possibility of not reaching the summit very real and had forced him to realise that reaching the top of Kangchenjunga was of paramount importance to him. The motivation he had had to summon up then to get himself walking and fit, and then to drag himself upwards with constant pain in his wrist, was not susceptible to any eleventh-hour uncertainties.

For myself, having been given back the chance of reaching the top when I had thought all was lost, I was keen too to carry on with the attempt. I did feel, however, that we needed a day or two of recuperation down at the tents on the North Col.

In the morning Doug woke us to say that he had had the most refreshing night's sleep full of dreams which had inspired him with the conviction that he should go on to the summit. He went outside to relieve himself and shouted in to us that it was the clearest of mornings and that it would be a pity to waste such a good day going to the North Col when we could use the good weather to go up again. This was the other side to the man wracked with doubts; this was the side of him which drove him on to climb more and more mountains.

It was a jolt to wrench one's thoughts upwards so soon again. We were low on food and had only one spare cylinder for the gaz stove. Our intention had been to descend to Camp 3 on the North Col to bring back up food and more fuel. Certainly the idea of going up again instead was more attractive than the long trail down and the climb back up to this cave, but I doubted if I had recovered enough to go all out for the summit. Pete was cautious too, torn between the opportunity of capitalising on this new enthusiasm and the risk of finally pushing ourselves to exhaustion if we were to meet bad weather and run out of food high up.

The discovery of a second cartridge of gaz tipped the balance. Upwards it was to be. Doug turned to Georges, who was still in his sleeping bag: 'Georges, would you like to come with us to the top?' He said it as if nothing would please him more than to have Georges's company.

'No. I am going down, but I think you should go for 'eet from here. It is better than delaying further.'

So we left to go upwards and watched Georges's figure dwindle to a speck. We watched until he was down the crest of the ridge to the start of the ropes at the top of the wall and we knew that he would be safe. It was the saddest of sights. Forever volatile, Georges was as easily despondent as he was enthusiastic. There was no ill-feeling. He had made a decision for himself and we for ourselves. He expected to get back to Base Camp that evening and he promised to light a fire as a signal to us if fine weather was forecast. No fire would mean bad weather.

Pete and Doug stood aside to let me break trail to the bottom of the rope leading up to the plateau. The storm which had caught us out the night before had covered the slope thickly with new snow.

'It's about time you broke trail to here, Joe,' said Doug, aligning himself with Pete in a self-righteous stance of having done their share of work other times when they had been this way.

The snow was knee-deep and though it was only 200 feet to the rope, my legs were leaden with fatigue. I reached the rope where it hung clear on bare ice and expressed my doubts to Pete and Doug about whether we had had enough rest. Pete was sympathetic to the idea that we should rest for another day but Doug wanted to press on and Pete was prepared to push himself to ensure that the chances of reaching the summit did not begin to dwindle once more.

Pete encouraged me on. He knew me more than anyone.

'Just make your way as slowly as you like to the cave in the crevasse. We should be there by early afternoon and you will get a good rest. You can make your own pace once we're on the plateau.'

Every inch of the 500 feet of rope up to the plateau was exhausting. My spirit seemed crushed by the impossible effort. On the plateau Doug was already far ahead, piling stones one on top of another to mark the way back in darkness or storm. If he had doubts about why he was on the mountain, they were not doubts about his strength, he seemed to have energy to spare. I hobbled along in company with Pete. We sat down often to rest, watching the afternoon clouds roll in, until Pete too went on ahead and I plodded with infinite slowness up the last incline to the snow cave.

Inside, Doug and Pete were already at work, levelling out the floor for us to lie on. I shovelled half-heartedly at the piles of ice-chippings, sending them down into the dark crevasse where the ice was parted from the rock wall.

A minor storm was sending showers of hailstones down the tunnel, so Pete sealed it with carefully fashioned blocks of snow. There was enough air, streaming up from the depths of the crevasse, for us to breathe comfortably.

We settled in for the night, Doug seizing the prime place, and promising to cook in compensation. His fingers still hurt too much, however, and he had to abandon the cooking to avoid the painful contact of snow on his bare hands.

Pete and I had less room, but it was better being squashed close together as we could share body heat. When one side of me grew cold, I would turn over so that I was warmed against the extra insulation of Pete in his sleeping bag.

At the arranged time of 8.00 p.m. we were reluctant to break open the protective cover on the tunnel to look for the light of the fire which Georges

had promised if the forecast were good. Any movement at all was dispro-
portionately tiring and therefore unwelcome. We resigned ourselves to
making our own judgement about the weather next morning.

I had a terrible cough which was caused by the heavy breathing-in of the
cold, dry air. My throat had become inflamed to such an extent that the
slightest irritation would send me into an inescapable, noisy bout of coughing, which Pete and Doug found alarming and I was concerned would keep
them awake.

We achieved a comfort of sorts. Doug, in the widest part of the cave, was
exposed to draughts which disturbed his rest. Huddled close to Pete, any
discomfort softened by the influence of a sleeping pill, I slept soundly.
Doug woke me to find the time, then again to ask for tablets to ease the pain
in his fingers and to help him sleep. But Pete was already fumbling for his
canister of pills and I dozed off again.

We were awake at 4.30 a.m. All three of us were slow and unenthusiastic
about stirring from the delicately achieved equilibrium between warmth
and cold. I started the stove, feeding lumps of ice into the pan and lying
back in my sleeping bag waiting for the liquid to heat. We shared a mugful
of granola, drank a mugful each of fruit drink and a mugful of tea, and then
there was no reason to delay further.

We left everything behind except a bottle each of water, spare mitts,
cameras and sweets. I thrust my share into my pockets but Pete and Doug
took their rucksacks. We burst out of the tunnel, pushing the protective
blocks aside. The sky was clear blue, mountains far below were in view as
far as the horizon, which was marked by the dominant shapes of Everest
and Makalu. A slight breeze was blowing but it was as perfect a day as we
had known on the mountain.

I needed to relieve myself before we started off and remember being
pleased that my body was functioning so regularly, even so high up and
under the duress of such effort and minimal diet.

We strapped on our crampons and moved off up a slope of snow, all three
of us on a length of rope 120 feet long. As soon as we started upwards I
felt the deadly fatigue again; we hardly talked, every breath was needed for
the strength it gave for movement. I could not know of the doubts Pete or
Doug might have, but in their silence assumed that they had none. I could
not imagine myself going on upwards all day if after every few steps I was
needing to rest. I resolved to go until I ground to a halt, then I would return
to the cave on my own, leaving Pete and Doug to continue together. I did
not want to hinder their progress, they seemed strong and purposeful, and
would turn back if I held them up.

On the earlier attempt overnight, Pete and Georges had gone straight up
a gully of snow and lost their way in the dark. Doug and I had talked about
taking a line which zig-zagged up through the rocky area, following two

distinct runnels of snow up to an unavoidable step of rock, the narrowest part of the barrier above. We took it in turns to go first, although we were moving together. The slope of snow was not steep but sometimes steps needed kicking in the crusty snow and this was tiring, so we shared the work, and as second or third on the rope one could easily rest mentally from the extra attention needed to decide which way to go.

At the step of rock it was my turn to lead. Judgement can be clouded at altitude and I distrusted the impression I had that this step of rock looked easy to climb. It appeared to be only about sixty feet high, and lay back in a series of slabby steps. Cautiously I set foot on the first holds, levered myself upwards and fingered each hand-hold suspiciously. I felt as if difficulty was personified and was going to grab hold of me at any moment. Pete safeguarded the rope below me, watching my every move and waiting till I reached the top of the step before starting up himself. Warily I glanced about; I had thought this was going to be as big a struggle as I had read that Nick Estcourt and Tut Braithwaite had had to break through the rock band on Everest, but it was no more of a struggle than was any other minute of survival at high altitude. If anything it was more interesting than the repetitive plodding up snow slopes and ice. I reached the top, where the rock shelved into snow bands which ran into the great diagonal swathe of snow, 2,000 feet across, towards a notch on the ridge 300 feet below the summit. That diagonal ramp of snow was clear of obstacles. My doubts had disappeared.

The interest and excitement aroused by solving what had been long considered an imponderable obstacle had subdued my feelings of fatigue. The weariness remained but the interest and desire to look over that notch in the ridge, down the far side of the mountain, to look round every remaining obstacle until we were looking at the summit, this eagerness to explore purely to see was what kept me going. I knew now that I could keep on putting one foot in front of another for as long as daylight lasted. No illness marred my feelings, only if time ran out would I turn back now. If my emotions had not been in a state of 'shut down' I would have felt enthusiastic. I turned and shouted down for Pete and Doug to come up.

They came up together, then Pete led on for a while. There were no stages, each of us led the way for as far as he felt able. Every few steps we stopped to gasp and pant for breath. We went at the pace of whoever was slowest, but the slowest was not slow enough. Every stop was welcome, something indefinable had taken over to keep us moving upwards when all stimulus was swamped by the distress of muscles and lungs starved of oxygen. An urge beyond description got us to our feet after every halt and made us go up a few more steps.

Doug went first for a while, but his painful fingers and feet which were growing numb slowed him up and he asked if he could bring up the rear.

We were well wrapped in red suits of down, so that to look at we were barely distinguishable, individual size and shape being lost in the rounded contours of the padding.

I took over the lead. Sometimes the snow was firm and the forward points of my crampons bit firmly at each step. Where soft snow was packed on the surface by the wind a kick was needed to bury the foot in the snow and make a step. Always we worried that this soft snow would slide away, taking us with it, but we had to climb up it in places. I set my sights on a rock protruding from the snow some distance away. The distance did not mean very much, it was impossible to gauge with nothing to give it scale. It was the time that counted, but that was difficult to judge too. Between one glance at my watch and the next, time would have moved on with little to show save a few, very few, steps upwards and a long gasping for air. The notch on the ridge below the summit was an inestimable distance away in the time needed. In memory there is little left save a series of cameos, telescoped together, of panting figures in red, or figures in motion, shuffling upwards, six steps at a time.

I reached the rock, the target I had set myself, with no idea how long I had been in front nor how far we had come. Doug asked for a halt. His feet were still cold and he wanted to warm them before they became numb and frozen. He took off his boots and I let him place his stockinged feet inside my down suit, on my stomach, where the warmth of my body restored feeling to them. Pete and I were benefiting from the use of the new boots made of plastic, with a thin foam inner boot, which we had found to be far more effective as insulation than the traditional leather double boots. Doug's feet were too large for his plastic boots and he was suffering as a result of having to use his old leather ones.

Pete led on. The notch on the ridge was appreciably nearer. It was early afternoon and shadows were lengthening towards us. He came to a patch of snow which hardly seemed to adhere to the icy surface beneath. He gathered all his strength and rushed upwards for fifteen steps without pause. Doug and I, caught unawares, struggled and choked in pursuit. Pete reached a rib of black, shaly rock alongside which he climbed and then the notch was in reach. He climbed to the crest, catching the sun as he moved out of the shadow, and shouted back in a cracked voice that the view was fantastic. I joined him on the rock where he was perched, with the South-West Face sweeping down below. It was at this point that the first people to climb the mountain had arrived in 1955, after ascending the South-West Face. Our route up the unknown north side was over; from here 300 feet of ground which we knew had been climbed led to the summit. It was 4.00 p.m. with two hours left before darkness.

Pete was looking content. We hardly communicated at all, but in these minutes of waiting till Doug joined us a little relaxation and self-congratulation was permissible. The weather had remained fine all day, the wind had not reached its usual ferocity, and now what had seemed an endless struggle was all but over.

It hardly seemed possible that we could reach the top from here and descend to the snow cave and safety before dark. We knew that we would be lucky to reach the cave, where we had left our sleeping bags and food, if we started back immediately. But the altitude or ambition or the innate drive which had borne us so far precluded rational decisions.

'Do you think we should press on?'

'I think so. Do you?'

'Yes. Let's wait till Doug gets here to make a decision.'

Doug hauled himself out of the shadows into the sun. We were only separated from each other by sixty feet of rope but it could take five or ten minutes to close that gap even on the easiest slope. Doug grinned broadly: 'That's it then. Cracked it. We'll never get up this last bit and down again before dark.' It was the voice of reason.

Pete said we would kick ourselves for the rest of our lives if we did not do this last 300 feet and urged that we go on. Doug was persuaded.

'All right. My turn to lead for a bit then, but I want a rest.'

We knew that the vertical interval was 300 feet but what that meant in distance we did not know. It was a chaos of rocks, snow and ice covering the slopes below the summit. A steep wall of rock barred the way to the summit cave. Joe Brown, a brilliant rock-climber, had forced his way up there with his oxygen turned to full flow on the first ascent. The second party of their team had avoided the steep rock by traversing below on bands of snow. We could not tell whether we were looking at a distance of one hundred feet or several hundred feet. Clearly we could not go on forever. Behind a huge spike of rock on the skyline we could see the foot of a bank of snow.

'Let's go as far as that snow,' said Pete.

'We'll go on until we have pushed the patience of the gods to the limit,' said Doug, and he began threading his way across the slope, over rocks, down a chimney and gently upwards.

Clouds were beginning to fill the valley. Jannu, 3,000 feet lower, was almost obscured by cloud, and behind it more clouds were banked up, resembling the mushroom-shaped columns of nuclear explosions. A storm seemed to be approaching.

We traipsed on, the time forgotten once the decision had been made. Up and down, wending an erratic path to no one knew where. Doug ducked beneath the projecting spike of rock and stepped onto the tongue of snow. With laboured movements he turned to face us: 'It's just up here. Fifty feet away.'

The snow bank was easy. The nearness of the much-longed-for summit inspired a last big effort and we stood all three of us on a prow of rock which jutted out from the snow dome of the summit itself. It was 4.45 p.m. Far below, Jannu drifted in and out of cloud. Everest and Makalu could still be seen standing above all else. To the east the mountains of Sikkim were softening in the light of the setting sun.

We had given no promises to avoid standing on the summit itself, yet none of us made a move towards the rounded dome only ten feet higher than where we stood. The obligation to respect what was sacred to another people was beyond promises. Doug tried to skirt below the summit to look down the eastern face but the slope was too steep.

We all took photographs and crouched down together as Doug set the time control on his camera to record the three of us against the summit. The dark form of an Alpine chough flew over us – an omen, a messenger of the gods whose home we were threatening to desecrate. The heavy cloud had risen from the valleys, homing in on the mountain where we stood. It was time to go.

'Just a moment while I take some black and white photos,' said Doug and we waited. I was impatient.

'We must get moving.'

'You'll be glad of these when we get back. Just hold on while I change the film.'

'Pete, start moving. It will be dark soon.'

It was 5.30 p.m. as we moved off. Half an hour before dark. As we made our way back to the notch on the ridge the belly of the heavy cloud now hanging over the mountain was aflame with the orange glow of the setting sun. The distant mountains were blanketed from sight by this apocalyptic curtain-fall. Darkness covered the mountain and the snow started.

We picked our way down the ramp from memory, glad now of the marks in the deeper snow showing us the way and vainly peering for traces of crampon points where the snow was hard. Doug was descending first. It was not easy to keep on line. All our instincts were to climb straight downwards but we had to stick to a diagonal line. I heard a cry in the darkness and felt a tug on the rope as Doug, deceived by the shadows cast by his torch, tumbled over a step in the ice to land in soft snow. I could sense a weary fatalism taking hold of me. I was becoming too tired to take sufficient care when every groping step in the darkness needed fullest concentration. Doug kept going off course. I could remember better the line we had come up but Pete's sharper eyes were able to pick out the slightest traces in the surface of the snow. He went first then and for what seemed like hours we climbed down by touch and luck alone, the weakening pools of torchlight often hindering rather than helping.

In the deep blackness below we saw the flickering pinprick of light from a torch at Base Camp, then fires flared in signal that our torchlight was observed and they knew that we were on our way back from the summit. It was no sort of reassurance, Georges was signalling from another life, and his pinpricks of torchlight would only have meaning for us if we survived.

What had been a breeze became a savage wind which flung snow in our eyes as we tried to see in the dark. Doug's hands were almost insensible with the cold and a note of panic and urgency marked his voice as he insisted on stopping to warm them. At the rear my whole being was tense with cold and as I waited to move on I wanted to plead with Doug to keep moving so that we could reach the cave sooner. Pete was too far away for me to see, careful and capable; I was confident in his ability to keep on the right line.

There was some confusion when we reached the rock step, until we realised where we were and the nearness to safety gave me strength for a last effort.

The slabby step of rock was slippery with the new snow, but I felt at home there, sliding down confidently on what I had climbed up so warily. Only a long, sweeping arc down the slope below remained before we were at the cave entrance. Doug disappeared inside to massage his hands back to life. I felt all the tension drain away and I paused outside to take off my crampons and coil the rope. I was warm now from exertion and I felt a reluctance to break the spell of these moments, savouring the fury of the elements lashing the mountain, knowing that for a brief interval we had been allowed to master it.

I chatted to Pete for some minutes. We were still at 26,000 feet with a long way to go before we were in complete safety but nothing could take away from us the fact that we had climbed Kangchenjunga, we had stood just a few feet short of the third highest mountain in the world and we had done it all ourselves, without a massive pyramid of support from other selfless workers who had paved the way for us. I thought of the lady who had become my friend, Mrs Beaumont, who had had such trust in first lending me support in efforts to come to the Himalayas. She had had confidence in us when we least felt it ourselves and I thought now that climbing this mountain would be a justification for her of all her earlier trust.

'Mrs Beaumont will be pleased, Pete,' I said.

'Yep, it's going to be great to get back, isn't it?' and we crawled inside to join Doug. It was 8.00 p.m.

I felt relief and cautious satisfaction that the hardest part of our task was over, but the relief did not help me rest. Though my body was weary, my mind was still stimulated by the long day's need for total concentration and awareness. Sleep was fitful, but without anxiety for the energy needed for another day of upward struggle.

The morning chores of making tea and packing sacks were undesirable duties postponing departure. The departure, when it came, was more discomfort, an endless trail for limbs moved by a spark of life from inside. Doug seemed to have strength remaining. He drew ahead on the plateau, while I hobbled on in company with Pete, finding the uneven ground awkward under foot. My muscles no longer had the power to hold my limbs steady, and I sank down to rest at every excuse, revelling in the moments of ease stolen from the time needed for the descent. It hardly seemed possible that the plateau should stretch on and on as it did, and I worried that Georges could well have been right, that we had pushed ourselves on to our physical limits in reaching the summit and now had not enough reserves of energy to bring ourselves back down in safety.

Doug disappeared over the edge where the ropes led down to the cave and gradually we too came to the end of the plateau. Doug had already been into the cave when we arrived and had retrieved all belongings left there. The ceiling had sunk more in our absence so that there was only two feet of clearance left. The dark cleft looked more claustrophobic than ever and did not invite entry for a last nostalgic visit. We were sheltered from the breeze beside the cave entrance and we lingered for a while, warmed by the sun and melting snow to make tea. The loss of 2,000 feet of altitude and the sweet tea restored some energy. We roped together and started down the ridge to the North Col.

The wind was stronger once we were out in the open, mist-like streams of snow scoured the ridge and stung our faces. The rope between us stretched in a taut bow as we moved together downwards, trying to keep pace with one another.

The tents of Camp 3 at the North Col were frozen to their platforms. We tried to free them but the fabric tore and we had neither the time nor the patience to ease them free. We decided to abandon them, packing all the remaining gear which we could not carry into two rucksacks to toss down to the glacier below, from where we hoped to retrieve it later. We had more to drink and debated what to do with the oxygen cylinder. It would cost as much as it was worth to transport back to Kathmandu so it was a choice of leaving it or throwing it down the mountain. I had never used oxygen on a climb and asked Pete and Doug what it was like. I said I fancied trying some before we abandoned the bottle but they discouraged me by threatening to put it about that I had used oxygen on the mountain when they had done it without. It was all in jest but I was put off the idea. Doug wanted to throw if off the ridge to clear the mountain and enjoy the spectacle but Pete was in favour of leaving it just in case someone might come this way again and find it useful. So we left it and dragged the two sacks of gear up to the crest of the ridge. We sent them off, sliding down the gully above the line of ropes, hoping that they would stay intact for recovery once we reached the glacier ourselves.

Our own sacks were heavy enough. We were clearing everything we could from the mountain as we would not be coming back up. The wall had changed in the week that we had been above the Col. There had been a change in the season as the year advanced more towards mid-summer and the ice of the wall had become softer and wet with the rise in temperature. The day was well on as we started down and the warmth of the sun had brought rivulets of water from the ice which soaked the rope, soaked gloves and clothing as we slid down. Sometimes I sucked up mouthfuls of the dirty water to slake my thirst. We had eaten little in that week and I could feel all the more the weight of my sack through the straps which cut into my shoulders from which the flesh had gone. More loose rock was exposed by the receding ice. I dislodged some inadvertently and saw some dislodged from above. When I reached the bottom, where the ropes ran onto the glacier, I freed myself and scuttled down to be clear away from more stones from above. I heard Doug shout but could not make out if he was calling a warning or venting his displeasure at the awkward descent. Then I caught his meaning. Suspended part way up the wall near to him was the shape of a red figure, arms stretched wide, legs together. I was shocked moment-arily as my mind seized on, then discarded as impossible, the thought that there was a body stuck to the ice. It was only a down suit, part of the gear we had thrown from above. I looked around me; a few hundred feet away were other objects. One of the sacks had burst open and the glacier was strewn with other items of clothing. The down suit had opened out and drifted on its own to catch on a rock projection. Doug eased himself across on the rope and tugged it free, so that it sailed on to the bottom of the wall.

I forced myself to go about gathering up the scattered objects, retrieving all but a suit of my own. There was no sign of Ang Phurba or Nima, whom we had asked to come to meet us. We took what we could and made a pile of the rest for them to collect.

It was 5.00 p.m. There was only an hour of daylight left, but the return to Camp 2 had only ever taken half an hour so we were confident of reaching it before dark. Pete insisted that we use the bit of rope we had remaining to tie ourselves together, cautious to the last, lest the mountain should strike back, swallowing one of us up in a crevasse just as we were thinking we were safe. We spotted the two Sherpas just as we were leaving. They were a long distance away and were moving very slowly. We were angry that they should be so leisurely when we were so tired. They would have seen us the moment we had started down the wall and could have been almost with us by this time. I started first; the snow was wet and deep. I looked forward to reaching the more level part of the glacier where the snow was usually firmer, but it never became firm. At first I was up to my knees, then up to my thighs, and sometimes I sank up to my waist and floundered helplessly trying to move forward when there was nothing solid to step on. I looked back at Doug and Pete, they were no better off following in my tracks. Doug seemed to sink in even further with his greater weight.

Sometimes a dark, bottomless hole appeared when I withdrew my foot and I was glad of the tenuous reassurance of the line attaching me to the other two. A couple of times I could see a crevasse in the way and crawled, spreading my weight over as wide an area as possible and lunging over the dark gap, in the hope of landing in the snow of the other side. Sometimes I could not tell that a crevasse lay hidden beneath the snow and I felt the stab of fear in my stomach as the ground gave way beneath me and I would throw back the upper part of my body to bury my sack in the snow behind, and wait, suspended over nothing, till I had caught my breath and could haul myself out.

This was the glacier we had walked up and down so easily, in snow at most ankle-deep, on a track well beaten by our own footsteps. We had usually worn the rope in accordance with the precepts of safety rather than because there were any clear indications of the dangers below. Now we could see that this whole glacier basin was seamed with crevasses and only the firmness of the snow had facilitated our passage in those earlier weeks.

We resorted to crawling in many places and dragged our sacks along the snow beside us trying to take more weight off our feet. Darkness was drawing on and in these conditions it seemed as if it would take us hours to get back to the camp. We realised now why the two Sherpas had not reached the foot of the wall in time to meet us, and saw too that this deep snow must stretch all the way to Camp 2. At the mound where the avalanche debris lay across our way the going was only slightly firmer. Ang Phurba and Nima were closer and to keep up my spirits I consoled myself with the thought that we would be able to walk more easily once we reached their tracks.

We were all wet and cold from contact with the snow. Doug complained bitterly as if the cold was singling him out for special attention. His fingers and toes were giving him great pain.

Unannounced, Ang Phurba and Nima loomed up out of the gloom, and I felt we were saved. We told them of the rucksacks of gear we had left for them to collect next day but they wanted to collect them immediately since they were halfway there and they continued on by the feeble light of an almost exhausted torch.

They gave us some directions but night came on and the wind brought snow. The going was slightly better but I lost the way and came up against a large crevasse. Their footsteps were indistinct in the darkness, but I remembered Ang Phurba's description and got back on course. Pete was better in the dark and took over the lead until at last we reached the camp.

The sole tent remaining was covered in snow and indistinct against the whiteness of the now furious storm. We almost missed it but had realised our error when Ang Phurba and Nima reappeared out of the dark, carrying the heavy sacks we had left. The speed with which they had gone up and come back emphasised how weak we had become and how little able we were to continue fighting against the elements.

Their arrival meant we could now surrender all duties to them. We three piled into the tent, making ourselves comfortable, taking off wet clothing and slipping into the luxurious warmth of our sleeping bags. We lay back, letting the two Sherpas hand back hot drinks and food to us, as the cosy drug of near safety made heavy our eyes. I fought off sleep for as long as they were administering food to us, enjoying the delicious sense of fatigue without responsibility. When all was finished we took a sleeping pill each, Ang Phurba and Nima squeezed into the tent, and we slept in such comfort and warmth as had been long forgotten.

We were woken at 3.30 a.m. by Nima with a cup of tea. He and Ang Phurba were anxious to be moving before the snow softened again in the heat of the sun. It was only the first stretch, down to our old Camp 1, where the snow was deep. It was not yet as soft as the previous evening and once onto the bare ice of the lower glacier we could walk freely. Only new streams of meltwater signalled the advance of the season and, once clear of the slopes from which avalanches might come, we knew we could relax. At last we were down off the mountain and could truthfully say we had climbed Kangchenjunga.

Doug's pace quickened again. I could not hurry, not even to share the good news with those at Base Camp. I needed to guard my strength to keep my footing on the unstable mounds of rocks over which we had to climb. Pete and I talked shamelessly of the cigarettes we would let ourselves smoke in arrogant defiance of all the doubts and anxieties which the mountain had inspired before we climbed it. Neither of us would confess to 'smoking' in normal life, and knew that smoking was antithetical to the excellence of health we needed to climb mountains. As a symbol it represented all that was forbidden to us, and having succeeded we wanted the forbidden.

I fell several times, too weak to keep my footing on the boulder slopes leading up to Base Camp. By the time I saw Georges rushing down towards us, my arms were cut and bloodied from these falls so that I looked to have had an accident. Then Georges was hugging Pete and then me, and kissing my cheeks, smiling his pleasure that we were back, successful and well. Doug had already confirmed what he had seen through the telephoto lens on the camera. He had seen us as three tiny dots under a magnification of twenty times.

'Did you get a photo of us on the summit?' I asked.

'No, I was so excited, I forgot. I am so glad. I felt I was up there with you. I am so pleased.'

Base Camp was a place of blissful ease and safety. There was a festive atmosphere which made an ordinary meal seem like a celebration. It was 18 May. Georges had sent down for porters as soon as he saw us on the summit. They were due next day. I calculated that we should be back in England by early June.

Suddenly the mountain had been climbed and all our attentions were focused in the opposite direction. There was a whole new variety of preoccupations of a lesser order of importance. I had a sore throat to nurse, stinking clothes to change, a beard to shave off. I had worn a beard for almost ten years so that I had forgotten what I looked like without one. I decided to shave it off at Base Camp so that it had time to grow again if I did not like what I found underneath. One of my toes was very sore and appeared black beneath the nail. I did not know if it was due to compression in my boots over a long period or the freezing cold of the previous night of floundering in deep snow with soaking socks. I wondered if the black-ened toe-nail qualified me for the status of one who had had frostbite.

Even the simple food of Base Camp was too rich. For the previous two days we had eaten hardly anything and prior to that our diet had been minimal. No sooner did I eat something than I had to rush off to the toilet area.

This had been a long expedition and still it was far from over. The long walk back was unavoidable and once the thrill of returning to Base Camp had dissipated into normality I perceived how remote we were. At home, when distances are calculated in the hours of car or train or plane journey, it is hard to comprehend the isolation of knowing that only after many days of walking up hills and over streams will one reach a destination. It was difficult for me to conceive of life at home. We had been through depths of feeling and profound experiences which only we as a group had shared. I had become accustomed to facing my innermost being on my own, of coming to terms with hopes and fears, had realised where my real wishes lay in spite of the pain of reaching that place. The emotional and physical yearnings of the early weeks had been anaesthetised by the catharsis of the drama in which we had been the actors. I could hardly visualise what it meant to have a relationship with a girl. I looked forward to female company but without the urgency I had expected after so long away. The lovely village girl, Dawa, arrived as one of our porters and instead of the avid attention we had paid her on the way in no one took any notice of her. We were still influenced by the mountain which had dominated us and soaked up all our energies. In time, as the ascent receded into a memory, as we grew accustomed to knowing that we did not have to concentrate single-mindedly on the mountain any more, the ties of home would re-awaken and wax stronger, drawing us irresistibly back.

In a way it was fortunate that the pull was not at full strength, or the isolation now perceived would have become unbearable with still many days, if not weeks, between us and the return home. We came back to full strength only gradually, feeling the punishment of the long marches for the first few days. Then we would stride on, making our own paces, until the evening halt. We walked long and hard. My feet were tender from the cold they had felt and every step was uncomfortable, but the air was rich, the days warm and the food plentiful as we passed through the lower valleys. We came upon our mail runner, long overdue, dawdling in his home village instead of bringing us the mail he carried. We paid him off and pressed on, retracing our steps along a pathway scarcely remembered after all these weeks, and down into a tropical valley, after nine days of walking, from where one last hill had to be crossed before we reached the road.

There was a compound of huts where a road-construction project was under way. A solitary Peace Corps worker in a village had told us that the foundation for the road was almost complete and sometimes lifts could be obtained over that last hill. Doug and I went into the compound and knocked on a door. A clean, white-clad Englishman opened the door to us.

'Would it be possible,' said Doug in his most persuasive manner, 'for you to save us any more pain in our feet by giving us a lift over the hill to Dharan?'

The face of the man, puzzled at our dishevelled appearance, lit into a smile.

'You must be the Kangchenjunga team. I'm sure we can arrange a lift for you. Are you in a hurry or would you have time for a spot of lunch with us before you go?'

SEVEN

Apocalypse

K2

I

My beard grew back by the time we arrived in England. Pete went off to Switzerland and Doug started immediately preparing to depart again. Georges came with his wife, Norma, to stay with me for a holiday. They were good company and I got to know a different side of Georges. When we were laughing and joking round the table he would stop me and ask a joke to be explained far more often than he had ever done during the expedition. I asked him how it was that he had understood things during the expedition and seemed to have lost that understanding. He explained that he had not understood many things but had not wanted to be a nuisance by interrupting all the time for explanations when everyone else was laughing, so he had laughed too, just to join in.

He became converted to music too and would walk in, if the flat was silent, with a 'Hey, Joe, let's put a record on,' and I came back late a couple of times to find that he had fallen asleep on the floor with music still playing.

Georges and Norma returned to Chamonix, where they normally spent the summers, so that Georges could guide and I tried to spend some time paying attention to the business of running a shop before becoming totally embroiled in preparations for the return to K2.

The ascent of Kangchenjunga mellowed into being an achievement that nothing could usurp. Above all the setbacks, the doubts and the pain which each of us had had to face, the fact of reaching the summit stood out and would remain with us forever. The ascent might not have brought peace of mind but it did bring confidence to go on further, to take on something new and more difficult. There was nothing lacking in that the objective so long striven for should not, once achieved, be sufficient in itself. It was in the nature of such objectives, and of us who sought them, that one horizon reached should lead to the next.

The ascent of Dunagiri had shown that two people was a viable team for a difficult Himalayan peak and the next logical step was to attempt Changabang by its West Face, which seemed to border on the edge of the impossible. Succeeding on it was in no way disappointing but as a mountaineer the essence of life is in the struggle, the contest against great odds. Climbing Changabang's West Face demonstrated the level of technical difficulty which could be successfully attempted even by a very small team. The challenge lay in even higher peaks. On Kangchenjunga the problem was clear, with no room for compromise: could our bodies cope with the lack of oxygen we would have to endure to reach the top? However erratic a course we each made in reaching the top, nothing could ever invalidate that we had done so, and each of us by the strength of his body alone.

To go on from there, to progress, the three of us who had reached the summit of Kangchenjunga were already planning to attempt a mountain which was higher, and a route to its top which was harder. The success on Kangchenjunga gave us confidence to dare to return without oxygen equipment to the West Ridge of K2 from which we had retreated in 1978 after the death of Nick Estcourt.

Then there had been eight members on the team and this time, for the renewed attempt, we decided to have a team of four. It was a bold idea to go as a foursome to climb the second highest mountain in the world, by a route which had defeated eight of us, but we rationalised that the mountain, although 28,253 feet high, was only forty-five feet higher than one we had already similarly climbed. The real problem was that the route appeared to have difficulties for most of the way, and the big unknown was whether we could continue to overcome those difficulties of buttresses, walls of rock and runnels of ice at altitudes where every step would be a deadly effort. And whether, where all movement is painstakingly slow, we would be able to descend safely if an accident occurred or one of us became ill.

The unknowns were what gave flavour and attraction to the idea, and we believed that we could safely avoid the slope from which Nick had been swept away by climbing a faint rib of rock directly to the crest of the ridge. This would bring us out above the camp where Pete and I had spent four nights confined by snow-storms, the way to which was menaced, we now knew, by avalanche danger.

The loss of Nick was not something I had forgotten, nor an incident whose impact had lessened. It was a tragedy which had become absorbed into experience, the memory of which was a constant reminder of the need for caution in continuing to follow a pursuit which owed much of its value and compulsion to the risks entailed. Without the danger it is hardly likely that the superlative performance needed to overcome the difficulties would be stimulated.

Pete and I had applied to the Ministry of Tourism in Islamabad on our arrival back there in 1978 for permission for another attempt on K2. A few months later Doug said that he too had come round to thinking of going back and we joined forces. On our return from Kangchenjunga in 1979 we started looking for a fourth person, and I was keen to invite Dick Renshaw, who had recovered completely from his frostbite.

Since Dunagiri he had regained the confidence which had been shaken by the possibility of losing his fingers frozen during that harrowing descent. In keeping with his nature, he had quietly pursued a very active life in the mountains, climbing in winter in the Alps, in Canada, in South America. Whilst his fingers were still recovering he had gone off for a trek across some mountain passes in the Karakoram range. A year after the mishap, the doctors treating him had managed to save all but a few millimetres of bone which had had to be trimmed from three finger-ends. The miracle had been that, when his fingers had been black with frostbite, he had managed to avoid infection through all that long descent, the walk back to the road, the journey to Delhi by crowded bus and train and treatment in a hospital where the nurses were too shy to wash him.

Now he told me he was much more careful with his hands, always taking several pairs of gloves, to ensure that he had a dry pair lest his hands get cold with the damp. He was delighted to be asked to go to K2 with us, seeming to see it as the answer to that blind love for mountains which I knew he had not lost. Since I had last climbed with him, Dick had become a vegetarian, and as such would complement Doug, who had so far been in a minority in his eating habits.

In the autumn of 1979, Pete went off on an expedition to a beautiful mountain called Gauri Sankar and Doug went back to Nuptse, which I had tried with him in 1978. I was relieved not to be going away again so soon. After three expeditions in thirteen months I savoured the prospect of almost a year at home. I knew that Pete was ambivalent about going off again so quickly, but an expedition is so complex to organise and is arranged so far in advance that alterations in the arrangements are hardly feasible. For once I had the chance to relax, to return to rock-climbing in Britain, to organise my life better, but the summer was gone, and the long, cold nights of winter drew in before I realised that the departure for K2 was only a few months away and that we had not raised any of the £16,000 we had estimated to need for the expedition. Most of the £9,000 we had needed for Kangchenjunga had come from our own pockets, and none of us had money left in such quantities. Expeditions to the Karakoram, in Pakistan, cost very much more than in Nepal and India because rates for the porters are much higher and the mountain regions are less inhabited. One cannot rely upon obtaining food or fuel in villages, even where they exist, so supplies for porters as well as for the expedition have to be purchased and carried for long distances.

Whereas Mount Everest is well known to the general public, and the wish to climb it needs little justification, the same is not true of K2, a mountain only a few hundred feet lower. Because the cost of the expedition was beyond our personal means, we needed to attract some form of sponsorship beyond the amounts we could expect from the Mount Everest Foundation and the British Mountaineering Council. Most companies, however, need more justification to act as sponsors than the wish to further a sport for its own sake. The sponsorship usually has to be seen as beneficial to the company itself. With climbing the mountains we were familiar, but in raising the money to do so we were amateurs. It was part of the conflict of any climber between the need to establish a reasonable life-style and the desire to have the freedom to climb. Often one has the means but not the time. We had the time but not the means.

A few weeks before we were due to leave, Doug had gone off to Australia and New Zealand on a lecture tour, Pete was living in Switzerland and Dick was based in Cardiff. Arrangements were well in hand but we were still £10,000 short of our budget. Because I was the only one of the team available, I was asked to appear on the BBC 2 *Newsnight* programme to talk about the expedition and from there more requests for interviews sprang up. Out of the blue one day the telephone rang and a Mr Swain introduced himself.

'I heard you speaking on the *Today* programme while I was driving to work. The company is Sadia Aerofreeze, and we make freezers. How much money are you looking for?'

The weariness with which I answered the many phone calls disappeared. We talked further and though he could not promise all the money we still needed, he was sure his company could be of assistance.

'By the way, how much will your total baggage weigh?'

'About one and a half tons.'

'Oh. We have a new model freezer which happens to be called the K2 model, and I was wondering if you could carry one to Base Camp to take some unusual photos of it.'

We agreed that since their freezer weighed a ton in itself, it was impractical for us to take one with us. I mentally tried to imagine the porters struggling with this object along the crumbling footpaths, over swollen rivers which we would cross by rope bridge and up the long Baltoro glacier with its unstable mounds of rubble and concealed crevasses. It brought home to me how little was understood by many people about climbing mountains. Mr Swain was not deterred, and the financial support of £3,000 which he offered on behalf of his company was of enormous help.

Of similar amusement was the request by Bass Ltd, whom we had also approached for support, to take with us some of their non-alcoholic beer. The beer had been developed for Saudi Arabia where, as a Muslim state, alcohol is prohibited. When it was realised that the beer had been brewed in a conventional manner, then had the alcohol extracted from it, the resulting alcohol-free beer was regarded as being contaminated still by the contact it had once with alcohol. Bass were left with vast quantities of the now unwanted drink and our visit to K2, itself the highest mountain in the Muslim state of Pakistan, was viewed as a suitable means of disposing of some of the drink. It was the only 'drink' we would be allowed to take into the country. Bass had long been associated with mountaineering in that they had raised a huge sum of money for the Mount Everest Foundation by a lottery run in their public houses. Peter Sherlock of Bass took an interest in our plans for K2 and promised to find what money he could.

From these two sources the sum needed was almost found and the final amount came with a request from *Newsnight* to send them back news reports, for which they would pay, during the expedition.

Only days before we were due to leave, the financial problems had been solved, and with £1,000 from each of us the total of £16,000 was reached.

I had another phone call before we left. It was Dick asking me when I thought we would be back from the expedition.

'I'm going to be a dad, you see. The baby is due at the end of August. We should be back by then, shouldn't we?'

We were due to leave on 31 April. August was four months ahead. Certainly we should be back, but Dick would be absent through the most trying time of the pregnancy and his girlfriend would have all the anxieties of knowing that Dick was out of contact, attempting a most difficult and dangerous mountain.

I had become friendly with a girl called Maria, whose brother was a climber but who had never appreciated the full implications of having a boyfriend who was committed to climbing mountains. The prospect of my being away for so long on this uncertain venture began to alarm her more as our departure drew near.

One afternoon I was in the process of booking our flights over the phone with a travel agent in London. Allen Jewhurst was visiting me for a few days. He had hovered on the fringe of involvement with mountains since he first took an interest in making a film of a climb. The march-in towards K2 in 1978 had whetted his appetite for the rough life of the mountains. Often he had hinted to me how much he would like to come on an expedition again. Now as I spoke on the phone he whispered to ask when we were leaving.

'Book me a ticket to Pakistan. I might come with you for a few days.'

I never knew when to take him seriously. He was impetuous in everything and I booked a seat for him, expecting to know for certain whether he was coming only at the last moment.

'It's "ma" business commitments. If I can sort them out I'd fancy a bit of sun. I think it's really lovely out there.'

He did come and flew with Dick, Pete and myself to Karachi. Doug was delayed a few days by his late return from New Zealand and planned to join us in Islamabad.

We had fifty bags and boxes of equipment and food, and expected endless hold-ups at the customs, but there was not a moment's delay. A truck was waiting at the airport, hired by us from England through the continuing assistance of my good friends, Mr and Mrs Beaumont. They had telexed our needs to the company office in Karachi and all was waiting for us. We threw all the baggage aboard, piled on ourselves and the truck drove off into the night.

We travelled for three days and nights across the Sind desert on the back of that lorry, and our whole world seemed to be centred inside those wooden walls, protected from the sun in the hottest part of the day by an awning tied above. Our rucksacks and kitbags provided uneven seating and the jolting progression of the lorry prevented any rest. From civilised, elegant airline passengers we were reduced in a matter of hours to bedraggled scarecrows, choked by the dust of the road, hanging onto the side of a wagon as yet another jolt flung us into the air.

The journey served to decondition us from the life of the West. By the time we reached Islamabad we had become attuned to the idea of being once more in the East. We made for the haven of the British Embassy residential compound where we had been invited to stay. Elspeth, a secretary whom we had met in 1978, had put her air-conditioned house at our disposal. After the bumpy ride it was an oasis of cool comfort where we could re-sort our equipment and complete formalities. Doug arrived, and together the five of us seemed to have taken over the whole house. There were not enough beds for all of us but Dick was content to sleep on the floor, telling us that he found the beds too soft for him. It had been almost five years since Dick and I had climbed together and had shared those bleak days when all our strength and life itself seemed to be dwindling away as we retreated down Dunagiri. He had not changed, still accepting with reluctance anything but the barest essentials for living. He stayed in the house only because we wanted to and he needed to be with us, but he accepted its comforts uneasily and suggested at one point that we should all bed down in the garage rather than crowd Elspeth out of her own home.

We divided up to attend to all the different tasks necessary before we could leave. Pete and I sat through the detailed procedure required to arrange a bank guarantee against the need for helicopter rescue, while Doug and Dick went off to purchase the 60,000 cigarettes needed as part of the rations for our porters. Allen relaxed by the swimming pool waiting for the formalities to be completed. He was not on the expedition proper and as such was not allowed to come with us further than the village of Dassu at the end of the first day's walk. He was disappointed but the regulations concerning movement in the mountain areas are very strict and even to obtain a trekking permit would have taken him several weeks.

We met our Liaison Officer, Major Sarwat, from the Pakistan army. It was a mark of the high regard in which our expedition was held that a major instead of a captain had been assigned to us, but we sensed that Major Sarwat was not impressed with our small group, with its lack of pretensions and its informality. Once again there was the dichotomy between the public image of expeditions, based on the well-publicised, large-scale ventures, and our own more intimate, loosely structured approach. I found I was comparing Sarwat with Captain Shafiq, who had been with us in 1978. He had been liberal in his attitudes and had seemed more of a companion than a supervisor. Major Sarwat seemed more rigid in his interpretation of the rules by which we had to abide. He was a strict Muslim and could not understand how five men could innocently stay in the house of a single girl. According to his religion such familiarity between the sexes was taboo. We had to get to know the man who was to be with us for many weeks and we each attempted to establish some familiarity with him. Major Sarwat was earnest and energetic in his wish to help the expedition to which he had been assigned even though it did not fit his preconceptions of what an expedition should be. Pete was the official leader but he did not behave like one. Amongst ourselves we came to a consensus on any decisions, but for official purposes one person had to have the title of leader. Major Sarwat needed one person to whom he could look for orders and the resolution of problems but Pete was as informal as any of us. He jested with the Major that we had friends in China to whom we would sell photographs of bridges when we returned home, but the jest met with the cold reply that the Chinese probably knew everything about the border areas anyway. It was as if the luxury of the Embassy quarters and our irreverent attitudes were a slight on the standard of living in Pakistan and an indication of a feeling of superiority in us. Our relations with the Major held little promise of being anything but a strain in the weeks ahead.

On returning from their shopping round, Doug and Dick discovered they had left the case of 60,000 cigarettes in the boot of a taxi, and had no means whatever of distinguishing it from any of the hundreds of ramshackle cabs which cruised the dusty streets. Doug regarded the mishap with philosophical resignation. Dick raged at his own stupidity and forgetfulness, feeling the loss as a personal blow to his normal sense of thrift. They reported the loss to the police without any great hope of recovering what would be an enormously valuable and untraceable booty for any taxi driver. But Mr Awan from the Ministry of Tourism rang the next day to say that the cigarettes had been handed in and Major Sarwat's face shone with joy.

'This day I am proud of my country,' he said with evident satisfaction.

At the airport, where we queued for seats on the flight to Skardu, there were two men from Hunza who made themselves known to us. One of them claimed to be a cousin of Quamajan, who had been with us on the 1978 expedition. We had written asking him to come and work with us again but his 'cousin' Gohar said he had come in his place as Quamajan now had a steady job as watchman in a government rest-house. Gohar was well over six feet tall, an unusually big man for the East. He was keen to join our expedition as high-altitude porter and with him was a man called Ali, who asked to be taken on as cook.

The men from Hunza have a reputation for reliability and resourceful-ness, but we did not wish to hire two full-time attendants without having a chance to assess their capabilities. In 1978 we had taken on a cook through someone else's recommendation and were subsequently disappointed in his performance. We did not want the same to happen again. The flight to Skardu was full anyway, and there seemed little chance that they would arrive there in time for us to sign them up. Our own seats had already been assured.

On the flight we noticed that Gohar and Ali had somehow managed to wheedle their way in and were sitting in a front seat, studiously avoiding imposing their presence upon us.

Little had changed in two years. The same motley assortment of ragged Baltis filled the baked mud compound outside the town gaol, jostling each other in the heat of the day, anxious to be hired. Similar police were in attendance, controlling the eager crowd. There was an order underlying the apparent chaos; there were groupings of men under appointed leaders and instead of suspecting, as in 1978, that this was another attempt to fiddle us, we found that these leaders were the instruments of control. We were no more admirable in our behaviour than we suspected them to be. We tried to reduce the number of porters we needed by increasing the weight of their individual loads, but the subterfuge was detected and we were diminished somewhat in their eyes.

We had learnt in 1978 that the men who congregated in Skardu, the men from Huche and Paphlu, were the most reliable as porters. They had to walk far to be hired and seemed to have more commitment to the work they took on than the porters from the villages along our way, who took it for granted that they would be hired. We tried to select all ninety porters we needed from the more reliable villages, but the local laws decreed that the work had to be equably distributed between several villages so that as wide an area as possible could benefit. We surrendered to the prevailing norms. Any attempt to change the order of things only meant more worries and frustrations for ourselves. In the end we knew we would reach Base Camp, no matter how trying circumstances might seem at times. Argument, discussion and compromise are all part of the tradition of these mountain areas and our Western ideas on efficiency and conformity were out of place.

The leaders of the groups of fifteen or twenty men were the Naikes, who expected to carry nothing, but were proud overseers of the groups. It was better to go along with this established practice, since it meant we had only five or six people to bargain with rather than close on one hundred.

We came together more as a group when we were held up by heavy rains in the village of Chakpoi only two days out from Skardu. Porters and team alike were confined in a muddy clearing waiting for the rains to stop before entering the Braldu Gorge. The track runs along the edge of the river for a number of hours and the hillside above is a steep slope of mud and boulders. The rain softens the mud and boulders are released, crashing down onto the track and threatening the passage of all below. In 1978, shortly after we had abandoned the expedition to K2, a member of another expedition in the region had been killed in the gorge by falling rocks and only a week previous to our present arrival a villager and a porter had been similarly killed. Only a couple of days after starting, we had come to a halt, worrying about the danger to the porters in our employ and the high cost of keeping them static for days at a time.

Allen had left us. He had gone back reluctantly but unable to come further, since Major Sarwat was with us as guardian of the laws of his country and so far had seemed unlikely to bend any rules. All four of us were sad to see him go. He was not overshadowed by the problem which affected all our thoughts, that of climbing K2. I felt that he was buoyant when we were intense, lively when we were reflective.

Since that first time in the mountains in 1978 he had come to know what to expect. The physical effort and discomfort had not shocked him into silence this time; on the contrary he seemed at home with the rough way of life. The weight of organisation was not a pressure on him but he had thrown himself into any work necessary to get the expedition under way. Each of us could laugh and joke with him because he seemed to possess a levity which the task ahead precluded us four from having. We said our goodbyes and I could see he was sorry to go. His heart was still with us. With him went some of the chirpiness of the expedition and I wondered if we were destined to have a serious time, since none of the four of us had Allen's gift for creating humour out of any situation. We seemed a more serious group when he had gone.

II

The porters hired a local holy man and made a prayer-offering with a chicken to halt the rain. They were as irritated as we were by the rain, since they preferred to complete their work for one expedition in order to rush back and work for another. 'Waiting days' were only at half pay.

When at last we exited safely from the gorge, the porters broke into song.

The sun came through the clouds and the heavy depression which had hung over the expedition lifted away. The song of the porters was a long traditional ballad of courtship and romance. The whole recitation takes several days but our porters would sing parts of it at night or on this occasion when there was cause for celebration. A dance was performed by a gaunt scarecrow of a man, partnered by a short, mischievous porter who called himself Mahdi. They danced in time to the song, performing an interpretation of the eternal confrontation between man and woman, a mime so well executed that we had no need of words to follow the story. I filmed some of it but the camera jammed and I was left to record in memory only the delightful scene. One of the Naikes, Ali Hassan, did a solo piece, revealing an unsuspected elegance of poise. His extended arms waved sinuously and his hands flicked expressively as he responded to the chant of the song. I felt that we were privileged to glimpse another side to the life of the people we were employing and that afterwards we had more rapport than on our first mutually suspicious encounters.

There was a slight tinge of green on the barren land we were passing through as if the heat of summer had not yet reached its full strength. Certainly the days were easier than I remembered. It seemed as if we were enjoying a spell of relaxation before entering the long, hard weeks above the snow line. Dick let slip details of the trek he had made this way in 1976 when he was waiting for his hands to heal. His two partners had turned back and he had taken over the tent and the food so that his sack weighed ninety pounds. He could not afford to hire porters but sometimes villagers had taken pity on him and carried part of his load for nothing or for a minimal charge. Once he had tried to cross a rotting bridge made from creepers, but the strands had parted and almost deposited him in the torrent below. He had a store of tales such as these which testified, if he could be enticed to speak, to a determination and resolution which assigned no value to comfort or ease. He busied himself about tasks in the evening which Pete, Doug and myself had grown accustomed to seeing done by the porters or the hired cook. He had not lost that self-sufficiency which made him do everything possible by his own efforts and which now made him uneasy to have a meal cooked for him or a cup of tea brought to his tent in the morning.

I knew the extent to which he felt uncomfortable at what he saw as undeserved luxury and I used to lead him on by exaggerated displays of laziness. I would ask for the sugar and let the cook put two spoonfuls into my mug, stir it and then pass it to me. Dick would look on in shocked disapproval, sometimes letting me know that I was living up to his worst memories of my indolence.

Pete knew how thrifty Dick was and he too would tease him with suggestions of extravagance. 'I don't want to spend more than £300 on presents in Islamabad on the way back,' he said to me once, knowing that

Dick was listening. And Dick, who could live for half a year on £300, responded with the expected incredulity at such profligate intentions.

For Doug, Dick was a welcome addition to the team. At last, after two years of enduring the scepticism and incomprehension of companions at his vegetarian diet, in Dick he had someone who was even more confirmed in the belief in vegetarianism than he was himself. Dick avoided eating not only meat but fish as well.

Ali and Gohar had worn down our resistance and by the time we were leaving Askole, the last village on the way, we had agreed that they should stay with us for the whole of the trip. Ali was to be cook and Gohar was to lend a hand with any load-carrying we might need.

There was none of the tension that had seemed to exist in 1978 between the expedition and the porters. I could not tell whether the porters had changed, had become more accustomed to the procedure of expeditions or whether we were more experienced and therefore more relaxed so that we did not suspect conflict where none existed. The only real confrontation came at Urdukass, a camping spot on a promontory above the Baltoro glacier, after nine days of walking. From here we had to drop down onto the glacier to find a way along its rubble-strewn surface for four days up to Base Camp.

The porters were demanding socks, footwear, rain capes and sunglasses before they would go onto the glacier. The supply of these items has long been a point of contention. In theory the porters have to buy them from the expedition, in practice none wishes to do so, preferring to keep all their wages for their other needs. If the expedition provides them free of charge, it is normal to see the porters walking barefoot, carrying the new footwear and storing the other items away to keep as new to re-sell later. Transportation alone of boxes of footwear, socks and clothing is very expensive and since the porters are expected to possess clothing and footwear for glacier travel we decided to hire only those porters who were equipped already.

At Urdukass it transpired that Major Sarwat had not after all translated this condition of employment and we were faced with the impossible demand to equip our ninety-two porters before they would go further. We had brought stockings and some cheap sunglasses, knowing that some such demands would arise however well equipped the porters all were, but the numbers we had employed were greater than I had envisaged when organising the gear. All told we only had seventy-five pairs of stockings and a similar number of sunglasses. Major Sarwat was insistent that I, as gear organiser, should solve the problem of finding another seventeen pairs of stockings. His demands seemed completely illogical as he knew how long it had taken to reach this place and how long therefore it would take to send back to Skardu for more stockings. I grew angry as Sarwat restated the impossible problem, looking to me for a solution. I knew that we would

21a. Pete leaving the snow cave in the crevasse at 26,000 feet for the final attempt on the summit.

21b. Doug on the summit of Kangchenjunga at sunset.

22a. K2 as seen from Concordia. The West Ridge is on the left, the Abruzzi Ridge is the right-hand ridge from the summit becoming lost in the cloud. Base Camp was beside the rock buttress in the low left of the picture.

22b. Gohar bringing us cups of tea in the morning.

reach Base Camp and that some confrontation was inevitable owing to misunderstandings or cultural differences, but I did not like having to take part in what seemed an almost ritual scenario of argument, deadlock, ultimatum and capitulation. Pete intervened, playing the role of moderator but no more able to solve the problem.

Partly I suspected that such scenarios were as essential an ingredient in the lives of the porters as their ballads and mimes. The confrontation at Urdukass occurred during a day's halt agreed upon so that the porters could cook their food prior to the journey over the barren glacier. In 1978 the violent scene between our Liaison Officer and a porter, with the subsequent threat of a strike, had also occurred on a 'rest day', leaving one to conclude that arguing was all part of the entertainment.

The Naikes were the mediators and the solution to any conflict was in their hands. We were on good terms with them and Ali Hassan especially made a point of sitting with us and recounting tales, interpreted by Major Sarwat, about other expeditions he had been on. We were in sight of the colossal Trango Towers, granite monoliths which would inspire any climber. Ali Hassan had been with the British party in 1976 which had first climbed the Nameless Tower and he made us laugh with stories about the members of the expedition, all people we knew well. He had been impressed by the ascent of the huge tower but he remembered most the cameraman named Jim who ate enormous amounts for breakfast then after a few miles of hard walking would vomit up all his food and say he was hungry again. He would then eat more and repeat the procedure further on. It struck me how observant and humorous these people were and how much we could widen our experience if only we could speak their language.

He had been with the Polish women's expedition to Gasherbrum III under the leadership of a woman called Wanda. He thought she was a good climber but had problems as a leader. His favourite memory from that trip had been of crossing the Punmah river when all the women had had to be carried across by the porters. The Liaison Officer had wanted to be carried too until he saw his chance of carrying a woman across himself. Every couple of days, according to Ali, the women had crowded into a tent to have a good cry from homesickness. At one time the porters had gone on strike for more money (this was in the days before the rates were fixed) and Wanda had fled into her tent and cried. The Liaison Officer had discovered her crying and berated the porters for their unmanly behaviour. The porters decided to carry on.

As he was telling us these slightly scurrilous tales I warned Ali Hassan that Wanda was a friend of ours. He replied that he did not care if we repeated these stories to her, they were all facts, none were invented.

Wanda seemed, in fact, to have the leadership business sorted out. We suggested to Ali Hassan that going off and weeping in our tents might be a way for us to solve our problems. He said that we were welcome to do so if we wanted similar stories to be recounted about us to subsequent expeditions.

The impossible was achieved. Seventy-five pairs of stockings were divided between ninety-two porters and we carried on our way over the rough glacier. We had had a strange encounter at Urdukass with a French climber, Ivan Ghirardini. He is well known for his solo ascents of some of the most difficult routes in the Alps. He had permission to solo Mitre Peak, a small but steep mountain a few miles from K2. His wife, Jeanne Marie, though not a climber, was with him, intending to stay in camp whilst he was on the mountain. He asked, without preamble, if he could join our expedition to K2. There was no warmth in his manner, he seemed intense and serious, without any sign that he was pleased to meet us in this remote spot. It was not in our power to grant him permission to join us, for such a move could only be made, unless one risked expulsion from the country, with the sanction of the Ministry of Tourism in Islamabad. He knew this as well as us. Even so it was a strange request to make. There were many people whom we knew much better than this stranger whom we would have asked along if we had wanted a larger team. He had been on a French expedition to K2 the previous year which had been foiled just short of the summit. He wanted a second chance to climb it but he must have known how drastically it would alter our complex and carefully made plans for us to invite a stranger to join us.

He accepted our refusal and went off to ferry loads up the glacier. To save cost he was employing only one porter and spending several days going backwards and forwards to stock up a camp below his chosen peak. His wife stayed on the grassy spur of Urdukass, dining with us whilst we were there and content to continue the study of the only book she had, a book on shorthand and secretarial work. They had not long been married but it seemed a strange way for her to spend a holiday, camping in a remote, bleak spot while her husband was off climbing. We told her that Nepal was a much more pleasant Himalayan country for a holiday but she protested she was not on holiday, she was simply following her husband. The porters, influenced by all the taboos which circumscribed their relations with women, were intrigued to see a woman alone, with hair which to them was startlingly fair. The woman was a mystery to all of us and equally strange was her willingness to wait alone for her husband's return.

Mitre Peak stands at a junction of glaciers where we were to branch off to the north. It is an elegant peak but seemed too modest to satisfy the capabilities of the man we had met. The real motive for his presence in the area we suspected to be an intention to make a solo attempt on K2. Such a project would, we believed, be more in keeping with his past record and ambitions. It was a problem our Liaison Officer, as guardian of his country's laws, would have to face if the situation arose. Ghirardini's own Liaison Officer, he told us, had injured himself early on during the approach march and had had to go back.

Heavy snowfall made progress along the glacier miserable and difficult. On the second day on the ice the route was not always clear. I was walking with Gohar when we came to an awkward step. We turned back to circumvent it and Gohar, six feet ahead of me, disappeared from sight as the ground collapsed beneath his weight, revealing a crevasse concealed by the thick new snow-covering. There was pandemonium from the porters.

I could hear Gohar's voice inside the icy cleft and felt reassured that he was still alive. Dick was pulling on his climbing harness and I searched through the kitbags for a rope. Doug straddled the crevasse shouting reassurance down to Gohar and Sarwat shouted instructions, which no one heeded, as if he were commanding an army manoeuvre.

Dick made as if to descend into the crevasse almost before anyone was holding onto the rope he was attached to. Pete and I tried to pay out the rope in the disciplined manner of an oft-rehearsed climbing technique but the eager porters seized the rope, using the strength of numbers to hold the weight. Dick shouted up for us to pull and the porters heaved *en masse*. A shaken and bruised Gohar emerged from the dark hole. Dick was hauled up in turn and he told us that Gohar had been saved from falling irretrievably into the furthest depths by his rucksack which had wedged him in place twenty feet below the surface.

The dark mist and swirling snow increased the gloom which sprang out of the incident. Memories of accidents past and awful deaths in crevasses loomed large in all our minds. We reached Concordia, camping place for the night, cold from the wind and our feet wet from the deep snow. Gohar became silent and morose after his narrow escape and the porters, whose ragged clothing was poor protection against the weather, displayed a sullen resentment.

The porters carried their loads for the next leg of the journey but the stormy weather persisted. They refused to go any further. They had brought us to the foot of the mountain but we needed the loads carried up the Savoia glacier round to the west side to make a Base Camp at the foot of the West Ridge. They flatly refused. A porter had been killed the previous year on the edge of the Savoia glacier and Gohar's mishap had revived their fears. No matter how we tried to persuade them, cajole them, offer them three and four times the daily rate and promise to safeguard everyone over the dangerous areas, they were adamant. 'Please do not tempt us with money when our lives are at stake and we have families at home.' We gave in and paid them all off. Their viewpoint was valid but equally we knew that in 1978 hordes of villagers had returned, unroped, to loot our camps up to 20,000 feet on the West Ridge and that adamant as they were now, on another occasion a fine day would make all the difference to their willingness to go further.

The unexpected work which now fell to us had a marked effect on our plans to climb the West Ridge. Establishment of Base Camp near our chosen route took much longer than we had planned for and delayed our attempt on the ridge. When we were able to get to grips with it we made steady progress to 23,000 feet, with spells of bad weather occasionally slowing us down. We avoided the slope which had killed Nick in 1978 and reached the crest of the ridge. After following the ups and downs of the ridge we were forced back into the centre of the face when we came up to a steepening barrier of rock hundreds of feet high. A very difficult pitch of three hundred feet took most of a day to climb, but it linked us with an ice field in the centre of the wall. It had been my turn to lead on that pitch and I staggered into camp, an hour after the other three, utterly spent by the effort it had taken.

Time was running out for Doug. He had not anticipated being on the mountain for as long as we were going to need to succeed on this route. With more difficulties ahead, but much higher up, he believed we were too small a group for the siege tactics he was beginning to think were necessary. He had other commitments which were drawing him home, another expedition of which he was leader but which he would not be back in time for if we did not reach the top soon. He pressed for us to make an ascent of the route by which the mountain was first climbed, the Abruzzi Spur, on which we would not have to fix ropes and which we should be able to climb more rapidly than the West Ridge. None of the rest of us wanted to leave the West Ridge but Doug was going to have to leave soon anyway, so we abandoned the West Ridge for a second time. The Abruzzi Spur was not going to be an easy route at all. We spent three nights at 19,000 feet holed up in tents as storms lashed the mountain. We passed the time reading, having torn up the only book we had to share between us, and eventually we had to retreat. Doug had no time left, another life and another expedition drew him away; Dick, Pete and myself stayed on. For us, reaching the top of this mountain had come to assume an importance which outweighed any other obligations or considerations.

III

Tackling a mountain as big and difficult as K2 in a party of only three should have been a daunting concept but we had reached this point gradually so it seemed only a logical development. At Base Camp, back at the spot from where the porters had left, we amended our plans. Gohar and Ali were still with us, two mail runners periodically arrived after a round trip of ten days with news from home, and Major Sarwat was proving to be an encouraging and valued supporter of our efforts to climb the mountain.

Since the days when I had been perturbed by his serious demeanour and attention to the smallest of rules, I had begun to realise that he was wholeheartedly in favour of our expedition. In arguing with the porters he had worn himself out on our behalf to spur them on to help us. His job now was unenviable. He had to wait in attendance at Base Camp until we had finished the climb, however long it took. There was little for him to do, but he occupied his time reading and doing odd jobs about the camp. The vast pile of debris nearby from the previous year's French expedition provided a rich source of pickings for him. He unearthed several huge cylinders of gaz and put together a stove from discarded parts, providing for Ali a cleaner and easier means of cooking than the paraffin stoves we had brought. Sarwat always managed to appear immaculately clean when we were dishevelled and grubby. On the walk-in he wore a green tracksuit, appearing as neat and dapper as an athlete on a track. He preserved the ability to look neat and well cleaned throughout the three months of the expedition.

Ali had won his place as cook on the strength of his avowal that he had worked in an army mess. By the time we discovered that he had only been a waiter, we had not the heart to change our minds. The meals he cooked were excellent and he was always cheerful. Only when an aching tooth bothered him was he anything but busy and willing at every moment of the day. Gohar came to borrow some pliers to remove the aching tooth but we gave him some pain-killers and promised to send Ali to the Base Camp of a Japanese expedition three days away if the pain did not let up.

Dick had gradually come to accept that meals would be cooked for him. Ali as cook and Gohar as a general help liberated us from the daily chores and allowed us to concentrate our energies on the mountain. They were also company for Sarwat who, unlike many Liaison Officers, refused to slip back to wait in warmer quarters at Askole, insisting that his duty lay at Base Camp, to be on hand lest his help be needed. One day I noticed Dick, instead of jumping to do the job himself, passing a tube of Araldite to Gohar who was looking for some way to mend the cracked washing-up bowl. Misunderstanding Dick's instructions and gestures of mixing the substances together, Gohar started squeezing the tubes into the soup which Ali was busy stirring. The soup was rescued before harm was done.

We were waiting for a clearing in the weather before going back on the mountain. Little information could be obtained from the radio which Sarwat tuned in to each evening. A one-sentence forecast described the weather pattern for the whole of the country and we were having to make our own judgements.

On descending from the West Ridge, we had found Major Sarwat to be in a state of great distress. He was pleased to have our company again but

it was a full day before he could be made to divulge what was upsetting him.
I had developed a joking relationship with him, often being wildly outrageous in my comments so that he could see I was not serious. It was good
for him to see that there were differences between the three of us so that
when Pete took Sarwat's side in disapproval of some extravagant statement
I had made, Sarwat could see that he was not an outsider to the group, that
we regarded his opinion as of equal validity to any of our own. When the
mail arrived and he received letters I used to tease him that his wife should
still be writing and not have run off with someone else, an event which was
a near impossibility in a well-regulated Muslim state. I remembered to
enquire again what had upset him; he had not wanted to mar our return
immediately by his own troubles.

He described the amazing confrontation he had had with Ghirardini,
who had visited our Base Camp whilst we were away, and the arguments
he had had with him. It seemed hardly credible to us that such antagonisms
could have arisen to spoil the atmosphere of a region so remote that any
encounter should be a welcome one of people who have a love of the
mountains.

The same day that he recounted this tale we were visited by two
American friends who had come to climb the neighbouring peak of Skyang
Kangri. They had made their camp near to us and their jovial Liaison
Officer, Tim, turned out to be an old friend of Major Sarwat's. We were
sitting inside our large dining tent reminiscing and swapping yarns when
Gohar's face fell, and a strange dismay seemed to possess him as two figures
approached our tent. It was the Frenchman and his wife.

The ensuing scene was bedlam. The Frenchman vociferously insisted
that he was prepared to forget the earlier arguments if the Liaison Officers
would let him climb K2 on his own, and his wife offered her opinion and
supported her husband's demands in a strident French which it was
difficult to comprehend.

The scene seemed starkly out of place amongst the mountains, this
confrontation and dispute, and the forcing upon us of a dilemma which had
nothing to do with us but into which we were inevitably drawn.

Ghirardini wanted us to say that we did not mind him climbing K2 and
he seemed to think he could manoeuvre the Liaison Officer into turning a
blind eye to his activities. He intended to follow the ropes left in place by
the French party the previous year. But we told him that we had no
authority even to say that he could climb the mountain. We were in a
foreign country and had agreed to accept their laws, whatever we thought
of them.

The Frenchman had no time for such restrictions: 'If I see a beautiful
mountain, I want to climb it. It is my natural response.'

There was some point in his assertions but his attitude was very

simplistic and his peremptory manner did not inspire sympathy for himself
or his views. Even Dick was moved to voice his disapproval of the man's
attitude. In a quiet and sincere voice he said: 'But we all know what the
rules are before we come.'

'I have no time for rules. They make me sick. I don't like coming to
places with such rules.'

'Well there you are then. Don't come if you don't like it.'

'O.K.'

The man and his wife left to camp some distance away without saying
whether he was going on the mountain or not. What should have been a
period of rest before our return to the mountain had been more exhausting
than if we had stayed high up in the worst of storms. I was keen to get back
on the mountain but I felt annoyed at the waste of time and energy which
had sprung from both meetings with the man. He was certainly an odd
character and seemed to have the ability to introduce tensions and discord
where none should have existed.

On 2 July Dick, Pete and I returned to the Abruzzi Ridge. Ali and Gohar
came with us to the foot of the ridge, relieving us of the full weight of our
loads until the climbing proper started. The trek round to the ridge took
two hours, up through the complex maze of ice towers on the Godwin
Austen glacier. There was debris from the camps of earlier expeditions at
the foot of the ridge, including some oxygen cylinders and a decayed
breathing mask. Pete turned on a bottle of oxygen to test if it still worked
and sniffed at the oxygen: 'Smells good, do you want a sniff?' but Dick and
I refused and Pete felt outlawed by our refusal even to sample the invigora-
ting gas.

Ali and Gohar turned back from the small platform a few hundred feet
up a rocky slope from the glacier. It had been on this platform that we
had spent three nights confined inside our tents by storms during our first
foray on the ridge. This second time we benefited from the knowledge
gained during the earlier attempt and reached a camp-site on a snow shelf
at the head of a couloir at 20,000 feet.

Our movements were slow and weary. We had expected ourselves to be
fitter on this new attempt but it was six weeks since we had first reached
Base Camp and although we were well acclimatised the effect of living at
altitude and making strenuous efforts on the mountain must have had a
debilitating effect. Our rucksacks were heavy too. We carried fifty pounds
each, bringing up food for a prolonged assault and spare rope to fasten over
awkward steps to facilitate our eventual descent.

Since the route had been almost climbed in 1939 and 1953, then finally
succeeded on in 1954, we did not expect the difficulties to be too great. We
reasoned that our technical skills were probably greater with the general
rise in climbing standards since those days; the modern mentality now

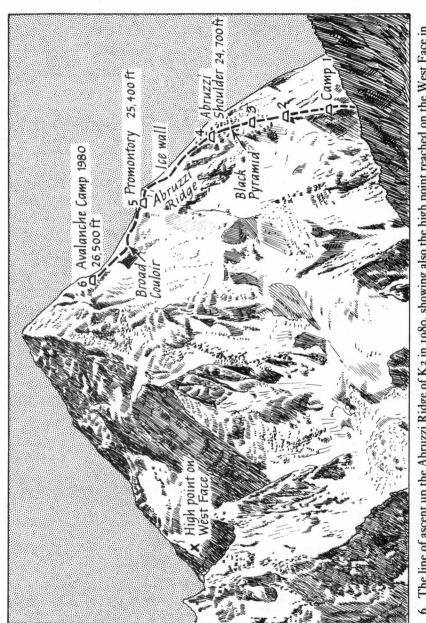

6. The line of ascent up the Abruzzi Ridge of K2 in 1980, showing also the high point reached on the West Face in the first attempt.

encouraged a more mobile attack on a mountain and our equipment was correspondingly lighter and better suited to this sort of approach. We could carry everything we needed for survival on our backs and, once fit and acclimatised, given that no obstacles caused long delays, we were now expecting to be able to start from the bottom of K2 and reach its summit in a matter of days.

We were not doing justice to the early pioneers. The route was extraordinarily difficult. Low down on the ridge, broken rocky slopes and snow couloirs were interspersed with awkward steps of rock. This was not unusual for the lower reaches of any route but on this ridge the difficulties increased as we climbed higher. Frayed remnants of ropes, sometimes over twenty-five years old, marked the route in places. Though only three expeditions had succeeded in climbing the ridge, the history of attempts, tragic accidents and hopeless retreats had left relics of former struggles along the way. We could always climb sections but were overawed by the perseverance which must have been needed in the days when ropes were made from hemp and when boots were heavy with the nails in the sole for friction. Our loads felt terribly heavy but they would lighten as we went on, as we consumed the food and left ropes on difficult passages. In those early days one rope alone would have weighed ten pounds, and much more when damp.

In theory, now that we were as acclimatised as we would ever be, we should have been able to climb the mountain in five or six days, even though it was the second highest in the world. We had worked out our projected camping spots on photographs and the stages into which we planned to break up the ascent.

In practice the difficulties were too great and our loads too heavy to make such methodical progress. The weather too played a major part and we became resigned to languishing in our tents for days at a time until the ferocious winds should diminish and the snow stop falling. We came to accept that we would have to climb in weather worse than we would normally have contemplated if we were to make any progress at all. Thus if it was possible to move we would climb up into the cloud, hoods drawn tight against the storm to explore the next section, fix short lengths of rope where necessary and dump food and gear up high ready for the next day when we would move up ourselves with the tents.

At 23,000 feet we spent four nights in the tents which were beaten flat by the winds, but the alloy tubes, forming hoops inside each tent, would spring upright once again when the storm allowed. Snow formed drifts against the tents but this was a welcome supply for melting into water.

We had with us two tents, weighing six pounds each. All three of us could squeeze into one but we carried a second lest one became damaged. During the enforced halt I had a tent to myself and Pete and Dick shared the other. I used to lie during the day with my rucksack packed, ready to evacuate the tent at any moment as the roof flattened against my body under the impact of the wind. I had used one rope to hold the tent in place, wrapping it round the poles and anchoring it to stakes driven into the snow. Pete and Dick thought I was better off then they and would shout to me to make them drinks of tea. For my part I believed my tent was more exposed and acted as a windbreak for them, whom I considered to have the advantage, expecting them to do the tea-making.

We had radio contact with Base Camp via a tiny, lightweight walkie-talkie. Major Sarwat could be relied on absolutely to pass on any information he could glean from the sparse weather reports on the radio. But K2 seemed to create its own weather pattern and the benefit of the walkie-talkie was the psychological advantage of a link with our Base. We had radio calls at 7.00 a.m. and 5.00 p.m. as a regular schedule, with a fall-back call-time every half hour after those times lest something prevented either party speaking then. We had brought lightweight walkie-talkies after realising on Kangchenjunga, when we had been separated and out of touch, just how useful they could be.

There were times when Sarwat was encouraging us on when the weather was clear at Base Camp and he could not suspect that the cloud, which he could see enveloping the mountain, was more than a light mist. From inside the cloud, for our part, we could not believe that the ferocity of the storms we were experiencing was having no effect at Base Camp only a few miles away.

On 8 July the weather allowed us to make our third camp. The ground was steep, complex and loose. The fresh snow further hampered us. We stopped earlier than intended as ledges large enough for a tent were infrequent. The third camp-site itself was only large enough for one of the tents. From there, however, we had a magnificent view across the border into the Sinkiang province of China and of Broad Peak, in profile, capped by plumes of cloud and coloured pink by the setting sun.

The most difficult part of all was yet to come. We knew of the Black Pyramid by descriptions from the earlier ascents but nothing prepared us for its sustained and improbable passages. The Black Pyramid is a distinctive area of dark, formidably steep rock, hundreds of feet high forming a rough triangle beneath a wall of ice. The rock was compact, with few foot-holds or cracks for pitons. This was one area where we took care to secure in place a life-line of rope for our descent. We did not have sufficient of our own rope to stretch all the way, so where the rock eased off into a slope of snow which ran up to the ice cliff we retrieved some remnants of ancient rope to use as a guideline.

Dick led the way up the wall of ice. I was pleased it was his turn in front, as the ice was hard and splintered at each blow of the axe. More remains of rope showed evidence of others who had passed this way but how the pioneers of the first attempt had climbed ice such as this I could not imagine. Dick went stolidly on. He had the ability to remain undaunted by any qualms about starting up such a repulsive section of ice, but he was exhausted by the time he reached the top.

There was an easy snow slope above and I went up it to scout around for our next camping site. Pete went off to the left and we had a heated disagreement about which way to go. The leftwards route proved best.

That camp-site, our fourth on the ridge, was the best so far. We had reached a shoulder of the mountain which went on upwards in an undulating incline of snow. We climbed up from the left edge of the ice cliff for another 300 feet to a level shelf, huge by comparison with any camping place we had so far used.

We had reached 24,700 feet. The effect of such sustained efforts at altitude was beginning to make itself felt, but all three of us were in good shape. For Dick it was the highest he had ever been. From this camp-site we could look over the edge of the ridge, only twenty feet away, at the precipice dropping sheer away down the South Face for 9,000 feet to the Godwin Austen glacier far below, and our Base Camp, invisible from this distance. Somewhere in this region two of the great tragedies in K2's history had taken place. In 1939 three Sherpas going up to rescue a sick American, Dudley Wolfe, disappeared. Bad weather closed in, preventing any other members of the expedition from returning to the mountain so that no one ever knew what had happened to the three Sherpas and the sick man. The second tragedy occurred in 1953 when another American, Art Gilkey, was taken ill from thrombophlebitis induced by inactivity due to the prolonged storms. The other members of the team attempted to lower him all the way down the mountain but, whilst the active members were recovering from a fall which had almost killed them all, the sick man disappeared from the side of the mountain. He had been wrapped in a crude hammock made from tent material and sleeping bag and was secured by ropes to the ice slope down which he was being lowered. On returning to continue the rescue his exhausted friends found the slope bare. The likely explanation was that an avalanche had swept him away but there was the lingering thought that he may have cut himself loose to relieve the others of a responsibility which would almost certainly have brought tragedy anyway.

The summit seemed within our reach, only one or at most two more camps, two or three more days and we could be on top. No illness or headaches had slowed our progress and there was every reason to hope that we could make it, providing the weather held out.

The next day, 10 July, the weather was magnificent. The sun shone in a clear blue sky, the snow under foot was mostly firm, and though the altitude made every step exhausting, forcing ourselves on was a discipline we had long since attuned ourselves to.

Before we left that spot on the shoulder we had sorted out only the bare essentials to take up with us. In a hollow in the snow we left the spare tent, extra food, a pan, spare gaz cylinders and any items of clothing we had found unnecessary. With the summit now in reach we intended to travel as light as possible.

The gentle incline of the slope steepened into a wall of hard snow topped by a cornice. We made for what looked to be a line of rope emerging from the snow. We were thankful for the direction shown by what we thought to be a relic from the past, but it was no relic, it was a shadow cast by the sun in a surface groove. We climbed on up nevertheless, me forcing a way past the overhanging cornice and Pete taking over to lead an unexpected wall of ice.

I hauled my way up the rope which he had led out and saw him striding upwards where the cliff fell back into a snow slope, into the sun and stopping to shout that he had reached the shoulder.

We came onto the end of a huge promontory jutting out from below the final 2,000-foot summit pyramid. The crest of the promontory was a broad, rounded plateau with hundreds of square feet of room in which to camp. The promontory rose gently towards a rocky escarpment which cut across beneath the summit, forming a narrow couloir of snow where it met the distinctive and enormous buttress of ice, the last barrier before the summit slopes.

Our fifth camp-site was at 25,400 feet, on the level plateau at the end of the promontory. The summit of Broad Peak was now only slightly higher than where we were, and most other peaks were much lower. I felt satisfaction at seeing the surrounding peaks dropping away below as we neared this mighty summit. We scrutinised and memorised details of the summit pyramid for the next day, trying to assess the remaining difficulties and the time we would need to overcome them.

But next day we were trapped in our tent once again by heavy snowfall and lashing winds. We lay dejected, with no means of passing the time except by daydreaming or cooking a meal. Our food was running short and after ten days on the mountain we ourselves were low in physical reserves. The illness which had afflicted Art Gilkey, arising from similar inactivity, preyed on our minds, and we discussed the pros and cons of continuing or going back down.

Over the radio, Major Sarwat was full of encouragement. He had come to have real faith in our ability after his early doubts about the likelihood of success for so unconventional a team. He exhorted us on as if he were a coach and we were his team of players. Reception on the little radio was poor but we could tell he was enthusiastic for us, mixing news of the weather with firm suggestions to press on.

By late afternoon the snow was deep outside and the weather showed no signs of let-up. I proposed that if the next day brought no improvement we should go down, recoup our strength and come back up with more supplies. Pete was against this idea and Dick was undecided. There were merits for both points of view. The summit was almost within our grasp and to go down now would set it back once again a long way from us. If the weather did clear, even if we had little food left there was a chance that we might be able to bring the expedition to a conclusion in one long, hard day of climbing, and thus avoid the uncertainty that a retreat all the way to Base Camp would entail. On the other hand there was the greater strength we would have in coming back up a route we now knew well after some rest and good food at Base Camp. With all the difficult passages prepared and little for us to carry except food, we could expect to regain our high point in perhaps four days. It is always hard to make a decision in such a situation, not knowing which will be best to achieve the desired outcome and not wanting to lose a position won against many odds. Though in reaching decisions we each propounded a more positive opinion than we actually felt as part of the process of thrashing out all possible angles on the decisions to be made, there was no conflict between us. Living in such close proximity to other people, when conditions are far from perfect, inevitably produces an abrasiveness of temper and curtness of manner, but we were all three experienced enough to recognise the tensions produced by the strain of the situation.

In the event, the decision seemed to be made for us. On the 5.00 p.m. radio call the Major informed us, with audible satisfaction, that he had picked up a detailed weather forecast. This had been transmitted for the sake of a Japanese expedition on Masherbrum, a mountain which we could see clearly in fine weather. The forecast, unusually specific in contrast to the norm, was for cloudy weather the next day, 12 July, with no wind or snow. The 13th was to be fine all day.

So the decision was clear. We would go up, using the day of cloud to reach a point as high as possible where we could camp in an advantageous position for the summit bid on the 13th. I slept with mixed feelings of excitement and reluctance at the test ahead. It was the nervousness of knowing that we were on the threshold of achieving something long desired and struggled for, but with apprehension about the test of strength, stamina and skill which the reaching of that goal would entail.

There was cloud next morning, thick and swirling up from a murky void which concealed the valleys below. We radioed down that we were setting off to make a sixth camp that day with hopes of continuing next day to the top. The wind was strong, blowing flurries of snow into our faces as we walked along the broad crest of the ridge. The forecast had said no wind but it did not strike us as unusual that high on the mountain currents of air should form localised turbulence. There seemed to be some snow falling as well as being blown from the surface under-foot, but even that was not a cause for concern in that such dense cloud could be expected to deposit a little of its moisture.

The ridge rose up gradually as we approached a wide couloir separating us from the main mass of the summit pyramid. The broad crest of the ridge sharpened into steep slopes and we picked our way carefully along one side, aiming for any rock which projected and offered a sense of security in the open expanse of snow. The crest of the ridge was to our right and to our left the mountainside dropped steeply away into a seemingly bottomless abyss of cloud.

We were roped together and moved simultaneously until we reached the couloir. The great channel was four or five hundred feet wide and had runnels scoured down it by the passage of avalanches. In the cloud above us we could sometimes glimpse the huge cliff of ice which guarded access to the summit slopes and which, we guessed, occasionally sent avalanches thundering down the couloir. The snow in the couloir was deep and instilled fear that it might give way at every step and that we would go tumbling down to the bottom of the couloir and be flung out into the abyss.

We aimed for an enormous boulder in the centre of the couloir which had clearly withstood the force of many avalanches. That was a halfway point, a breathing place from which to tackle the second part of the frightening gully. There was no technical difficulty in the crossing, the angle was gentle enough for us to walk upright, only using an ice axe for balance against the slope or to lean on in rest when fatigue forced a halt. Every step, however, was dogged by a presentiment of catastrophe, as if, out of the mists above, a white wave of death would engulf us. The altitude enforced its own pace of movement, but we urged ourselves on to reach the rocks at the far side with as few halts as possible. Only when we gained those rocks and climbed up out of that terrifying gully could we allow ourselves the frequent rests and slowness of movement which our oxygen-starved bodies were demanding.

I do not remember at what point in the day it became evident that there was a steady snowfall rather than an intermittent flurry of windblown surface snow mingling with light flakes from the cloud. It was early afternoon before we reached the safety of the rocks beyond the couloir and we certainly knew then that we were in another storm but we still had faith in the broader outline of the forecast and expected the next day to be fine. We carried on along a sharp, rocky ridge beginning to look for a place to put up the tent for the night. The altimeter told us that we had risen above 26,000 feet and, as on Kangchenjunga, we hoped to be able to climb those last 2,000 feet to the summit in one day.

It was another 500 feet before we did stop for the night. The rock ridge had few places where it would be possible to erect the tent and always we pressed on, enticed further by the illusion of a better ledge a little higher. The fear of an avalanche in the night kept us to the rocks well away from the snow couloir where we could have dug out a platform, and well away from the fall-line of any blocks of ice from the cliff above.

Pete seemed indefatigable. He led on in increasingly deep snow and Dick and I trailed behind, following his tracks but still not able to match his pace. Dick was experiencing the exhaustion of altitudes he had never before been to and that exhaustion worried him. The afternoon wore on and Pete still forged a path through snow as deep as his thighs. Time and again the promise of a ledge proved to be false until Pete forced his way up a shallow gully beside a rock and announced that he had found a usable spot.

With many more rests before closing the gap between us, the three of us stood on top of a rocky prow which stood out from the slope. All around more rocks protruded from the surface of the snow and a hundred feet above us stood a great wall of rock. The snow around us was anchored by the presence of so many rocks and the slope between the small prow of rock on which we stood and the great wall above was short enough to reassure us that no dangerous build-up of snow could form there. We believed the prow of rock to be safe for the night, but it needed two hours of work before we had chopped away enough ice to erect the tent. We tied the corners of the tent to aluminium stakes driven into the snow and hammered a couple of pitons into the rock as attachment points to give security to our precarious perch. We could ill afford the effort of cutting out the ice and it was night before we settled inside.

The ledge was barely wide enough for the tent and when all three of us tried to lie down inside, Dick, who was on the side of the tent nearest the edge, had to pad out the floor of the tent beneath him with the rucksacks. Half of his place in the tent was poised over nothing, but the alloy stays in the rucksacks formed a platform over that drop.

Radio reception was very poor. If the Major could hear us, we could hear nothing from him. Our location was probably as close to Base Camp as it had been at any time, and certainly in line of sight if the Major stepped out from camp a few hundred yards, but our proximity to the rock probably affected reception.

We were perched a mere 1,500 feet below the summit and, had it been a clear day, they would have been able to see us through the powerful telephoto lens from Base. The prow of rock on which we were camped was 500 feet up from the couloir we had so fearfully crossed. This couloir ran down for 2,000 feet before ending abruptly in the vast precipice of the South Face.

Across the slope from where we camped was the ice cliff which we would have to by-pass the next day. The rock wall above us spanned the rest of the slope, meeting the ice cliff at a narrow gully, the route past the cliff. That was the last remaining problem for us, and beyond we envisaged the slope easing off into the summit itself.

We hardly had energy left to make as many drinks as we needed; waves of sleep swept over me and I noticed that Pete and Dick too kept drifting off. Inside the tent, Dick was lying closest to the edge of the ledge, Pete was in the middle position and I was on the side closest to the ice and rock of the mountain itself, which we had exposed in chopping out the ledge. The tent was too narrow for us to lie all three shoulder to shoulder. Pete and Dick had their heads at the end of the tent nearest the tunnel entrance and I lay with my head at the opposite end. It felt airless inside the tent, lying with my head furthest from the door, and I fiddled with the vent, trying to let air in without an accompanying flurry of snow.

Outside, the snow was still falling thickly, the tent sagged a little under its weight and I could feel the pressure of snow building up between the tent and the wall of the mountain. I pressed against the side of the tent in an effort to close any gap and make the snow slide over the fabric and we talked about the safety of our situation with some apprehension about the persistent storm.

The snowfall was heavier than it had been all day and if it kept up we might find we could not make any progress next day, even if the day were clear, and retreat itself could be suicidal. We were stuck for the moment where we were, we needed rest and could not do much in the darkness anyway. We could not even find the energy to melt snow enough for more than one drink, in spite of all the knowledge we shared about the rapid deterioration in physical performance at altitude without plentiful food and liquid. We each went off to sleep without taking the customary sleeping pill lest we needed all our wits for any emergency which might arise from this storm.

I awoke to an instant awareness of the imminence of a sordid death. All was black, the tent was collapsed on top of us. A heavy avalanche of snow was pouring over the tent. I was lying face down, cloaked by the fabric of the tent, my body and limbs moulded and held in place by the weight of the snow, solid as concrete. I tried to rise, only my head and shoulders could move, but the snow crashed down on the back of my neck and my face was beaten inexorably closer to the ground. It was a brutal and implacable force of nature with no malice, which, impersonal and unfeeling, was bringing extinction. I felt awe at the power at work. There was no thought process, I was simply aware, knowledge without deduction, of all the implications of what was happening. I shouted to Pete and Dick by name; there was no reply. My arms were pinned down and I could feel, with my elbow, Pete's feet next to me, also pinned down. They were inert. Of Dick I knew

23a. Doug prusikking up the ropes – seen through the eye of a karabiner attached to a prusik clamp – during the attempt on the West Ridge. This was the route which avoided the slope on which Nick was killed in 1978.

23b. Pete on the lower part of the route up the Abruzzi Ridge.

23c. Joe on the radio to Base relaying news of their progress during the harrowing retreat down the Abruzzi Ridge.

24a. Pete and Dick outside the tent at the fourth camping place on the second main attempt on the Abruzzi Ridge. This is on the Abruzzi Shoulder. Masherbrum pokes through the clouds in the background. Our terrifying retreat was down the slopes to the right.

24b. Coming up from the fourth camp, the scene of our later desperate retreat.

nothing, could hear no sound. I presumed that they had caught the full force of the avalanche, had been struck by blocks of ice or rock, and were unconscious, if not dead already, and I knew I would not be long in dying too. The blows on my head from the avalanche went on and on, at any moment I expected the tent to be torn free and sent tumbling and cart-wheeling for 10,000 feet with us inside, thudding into each other, resenting the blows from the others' flailing arms and legs, not the slow-motion impression of death as represented in films, a scruffy end, but not suffering for long before the impacts and collisions of the fall brought oblivion.

I felt no fear, only regret that our death should be so paltry and that we were to be extinguished without trace, because no one would ever know what had happened and there would forever be questions and guesses about our disappearance on the mountain, though our bodies would land only hours away from our Base Camp.

The blackness seemed to be inside as well as outside my head. Fire points formed jagged trails and then the blackness took me.

The snow had stopped falling when I came round. I realised that the tent was still in place – the snow anchors must have held it – my whole body was held fast by the weight of snow and only my head could move a little in a pocket of air. The air was stale, my breathing shallow from the crushing weight on my chest, and a slight panic that I would die now from suffocation began to form inside me. I could see nothing in the dark but I knew that in the breast pocket of my windsuit I had a penknife with which I could cut an air-hole in the tent. My arms were pinned beneath my chest but one hand was near the pocket. My groping fingers failed to find the knife at first, and my breathing came faster, the panic growing. Then I had the knife and, one-handed, tried to open the blade, but fumbled it and the panic all but overwhelmed me. I opened the blade at the next attempt and twisted my arm awkwardly so that my hand could force the knife into the fabric of the tent, inches from my face. My arm movement was restricted and the slit was only three inches long, but cold air came in and I felt relief that I could at least breathe. With Pete and Dick both gone I had to keep myself alive first before I could decide on my next move. Whether I could emerge from under the deadly weight of snow with only one arm partly free I did not know. Whether there would be any life left in Pete and Dick if I could ever get to their bodies I had little hope.

Breathing came easier, then I heard voices and I realised that Pete's feet were no longer next to me. The weight of snow came off my back. I could raise myself and I had my mouth at the slit in the tent, sucking in the air and shouting to them, immensely relieved that the impossible had happened and they were still alive. I was eager for more air but refrained from cutting at the tent more, since if all three of us were alive we might need it as our only form of shelter.

The avalanche had struck us in the middle of the night. At its first impact the tent had been partly knocked off the ledge before the snow stakes and the weight of the falling snow held it in place. Dick was suspended, in the folds of the tent, off the edge of the prow of rock, only the tent fabric preventing him from plunging down 10,000 feet of mountain. Pete had been pushed to the edge of the ledge where there was less weight of snow on him. With his head close to the tent entrance he was able to pull himself out. The prow stood clear of the snow slope still and the entrance to the tent was clear. He pulled Dick out of the tent and back onto the ledge where both of them shouted for me for long minutes, hearing no reply. This must have coincided with my blacking out. They had begun digging for what they presumed would be my dead body under a deep, solid mass of snow, and perhaps the gradual easing of weight from my chest had allowed air to enter my lungs and consciousness to return.

I realised that I was no longer against the solid wall of the mountain. The tent was still hanging off the ledge and the pocket where Dick had hung was full of boots, stove, food and anything else which had been loose when the avalanche struck.

We conversed through the slit in the tent while Pete and Dick dug clear more snow. My sentences were fitful as I sucked greedily at the air in between words, until I could sit upright and open the tent door.

I passed out to them their gloves and torches. When I had gathered my breath I made ready to join them outside but Pete suggested I stay in the tent to gather up all the loose objects lest we lose anything vital. Each of us functioned automatically as if we had rehearsed for such an event. Few words were necessary.

The snow-storm of the previous evening was still continuing. Now that I was alive I began to feel cold and uncomfortably damp. Outside, Pete and Dick scraped away at the snow, clearing the ledge once again. I groped into the pocket which had held Dick and pulled onto the ledge inner boots, and boots, and realised only then that they were still outside in their stockinged feet. I pulled the whole tent back onto the ledge and was able to slide back against the wall of the mountain now that the snow had been cleared away. I leaned back, surrounded by chaos, wondering what to do next.

A dull, hissing thud started up again, and the heavy blows of falling snow hammered once more against my head. I could not believe that there was snow left to avalanche again but the snowfall was so relentless that a new avalanche had formed already. I pressed myself back against the wall to prevent snow forcing its way between me and the mountain and prising me off the ledge. I held tight to the tent with all its contents, lest boots and other vital clothing were lost. I wondered if Pete and Dick would still be outside when it stopped.

This second avalanche brought home to me how helpless we were, how tiny and insignificant our lives were on this mountain. There was no harmony with these forces of nature; we were specks in this colossal and uncaring universe. In my icy tomb I was terrified, fearing another death by suffocation, but I did not dare try to move from my position, embedded in the bank of snow over which the avalanche was pouring. Even if I had managed to move from the frozen mould the avalanche would have whipped me away once I broke through the smooth surface over which it was now sliding. I waited, unafraid, for an outcome which I could do no more to influence; unafraid of what death would mean but horrified by the suffocation by which it was arriving.

Finally the pounding stopped. I shouted to find out if the other two were there:

'Pete, Dick? You all right?'

'Yes.'

They dug me free again. Pete had had the wisdom to tie himself with the rope to the pitons embedded in the rock. When the avalanche had struck he had grabbed Dick round the waist and held him all the while the snow was pouring down. We decided that the avalanches must be coming from the summit slopes above the great wall of rock one hundred feet above us. I passed them their boots and we took it in turn to dress properly and gather individual gear together. We had been sleeping fully clothed, only boots and gloves had we taken off, but it took time for each of us to make ready. We packed our rucksacks and waited for dawn, hoping against all hope that we would be spared another avalanche, for we could not move from the prow in the dark without risking ourselves even more on the open slope.

At the first glimmer of light in a sky still a heavy grey with cloud and snow I led off down, trying to keep to the rocks to avoid triggering off an avalanche and taking all three of us in it. But it was impossible to follow the rocks. Deep snow covered everything and my crampons slipped and caught on unseen projections. I decided to plough straight on downwards through thigh–deep snow, just trusting that we would survive. Inside I had a feeling of hopeless desperation and, as if some almighty power were manipulating us, I wanted to plead that we needed a break, that we had suffered enough, that no more avalanches should be sent down on us.

The three of us were on one rope 150 feet long but I could barely see the other two. I could hear Pete shouting and knew that he would be critical of my going straight down the open slope of snow, thinking me mad to be running the risk of starting an avalanche. Equally I knew without doubt that it was impossible to try to follow the exposed rocks when many more rocks lay concealed beneath the intervening stretches of snow. I had slipped and fallen many times in trying to keep near the rocks and thought that was certain to lead to an accident. I went down the slope of snow knowing the risk I was taking, knowing that we would be lucky to survive at all, hoping that if the snow did give way beneath me, Pete and Dick might be able to hold me if they were on firmer ground in the trough I had made.

I recognised nothing from the ascent. The swirling cloud and falling snow obscured all but twenty feet in front and behind. I ploughed on in the knowledge that if an avalanche came from above the rock wall again we would be wiped out whether we were on rocks or snow.

I reached the top of the rocky ridge we had followed along the edge of the couloir and recognised where we were. I tried to go along the crest of the ridge but the snow was too deep and I kept losing my footing. Pete agreed that we did seem to be better off in the deep snow, worrying as it was. I carried on down the couloir, down through that zone of fear, trying to keep to the edge and minimise the risk of being caught in the open. We glimpsed in the middle a huge boulder remembered from our ascent only hours before, and we cut across, feeling naked and powerless in the path of any avalanche from all the vast space above. We reached the boulder and took a diagonal line to the far side of the gully. The snow broke away at every step and I knew we were running risks which we could never expect to escape from if anything went wrong.

The previous day I had broken trail up to the edge of the couloir but could still recognise nothing. Pete seemed to be in a daze, his normally powerful self broken as I had rarely seen him and accepting being led. Dick plodded on, equally weak, encouraging Pete.

It was well after dawn but there was no sun, only blizzard; I kept my sunglasses off to see better and my eyes were stung by the driving snow and hail. I wondered if I would go snow-blind, and if I did which medication my doctor had said I should use, eye drops or amethocaine.

I was slow but Pete and Dick did not seem to mind. I kept asking directions and was told to follow the line of rocks. Gradually the angle of the slope lessened and I ground to a halt, bewildered by the whiteness around me and utterly exhausted now that we were out of the worst danger.

Pete forged on, knee-deep in snow, revived from his former aimless state. Dick went next and I brought up the rear. Suddenly I was very weak and could hardly keep up with the other two. I trailed along, repeating to myself the fact that it was not far along this almost level plateau to spur myself to keep on moving. I kept glancing to left and right trying to recognise features which would tell me where we were. I thought the snow ridge to the left was familiar, and the oddly shaped rocks to the right. We were roughly in the right place, but the smallest distance seemed too far to travel. I was falling over snow, and tried to force my pace so as not to be too slow and a drag on the rope for the other two.

Pete waded through an extra deep patch of snow, Dick followed and I found I had collapsed in the snow inadvertently. I heard Pete's voice:

'I think this is the place where we camped.'

I stayed sitting for a while, the snow was over my knees when I tried to walk, so I crawled over to join them.

It had taken us six hours to descend 900 feet. It was only nine o'clock in the morning but we were completely spent. We had brought down with us the tent which I had cut into and which had been further damaged by the avalanches, and to recoup some strength before continuing down we decided to put the tent up as best we could and carry on after a proper night of rest.

We had not strength enough even to level out the snow. We pitched the tent on a slight incline, hoping the weight of our bodies would flatten the snow sufficiently. The poles were bent and broken completely in one place. I bound an ice screw to the broken section, we drew the tattered tent over the misshapen framework and we had shelter. There were many vents and tears in the tent fabric but there were two layers of material and most of the holes were offset from each other. Little spirals of snowflakes came in but the main force of the storm was kept at bay. The wind battered the tent remorselessly but it stayed erect despite all the damage it had received.

Inside we lay on the sloping ground, wounded warriors resting from battle. Our weight did nothing to level out the snow beneath the tent floor, but we were too tired to stir again. We laid out our foam mats and pulled on our sleeping bags. Everything felt damp and we were chilled.

We needed food and drink but most of the food had been lost in the avalanche, as had the pan and spare gaz cylinders. We had only one cylinder of gaz on the stove and the pan lid in which to melt snow. Laboriously I melted handfuls of snow and poured the liquid into my water bottle. When it was full I heated the aluminium bottle on the stove and made a drink to share around.

I tried a radio call on the chance that the Major would be listening in but there was no reply. It was a gesture of hopelessness, wanting someone to turn to, someone else to take charge, someone with whom to share our catastrophe. We craved liquid but even the effort of melting snow on the pan lid was too much. I used my Swiss Army penknife to cut away the top of my water bottle and make it easier to push in lumps of snow. It made the melting of snow a little quicker but all three of us relapsed into a comatose state and if we started up from a doze, disturbed by the memories of avalanches and near oblivion, it was to stare dumbly about and to fall back doing nothing.

We found ourselves talking about our chances of coming back on the mountain until we realised how stupidly presumptuous such a notion was. Lying still, the pangs of hunger and fatigue forgotten in the dreamy state of rest after extreme exertion, we sometimes forgot the peril of our situation. We did not have all our wits about us, for when someone mentioned that we had not reached safety yet we all realised how much we had left to go through before we were off the mountain. The snowfall had not stopped since the previous afternoon, we had thousands of feet of mountain to descend, many open expanses of snow which would now be far deeper and more likely to avalanche than when we had come up over them. There were all the difficult stretches of rock which would now be covered in snow and in the thick cloud we would have trouble finding the way. Getting down would be a nightmare. With only one cylinder of gaz, perhaps three hours' worth, and little food, we could not afford to stay where we were. If we waited until the storm abated we ran the risk of being too weak to get down at all.

I had no spirit left at all. I wanted to surrender. If there had been any escape, I would have taken it; if it had been the same as in the Alps, where rescue by helicopter is possible, I would have called one in, but we were way above the ceiling at which helicopters can fly anyway. I mentioned my thoughts to Dick and he was appalled. He said he would not dream of getting off the mountain by anything but his own efforts.

At 5.00 p.m. I made the scheduled radio call. It took Major Sarwat a long time to comprehend my message:

'Our tent was destroyed in an avalanche and we are back at Camp Five.'

Through the crackle of interference I heard him saying:

'I get that you have reached Camp Six and are going for another try. Is that correct? Over.'

I had to fight back the hysteria which was creeping into my voice. I could feel tears welling up in my eyes that we should be in such desperate straits and that there was no sympathy from below. The Major seemed pleased that we were sticking with the attempt to reach the top.

If the line had been clear I would have had no shame in saying: 'Please take pity on us. We are only just alive. We are trying to get down,' but I had to be blunt and clear; there was no means of subtle communication.

'The tent has been destroyed.' I exaggerated a little to get the meaning across. 'We are coming down.' At the same time I did not want to cause alarm.

Jeff and Mike, the two Americans who were camped near our Base Camp, were with Major Sarwat. When he had finally understood that there had been an avalanche and we were on our way down, he told us that Jeff and Mike were leaving and wanted to say goodbye. There was nothing that they could do to help us, good climbers as they were. They had no knowledge of our route and they would have been equally at risk from new avalanches if they tried to reach us. I did feel, however, disappointment that they should be going, even knowing that they were watching and waiting with us in spirit would have been a consolation. Obviously they did not know in what distress we were.

I understood from Major Sarwat something about them wanting to borrow our mail runners to be their porters. I consulted with Pete and Dick and they were equally aghast. I radioed down our refusal, feeling mean, but wanting the mail runners on hand for when we got down, if ever we did.

We all slept badly that night. I had pains in the back of my neck and realised only then that I had probably been concussed by the blows from the ice and snow on the back of my head rather than the suffocation.

It took a long time to get moving next morning. The storm still persisted. We packed our sleeping bags but abandoned the tent. I radioed down that we would like Gohar and Ali to come round to the foot of the ridge to meet us with food and a tent once we were off the mountain. If we were late getting off the mountain we could spend a night on the edge of the glacier and they could help us back to Base Camp with our loads. I promised to radio down every couple of hours to relay our progress and asked the Major not to let Gohar and Ali leave until we were sure we would reach the bottom of the Abruzzi Spur.

Pete led off over the crest of the ridge into a deep expanse of snow. He was making towards the ice wall which he had led the way up during our ascent. Dick and I waited, watching Pete making ungainly progress in snow which came up to his waist. He began expressing doubts about the feasibility of descending that way in all the fresh snow. Where the slope steepened he halted and finally shouted that he was coming back, to descend that way would certainly be lethal. He suggested we follow a route down some rocks. I looked about but did not understand which direction he meant. The cloud and snow limited visibility to a few yards.

He was a long time coming back, though he had only gone 100 feet on a gentle slope. The deep snow and absolute fatigue was affecting the movements of all three of us. When he arrived it was to snap at us for not moving.

'What's the matter? Don't you agree about the rocks?'

'No. I just haven't a clue where you mean.'

Pete had noticed a line of rocks a long way to the left of the ice wall he had led and it was this he was proposing as a safer descent. 'We should be able to get some anchors in the rocks,' he said, 'and in a few hundred feet we should be clear of the worst part.'

He went off into the blizzard and after 300 feet launched off down some rocks which disappeared into the mist and snow below. Dick and I followed, all three of us on the one rope. I marvelled at Pete's forethought and memory of this line, trusting that his sense of direction was accurate, because I could not visualise which direction we were facing.

Sometimes the rocks were very steep and Pete shouted his need for tension on the rope as he floundered and groped for foot-holds and hand-holds in the snow. When he could, he took up a stance himself, fastening the rope to a piton driven into the rock till Dick and I joined him, slipping and sliding, with little control over the unseen slabs and projections.

My hands were numb with the cold and my gloves soaking with the constant contact with the snow. We normally wore thin gloves under thick mitts with a waterproof cover. My inner gloves made my hands colder with the dampness, so I discarded them, and used only the mitt which kept my fingers together, generating more warmth. As the steps downwards went on and on, as the insane floundering, wet, cold and seemingly hopeless, persisted hour after hour, I knew then that we had been mad even to consider coming back up. I had had enough. Surely, I told myself, this was an honourable failure. Surely we had gone as far as could ever be expected. We had driven ourselves to the limit. I tried to make radio contact at the prearranged times but it was futile and the radio became packed with snow.

We could only see twenty or thirty feet at a time, and the descent seemed interminable. All the time my mind was full with the question of whether we were in the very place where Art Gilkey had been lost.

Eventually we came to the foot of a couloir alongside the rocks. Pete continued on in a diagonal line across a snow slope which I could barely distinguish in the mist. We tied two ropes together to give him extra scope whilst Dick and I still remained attached securely to the bottom of the rock ridge. The mist thickened and grew thinner by turns and after a while we could see that Pete was walking upright, facing outwards from the slope, and he was over the worst.

Together the three of us walked down the undulating slope looking for the small cache we had made, when we had left our fourth camp, of the spare tent, food and other superfluous gear. It was no longer superfluous. To descend 800 feet had taken us six hours. The afternoon was nearly over, there was no chance of getting off the mountain that day, and we badly needed to find the tent and food if we were to survive the night.

The white mist merged with the white snow so that it was difficult to distinguish one from the other, difficult to decide what was up, or down, or level. No shadows gave any shape to the slope. By sensation alone we knew we were on a shelf more even than the rest of the snow slope and we looked for any signs that this had been the place where we had once camped and had left the spare tent. The fresh, deep snow blanketed everything into a uniform whiteness.

We sat helplessly in the snow. There were hundreds of square feet to search even if it was the right place. Feebly we each poked at the snow with our ice axes, hoping to feel softness which could distinguish the buried tent from a rock or ice. Dick dug into a spot he was sure was the right location and uncovered a frozen turd, evidence at last that we were near, as we had not strayed far from the tent to relieve ourselves. We concentrated our search in that region and with mighty relief came upon the folded tent and the bag of food and spare gaz cylinders.

It was 3.00 p.m. Inside the tent we were able to relax a little more, reprieved for another few hours from the prevailing certainty that every step we took invited death.

On the radio I told the Major that we would not be off the mountain that evening and hoped to make it next day. Jeff and Mike had not left after all, and the Major had a surprise for us. He said he was passing the radio to a friend of ours and we heard a voice familiar in its expressions:

'Hey, you guys, this is Georgess. How goes it?'

It was Georges Bettembourg, who had been with us on Kangchenjunga, come to climb and ski down the neighbouring Broad Peak with a team of Frenchmen.

"Ow are you? You 'ave it difficult. When will you be down?'

It was the same old Georges, bubbling with vitality, questions pouring out, not waiting for answers. I could imagine him bobbing up and down, running back and forth with the radio, impatient with the reception and trying to find a better location rather than concentrating on the conversation.

Pete was equally delighted and somehow Georges's arrival at our Base Camp gave us new heart. He was a friend who understood our predicament, but we told him there was nothing he could do for us. Pete spoke with him also and in spite of the feeling that we were in a condemned cell speaking on a telephone line to a free man we were able to exchange some of the banter and chatter we had enjoyed the previous year with him. The warmth of his company was a bonus to look forward to on our return to life.

There was food and fuel sufficient for our needs but we only had energy to melt a minimum of snow. We wanted to start early next day to try to descend all the remaining ground before dark, so we settled down early to sleep. We all took sleeping tablets, but I swallowed two to make sure that the drug deadened any discomfort and gave me the rest I craved.

I had a night of disturbing dreams. I was in the Vietnam war on a battlefield, standing beside a Colonel Kurtz. I had seen him in the film *Apocalypse Now*. The battlefield was a muddy mess of broken buildings and broken tents. Inside the fabric of the tents we could see the forms of people moving, and the Colonel took out his revolver and shot at point-blank range at the rounded shapes that were people's heads. The film had astounded me with the carefree manner in which the characters courted death. They were shown surfing off a beach whilst bullets poured out of the jungle, dropping napalm on villages to the sound of music from loud-speakers mounted in the helicopters, and sailing up the Mekong river into ambush as they danced to a song of the Rolling Stones, 'Satisfaction', on a cassette deck. I woke with the same sensation of capricious flirtation with death, as if death was not final as we tended to think, as if death was not to be feared, otherwise why should people court it so playfully?

One last traverse across deep snow for 300 feet brought us to the top of the ice wall which Dick had led. Pete went first again as Dick belayed the rope. I sat and filmed Pete disappearing into the mist. I had recovered enough composure to use again the small movie camera we had with us.

The snow gave way at every step Pete made. He shouted impatiently, with annoyance engendered by the dangerous crossing, and I was glad of the excuse of filming not to be going first across the slope myself.

Pete abseiled down the ice cliff and as Dick followed him he dislodged some loose snow which caught Pete unawares. The snow knocked him from his footing and he fell fifteen feet to be held by the frayed strands of the old rope we had knotted in place where we had thought it least important.

There remained 7,000 feet of descent, more difficult than the open snow slopes, but safer. The rock buttresses were too steep to hold much snow and we could hurry across the open gullies to the greater security of more rocks on the far side. We abseiled down some sections and in others the ropes we had fixed in place hastened our retreat. There was little energy left in any of us now but we had hopes of survival greater than at any time in the last three days.

I felt no wish that we had never started on the mountain in the first place, but now that we were reasonably hopeful of living I resented the long days of hardship that remained before we could relax. Even when our future had seemed bleak, there had been no space in my mind for consideration of anything other than how we could extract ourselves from our predicament. I knew then that I could not pretend to myself that I should have chosen some other way of life because I had had doubts before and had returned again and again to the mountains. Dreadful as our situation was, we had chosen to be in it.

I radioed down our position every hour, unable to say for certain whether we would make it down before dark. Gohar and Ali wanted to climb up to meet us but I ordered them not to. I lost time in making these radio calls, sometimes waiting for the call time behind a ridge which would shelter me from the wind while I spoke, and Pete and Dick drew ahead.

We were on easier ground now which was transformed by the new snow. Even on level stretches I could hardly walk upright. Where tattered remains of rope from the earlier expeditions hung in place I swung down on them, careless of their age, too weak to ignore them as we had done in ascent, and hoping to be allowed to escape from this mountain.

As we came lower, the cloud became less dense and the snow wetter. Sometimes the dark valley bottom was revealed and I was disheartened to see how far away it was and how far ahead Pete and Dick were.

Gohar and Ali were on their way round to us and late in the afternoon

I saw their tiny figures on the ledge to which they had come with us when we had left all those days before.

It was dark before I reached them. By touch alone I felt my way down the wet rocks, guided by their torchlight. Pete and Dick were already there. The ordeal was almost over. I straightened up when I reached the platform for the last few yards but stumbled and was caught by Gohar who leapt forward. He and Ali pressed close, wrapping their arms around me and squeezing tight their welcome. They held me for a long while and I wept with relief, surrendering myself unashamedly to the care of these strong, capable men whom we had hired to work but whose concern and affection for us was beyond what money could buy.

They would not let us carry anything ourselves. We had to descend a few hundred feet to the glacier where they had tents and food. The rock under foot was wet and in places icy, but we were alive. Gohar and Ali were solicitous for our every move and shepherded us, as they would their children, down to the place where we would spend the night. They had waited for us for hours, in the cold, in thin clothing on that ledge, forbidden to come higher but reluctant to go back to the tents where they had left their warmer clothing.

At the edge of the glacier we three settled into one tent while Gohar and Ali cooked and served us from a second tent. We were thoroughly damp but we slept in the comfort of knowing we were safe, and that our responsibility was over. We did not even need to carry anything back to Base Camp.

Gohar brought us tea in the morning and Ali presented us with a tiny flower he had picked from the desolate moraine. The ordeal was over.

Our steps were weak and faltering, even on the level part of the glacier. Gohar and Ali carried monstrous loads, refusing to let us take anything from them. For Ali this was the first expedition he had been on and he was unfamiliar with mountaineering techniques, but he was proud to be needed and insistent on doing more than we would ever have asked him.

The weather was clear for the first time in an age as we made our way to Base Camp. There were clusters of people outside our tents and as we came up off the ice they were looking towards us. I felt uneasy at meeting people who would ask about and revive the pain of our ordeal and then Georges was running towards us, his face wide in a smile, and my eyes were brimming with tears. I stumbled into camp blinded by the mist on my sunglasses, glad that their mirror-like reflections would save me explaining the tears, and Major Sarwat was shaking our hands, pleased that his boys were back.

IV

Gohar and Ali had brought us letters when they came to meet us but I had not opened mine. I felt cauterised by the experience of being so close to instant death and then the strain of living for three days in the knowledge of how close we still were at every step. The experience had rendered unimportant the other anxieties of life. Having been given back my life I felt no urgency any more, as if I had all the time in the world. Every moment was to be savoured, every sensation treasured and valued more than ever before.

The afternoon was bliss, worries were all gone, we were in safety with food and drink to hand. We relaxed in our large dining tent. Ali worked away on one side preparing the food and drinks. We had the company of some of Georges's friends from the Broad Peak expedition who were making a film of the ski descent. We shared memories and news of mutual acquaintances and exchanged stories about anything except what had just happened to us. They must have sensed that we were in a state of shock and were careful with their questions. Their camp was an hour away and they left at dark to make their way back, leaving us to return to our own tents to sleep for the first time in two weeks without the pressure of each other's bodies in the night and alone with our disturbing memories.

Deliberately I steered my mind away from that area of pain. The thoughts were all there, the encounter with myself, the view over the edge of the abyss of death, were present at any time for me to examine, but I covered it all up, like a wound bandaged over. The tears were still there and, unless I occupied myself with mundane things, I found them welling up again in relief, self-pity, delayed shock, the closeness of death, the tears for life – I no longer knew.

Jeff and Mike persuaded us to let them borrow our mail runners so that they could get away. Their mountain had beaten them and they had no purpose in staying. None of us three even thought as far as making a decision about whether to leave or not. We had to summon porters to carry our gear back, since we had much more than Jeff and Mike, so it would take a fortnight for them to arrive anyway.

We did a hurried news report to fulfil our obligations to the *Newsnight* team and I found I was speaking a formula of words which I had learnt in order to describe the events, so that speaking about it would not penetrate to the anguish inside. I scribbled a letter to my girlfriend Maria and all that came out was the raw pain. I could not find words to pretend. 'Hope to be home soon,' I finished. A deceit so that she would not worry.

We lay about for three days, weakly making the journey between our own tents and the eating tent, tripping over the rocks which littered the way because the strength was almost completely gone from our limbs. We teased Dick about going to be a father soon and I wondered if Alf, the manager of Magic Mountain, would have gone off for his holidays before I got back. Alf was due to leave on 9 August, and I did not know if I would get back to find my shop closed by his absence. Dick's baby was due in the latter part of August. Pete was worried about the climbing courses he ran in Switzerland and whether, having taken bookings for them, the clients would be turning up to find no one to guide them. It was now 16 July. Even if we could leave immediately we would not get back till August.

I borrowed a book called *Shōgun* from the Broad Peak team and became absorbed in its 1,200 pages of battles, intrigue and romance in ancient Japan. It was the perfect escapist reading so that Pete and Dick grew annoyed at my unsociable silence. I read the book at every moment, all day, through mealtimes and at night until my eyes dropped shut with tiredness. The willingness with which the characters embraced death in accordance with their Samurai code and the readiness with which the Samurai inflicted death, as one might stamp on an insect, exercised compulsive, horrifying fascination.

Major Sarwat, as a devout Muslim, was observing the fast of Ramadan. He was enjoined by his religion neither to eat nor drink between the hours of sunrise and sunset. He used to rise before dawn and Ali would cook breakfast for him. Thereafter he would sit with us at mealtimes but eat nothing, impressing us all with his dedication and making me have second thoughts about the disrespectful teasing I had indulged in with him earlier on.

I took a bath in a large plastic drum retrieved from the debris at the site of the French Base Camp. Ali heated great pans of water over his stoves and filled the drum outside. I sat in the tub in the sunshine, in the lee of the tent, delighting in the sensual pleasure of hot water on my wasted body which had not seen daylight for weeks. The surface skin was all dried and came off in flakes. My legs were ridiculously thin and my ribs protruded noticeably from my chest. I had lost an enormous amount of weight.

It was as if we were convalescing, patients to be treated delicately, but at some stage we had to make a decision – whether to abandon our attempt on the mountain or go back for another try. We did not discuss it at all. For three days there was no mention of what we should do, then on the third day Pete suggested that it was time we got together to decide our intentions.

It was immaterial who spoke first. All three of us had decided, on his own, that what he really wanted to do was go back onto the mountain and finish the task we had so nearly completed. In spite of all the pressing commitments, in spite of all the traumas of the avalanche and the retreat, what we wanted most of all was to try once more.

There would be time for only one more attempt because we had sent for the porters and they would arrive on the 29 or 30 July. Once they arrived, we would have to leave, since we could not feed or shelter them for more than two days. We estimated that if the weather held good we could reach the top in five days of climbing now that we knew the route well, had prepared most of the difficult pitches and, if we were weak, we were at least perfectly acclimatised.

We prepared to leave but dysentery hit all three of us in turn and we recounted tales at breakfast of waking in the night to vomit all the previous day's food. When we should have been gaining strength we were being further weakened by illness. The weather was still unsettled.

Dick sorted out enough food for a week and we left on the fifth day for our last attempt.

On the days when we could climb we made steady progress but the weather deteriorated on the third day, an ominous cloud cap on Broad Peak bringing early warning of the change.

On 24 July we reached Camp 3 above the first big ice cliff and were stuck there for four nights. The raging storms kept us locked in the tent as the snow grew deeper against its sides. After three nights the weather was worse than ever and with little food left we decided to stay for one more night and then descend. Any longer and we would have no reserves at all. Dick's rations had been parsimonious in the interests of saving weight but we could not blame him as I had spent all my time reading instead of helping him to sort out the rations and Pete had spent his time writing.

On 28 July the weather was less poor than it had been so we went on, up the rocks down which Pete had led the way, avoiding the second ice cliff. We went past the plateau where our abandoned tent was flattened and buried in snow. I wanted to camp there again but Pete urged that we should press on higher whilst we could and Dick voted for that too since he would allow himself no easy option.

We crossed the broad couloir which we had trembled to cross in the deep snow a few days previously and, though it had snowed since, the slopes were swept clean by avalanche or wind. Instead of climbing up the ridge on the far side of the couloir we descended it a little and camped on the broad back of the ridge where it stood out proud from the mountain. There we were safe from any avalanche and in reach of the summit next day if the weather permitted.

But the weather did not permit. We lay all day as the wind battered the tent and heavy cloud obscured the mountain above. Sarwat radioed to us that it was fine below and we should press on but we could not stand in the wind.

We lay with stomachs aching with hunger, ruefully regretting Dick's estimate of the food. We had expected to reach the summit in five days and this was the eighth. The sparse rations had already been stretched to the limit. We were saving used tea bags to re-use them again without sugar or milk to add. We could not last much longer.

Dick was doing most of the cooking. He had the self-discipline to make himself wake up and start the stove in the early hours of the morning whilst Pete and I agonised over waking to a new day. We were all feeling the cold much more since we were all so thin and the prime place in the tent for warmth was the middle position where a person could benefit from the body heat of the two on either side. Pete bargained with Dick for this place, but I preferred to be near the wall of the tent where there was more fresh air from the vent.

We rose at 2.00 a.m. next day to start for the summit should the weather be fine but the cloud was still there and the snow persisted. The wind had kept us awake all night. We had arranged a special radio call for 2.00 a.m. and even Sarwat had to admit that from his location too the prospects were not good. It was beginning to snow and more cloud was coming in. We had to start down.

This time we were in control. We left at dawn and were down by 9.00 p.m., infinitely weary but met at the bottom by Gohar and Ali again, who took us into their care. The last time we had rehearsed this play it had been a tragedy, this time it was just a sad little scenario. We had tried to our limits and could do no more.

We had the satisfaction of seeing that the weather had not improved. Heavy cloud still hung over the mountain and we knew of the maelstrom which would exist inside it. As we neared our Base Camp we met friendly groups of our porters who had been waiting a couple of days for us to descend. We had used up all the time available to us, now there was none to spare for a rest. We packed up that day and left next morning for home.

V

I felt no regret and neither Pete nor Dick showed any of the soul-searching anxiety about whether we could have succeeded if we had tried harder. We had the satisfaction of knowing that we had tried to the utmost and that whatever had been lacking it was not anything in ourselves. I had a sense, which I knew the others shared, that we were not giving up in our efforts to climb the mountain but simply taking a break in order to attend to other things which were necessary, and we started going over dates and opportunities of when we could return. The mountain held a compulsive fascination and without needing to talk about it all three of us knew that we all felt the same.

The journey back was partly delirium. We had food to hand but our stomachs seemed to have shrunk and we could not eat enough to sustain ourselves for more than an hour. Already thin, my limbs were now wasted away and all three of us took to carrying stores of food to eat when weakness made our steps falter. Sometimes one of us miscalculated and homed in on whoever had been more foreseeing in acquiring bars of chocolate and tubes of sweets.

My brain drifted in an intoxication induced by the privation; exhaustion was like an old aquaintance. I wanted to get home as soon as possible but I could look at my wishes calmly without the agitation I would once have felt. I knew that this expedition had affected me more profoundly than any other experience in the mountains; I shared the feelings of the Samurai brought back honourably from his suicide and knew the exalted state he would have been in on his reprieve. A whole new life was mine, as if the past was no more. I felt beyond the reach of anything as if I had total self-containment. I felt wealthy, blessed with fortune beyond measure. The body I walked in was weak but it did not matter, the pain of movement was only another proof that I was alive, a sign of the new life. When we stopped for the night, an unplanned halt in the schedule of our return, it made no difference to my peace of mind. As in the euphoria induced by a drug, I could be content to pass the time contemplating the day going by.

We had not planned to halt for the night at Urdukass, the grassy promontory above the glacier, but we were force-marching the porters and they insisted on a rest. It was immaterial to me and Pete. We had both sat in the dust at Skardu airport for days on end in 1978 and we could not summon the energy to hurry now when we were most tired, only to spend the time we had gained in that squalid place. But Dick did not know the reality of our remoteness and the impossibility of hurrying out. He did some calculations and realised that every day was precious if he was to arrive in England in time for the birth of the baby. If at all possible he wanted to share the experience with his girlfriend. He began making promises of extra pay to the porters if they would do double and treble stages and told Pete and me that he would pay them out of his own pocket.

It was almost as if we were being whipped on as well. The days were intolerably long and one day I woke with stomach cramps and diarrhoea which made me run off behind boulders to relieve myself every few minutes. That day we had to ferry the porters on a rope bridge across the Punmah river and I lay in the shade, weak from the sickness, until they were all across and we had to move on again.

We reached Askole that night after dark. I trailed in last, hoping for a cup of tea but Dick, always so unassuming, had not presumed to ask the villagers. I was angry because I was so ill and shouted at Ali to organise some tea which he did in minutes from a willing house nearby.

I lay on the ground in the dark and heard voices calling me by name.

They were some Japanese whom we had heard, from our mail runners, were ahead of us and whom we had now caught up. They were asking for Pete and Dick too, so I left them to it hoping that I was concealed in the shadows, but I had been to Japan and they wanted to say hello. I rose weakly to shake their hands and was embarrassed to appear so feeble before them.

Later there were more voices asking for me and I ignored them but it was a man I had met in Tokyo and he would not be put off till we had met and talked.

We travelled together then and stayed in the same rest-house in Skardu. It was 7 August. Our party was booked on a flight for the 9th but it was the monsoon period when the flights are most unreliable and we knew that we could be waiting for days and weeks.

We hired a jeep and had a ten-hour ride over the roughest of roads to Gilgit and then a transit van down the Karakoram highway which was not officially open to foreigners. Major Sarwat was on our side now and he ignored the petty objections of the officious Deputy Commissioner in Gilgit who was insisting that we return to Skardu, but we came up against a landslide and did not reach Islamabad for two more days.

Elspeth was out but we had cabled her from Skardu and her house was open when we arrived in the evening. Dick phoned England and we heard him promising to be on a flight the next day. He left, without washing, for the airport to try to transfer his ticket but the offices were all closed and he returned to the bar in the British Embassy Club later that night and joined Pete and myself drinking to the luxuries of civilisation.

There was no means by which Dick could leave sooner than us. We spent the next day in a tightly scheduled series of visits to the Ministry of Tourism to undergo the routine debriefing, a courtesy call to the British ambassador and a lightning shopping spree for presents. That night we flew down to Karachi and boarded a plane for home.

It was the Pan Am oo1 continuous round-the-world flight. I still retained the detachment which I had felt after coming down from the mountain. I wanted to return home but it was as if it were an intellectual concept, my emotions were still anaesthetised and I felt as if no hurt or anxiety could ever affect me; as if all extremes of pleasure and pain would be insignificant in comparison with the gift of life itself. Once on the plane I felt that I could just as easily stay on it until it had gone right round the world and I could disembark amongst the mountains ready to return to them once more. I returned to a girlfriend who could hardly recognise the stranger who disembarked to meet her.

Back in England, a few days after our arrival, Pete rang me asking for Allen Jewhurst's phone number. I had spoken already to Allen, whose tones of helpless concern told me how much his heart had stayed with us once he had left. I was vaguely puzzled and inquisitive after Pete phoned me to know why he had asked for Allen's number rather than asking me to pass on a message. Then Allen phoned me again:

'What's this about Boardman?' he demanded in his irreverent cockney manner. 'He says I'm to ring you and tell you he's getting married. Didn't you guys speak to each other on this trip?'

A day later the formal printed invitation arrived.

'Mr & Mrs Collins request the pleasure of the company of Joe Tasker at the wedding of their daughter Hilary to Peter Boardman. . . .'

The invitations, wedding, reception, had all clearly been arranged months beforehand and all through the expedition Pete had not said a word to us and had decided to go back up for another attempt knowing that there was every chance he might miss his own wedding. I realised then that the worry he had expressed for clients arriving for climbing courses before he was back had disguised his real concern at being absent on his wedding day.

Dick could not make it; his baby boy was born that same weekend. They called him Daniel, after the man who had survived in the lion's den.

Postscript

After the ordeal on K2, I felt, strangely, no sense of disappointment that we had not reached the top of the mountain, and I knew that Pete and Dick felt the same. We had done everything we possibly could to climb it. We had pushed ourselves to the limit mentally and physically and stayed at that limit for so long that we scarcely had strength left to drag ourselves back to normal life.

Physically we were completely run down and mentally I felt as if I was shell-shocked after a war. But the persistence remained, and I realised that I had changed or come to an awareness of self that was different from the perception I had had on first coming to the Himalayas when I had vowed never to return.

We had not reached the top of K2 but I saw more clearly than on any other climb that it was not reaching the summit that was most important but the journey to it, and though I would never have chosen such a trial as we experienced on that particular journey, having been through it I valued every minute.

Three of us had been united in a rarely experienced, single-minded determination, and when the going was difficult we had known we could rely absolutely upon each other. Since that first traumatic retreat from Dunagiri, descending with Dick, each of us almost oblivious to the other in our worlds of illusions and hallucinations, I had learnt how to cope better with hardship and exhaustion. I had learnt at least to recognise it for what it was and to separate the needs of reality from the fantasies of hallucination.

Many answers had been found to the questions I had had since first starting climbing. I knew now what karabiners were, knew why avalanches were lethal; I knew the mountains and some of the cities of the Himalayan countries so well that I felt at home in them; I knew that there was no closed circle of expedition people but groups of friends who chose to go away together as one would choose to go on holiday with people one knew, and now I had friends whom I knew I could rely on in the mountains, and would choose to go away with again, so that to someone starting to think about how to go to the Himalayas we too probably seem a closed circle into which there is no admittance.

I had never planned to go to the mountains so often nor to keep on going for a long time but I had come to see that there was something new and different there each time I went and that as long as that continued to be so I would continue to be drawn there. There are endless new challenges to face, endlessly alluring problems to solve, and difficulties to be overcome. Rather than being a matter of ticking off achievements or notching up a list of summits reached, visiting the mountains had come to be a way of life.

K2 had highlighted the extent to which we were prepared to push ourselves, and it must have seemed from the outside that we were suicidal or emotionless creatures. But we were only taking risks because the end we hoped to reach seemed worthwhile – reaching the top of the second highest mountain in the world purely by our own efforts – and so too with any objective in the mountains, the risks are only run because one believes the correct calculation has been made of how to avoid them in reaching a worthwhile goal. Rather than being suicidal, the climbers I know all love life and fight furiously to hold on to it, and the same restless energy and enthusiasm helps them overcome the problems of everyday life and is transmitted to those around them.

In some ways, going to the mountains is incomprehensible to many people and inexplicable by those who go. The reasons are difficult to unearth and only with those who are similarly drawn is there no need to try to explain. On returning from K2, we were planning to go back there some day soon, and there were other plans being formulated, other invitations being made to go to an unclimbed mountain in China, to attempt Everest in a small party, and for the foreseeable future, sufficient alluring prospects to keep on going back to the mountains again and again.

Chronology

The Eiger
Joe Tasker, Dick Renshaw.

1975 18–20 February First attempt.
   25 February–1 March Second and successful attempt.

Dunagiri
Joe Tasker, Dick Renshaw.

1975 30 June Permission offered for Dunagiri.
   5 August Dick passes driving test.
   6 August Departure overland for India.
   23 September Dick reaches Base Camp.
   27 September Joe reaches Base Camp.
   1–11 October (approx.) Ascent and descent of South-East Ridge of Dunagiri.
   End of October Dick flies back to UK.
   End of November Joe arrives back in UK.

Changabang
Joe Tasker, Pete Boardman.

1975 December First plans for attempt on West Face of mountain.
1976 May Permission received for expedition to West Face of Changabang.
   22 August Departure from Heathrow for Delhi.
   7 September Arrive Base Camp.

16 September	Establish Camp 1 on crest of ridge at 18,000 feet. First half of route completed. Ropes fixed to top of ice field in middle of face.
29 September–2 October	Attempt to make progress using hammock bivouacs.
5 October	Meet two members and Liaison Officer of American expedition to Dunagiri.
7 October	Return to mountain.
15 October	Reach summit.
16 October	Accident on Dunagiri to American expedition.
18 October	Return to Base Camp and meet Italian expedition and Ruth of American expedition and learn of accident to four of their members.
19 October	Climb up to 20,000 feet on Dunagiri to bury bodies of four members of American expedition.
1 November	Fly back to UK.

K2

Joe Tasker, Pete Boardman, Chris Bonington, Paul Braithwaite, Jim Duff, Nick Estcourt, Tony Riley, Doug Scott.

1977	Autumn	Invitation to join K2 expedition in 1978.
1978	10 May	Fly to Islamabad, Pakistan.
	15 May	Fly to Skardu.
	18 May	Start of walk-in to Base Camp.
	1 June	Siting of Base Camp on Savoia glacier.
	4 June	Siting of Camp 1 at 19,700 feet.
	7 June	Siting of Camp 2 at 21,400 feet.
	8 June	Pete and Joe occupy Camp 2.
	8–10 June	Snow-storms.
	11 June	Reach 22,000 feet.
	12 June	Nick swept away and killed in avalanche.
	13 June	All back at Base Camp. Decision to call off expedition.
	14 June	Chris and Doug leave for Islamabad.

22 June	Rest of team leave Concordia for Islam-abad.
29 June	Reach Skardu.
3–9 July	Various members obtain flights back to Islamabad.
September	Attempt on Nuptse, Nepal.

Kangchenjunga
Joe Tasker, Georges Bettembourg, Pete Boardman, Doug Scott.

1978	Autumn	Invitation from Doug to join Kang-chenjunga expedition in 1979.
1979	13 March	Arrive Kathmandu.
	18 March	Start of approach march.
	26 March	Pete breaks ankle.
	4 April	Arrive at Base Camp.
	13 April	Establish Camp 2.
	15–21 April	Climbing and fixing rope on wall.
	27 April	Reach North Col. Establish Camp 3. Pete injured by rock-fall, descends to Camp 2.
	30 April	Pete returns to North Col.
	1 May	Joe descends. Pete, Doug and Georges climb ridge and dig snow cave, Camp 4.
	4 May	Pete, Doug and Georges camp at 26,000 feet on ridge above plateau.
	5 May	Tent destroyed in early morning. The three retreat all way down off mountain.
	9 May	All four return to Camp 2.
	10–14 May	Attempt to reach summit.
	15 May	Georges descends. Pete, Doug and Joe set off for summit.
	16 May	Reach summit.
	17–18 May	Descend to Base Camp.
	28 May	Reach Dharan.
	29 May	Reach Kathmandu.

K2

Joe Tasker, Pete Boardman, Dick Renshaw, Doug Scott.

1980	30 April	Fly to Karachi (Pete, Dick, Joe and Allen Jewhurst). Journey by truck to Islamabad (3 days).
	5 May	Doug arrives Islamabad.
	10 May	Start of walk-in.
	24 May	Arrive at 'Dump Camp' of 1978. Porters leave.
	26–28 May	Ferry loads round to Savoia glacier beneath West Ridge.
	5 June	Reach site for Camp 1 at 20,700 feet.
	16 June	Reach high point of 23,000 feet.
	18 June	Descend to Base Camp.
	24 June	First attempt on Abruzzi Spur.
	27 June	Descend to Base Camp. Doug decides to return to UK.
	2 July	Pete, Dick and Joe return to Abruzzi Spur.
	12 July	Reach camp (6th) at 26,500 feet.
	13–15 July	Avalanche and retreat.
	22 July	Return for last attempt on Abruzzi.
	30 July	In camp at 26,000 feet, decision to descend.
	31 July	Reach Base Camp.
	1 August	Depart for Skardu.
	10 August	Islamabad.
	11 August	Karachi.
	12 August	UK
	End of August	Pete gets married. Dick's baby born.

Index

Index

L.O. = Liaison Officer, m. = mountain, mtr. = mountaineer, p. = porter, r. = river, t. = town, tr. = traveller, v. = village, va. = valley

Alf (shop manager), 253
Ali (cook), 221, 224, 228, 229, 231, 247, 250, 251, 252, 253, 255, 256
Ali Hassan (Naike), 223, 225–6
Alpiglen (v.), 27, 28
Alps, 13, 15, 16, 17–18, 41, 42, 55, 127, 216, 226, 246; French, 92
Andes, 40
André (Swiss engineering contractor), 20; Danielle (his cousin), 20
Ang Phurba (Sherpa), 164, 168, 170, 171, 175, 177, 179, 182, 183, 185, 186, 187, 188, 189, 190, 193, 194, 209, 210, 211
Annapurna (m.), 58, 129
Apocalypse Now, 249
Arun (va.), 167
Askole (v.), 224, 229, 256
Awan, Mr, 220

Badrinath (v.), 50
Baltoro: Cathedrals (m.), 142; glacier, 140, 217, 224
Balu, 120, 122, 123
Band, George (mtr.), 162
Bass Ltd, 217–18
Bauer, Paul (mtr.), 162
Beaumont: Mrs, 43, 44, 48, 94, 207, 219; Mr, 219
Bernese Oberland, 17, 20
Bettembourg, Georges, 161, 163, 165, 166, 167, 168, 169, 172–3, 174, 175, 176, 177, 180, 182, 183, 184, 185, 189, 190, 191, 192, 193, 194, 195, 196, 197, 198, 199, 200, 201, 202, 207, 208, 211, 212, 215, 249, 251, 252, 263; Norma B. (wife), 214
Blanc, Mont (m.), 14
Boardman, Peter, 92–126, 127, 128, 131, 133, 134, 135, 136, 143, 144, 145, 146, 148, 149, 150, 152, 153, 154, 155, 156, 157, 160, 163, 165, 166, 167, 168, 169, 170, 171, 172, 174, 175, 176, 177, 180, 182, 183, 185, 188, 189, 190, 191, 192, 193, 194, 195, 196, 197, 198, 199, 200, 201, 202, 203, 204, 205, 206, 207, 208, 209, 210, 211, 214, 215, 216,

217, 218, 219, 220, 223, 225, 227, 228, 230, 231, 233, 234, 235, 236, 237, 239, 240, 241, 242, 244, 247, 248, 249, 250, 251, 253, 254, 255, 256, 257, 259, 261, 262, 263, 264; Hilary B. (wife), 258
Bonington, Chris, 127, 128–9, 130, 132, 133, 134, 135, 136, 137, 140, 141, 143, 146, 147, 148, 150, 153, 154, 155, 156, 157, 262; Wendy B. (wife), 129
Boyson, Maggie, 135
Braithwaite, Paul ('Tut'), 130, 134, 139, 140, 141, 144, 146, 149, 155, 158, 161, 203, 262
Braldu: Gorge, 222; r., 138, 139
Breithorn (m.), North Face of, 20–1
Brigham, Ellis (shop owner), 16
British Mountaineering Council, 92, 94, 95, 118, 131, 163, 217
Broad Peak (m.), 142, 161, 180, 234, 236, 249, 252, 253, 254
Brown, Joe (mtr.), 162, 205
Buhl, Herman (mtr.), 152
Burke, Mick (mtr.), 58

Castaneda, Carlos, 181
Chakpoi (v.), 222
Chakravarty, 48
Chameleon Films, 132, 135, 138
Chand, Major Prem (mtr.), 162
Changabang (m.), 42, 44, 53, 55, 57, 62, 73, 77, 78, 81, 87, 90–6, 100–24, 127, 131, 132, 133, 134, 135, 150, 261–2; maps of, 50, 99, 103; West Face of, 94, 114, 116, 118, 124, 215–16, 261
Cheney, Mike (expedition agent), 163
Chogolisa, Bride Peak (m.), 152
Climb up to Hell, The, 17–19
Collins, Mr and Mrs, 258
Concordia (glacier junction point), 142, 143, 146, 227, 262
Connaught Circus (Delhi), 84
Covington, Mike, 159, 160
Crowley, Alistair (mtr.), 161–2

Danielle, *see* André

Darjeeling, 161
Dassu (v.), 219
Dawa, 171, 212
Delhi, 48, 49, 83, 84, 98, 99, 125, 216, 261
Dent Blanche (m.), 17
Dent d'Hérens (m.), 15
Devisthan (m.), 44
Dharan, 213, 263; Bazaar, 165
Dharansi Pass, 50, 124
Dibrugheta, 124
Don and Jenny (friends), 45, 90, 195
Donald (tr.), 84, 85, 86, 87
Duff, Jim, 124, 128, 131, 133, 138, 139, 140, 146,
  149, 154, 155, 156, 158, 225, 262
Dunagiri (m.), 44, 49, 53, 54–79, 91, 92, 93, 94, 97,
  101, 102, 106, 107, 111, 120, 124, 127, 132, 157,
  214, 216, 219, 259, 261, 262; the Col, 72, 73, 75;
  maps of, 50, 54, 61
Dyhrenfurth, George (mtr.), 162
Dylan, Bob, 46, 172

Eiger (m.), 14, 15, 20, 21, 29, 40, 58; Death
  Bivouac, 35, 36; Difficult Crack, 30; Exit
  Cracks, 37; First and Second Ice Fields, 33–4;
  Hinterstoisser Traverse, 32; map of, 30; North
  Face of, 15–16, 17–19, 22, 23–8, 29–38, 57, 261;
  Quartz Crack, 37; the Ramp, 36; Shattered
  Pillar, 24; Swallow's Nest, 33; Third Ice Field,
  36; Traverse of the Gods, 37
Elspeth (friend), 219, 257
Estcourt, Nick, 128, 129–30, 134, 136, 139, 140,
  143, 144, 145, 146, 148, 153, 154, 155, 156, 157,
  203, 215, 228, 262; Carolyn E. (wife), 130, 156
Evans, Charles (mtr.), 162
Everest (m.), 43, 92, 93, 98, 128, 129, 130, 131,
  133, 146, 155, 159, 161, 162, 164, 179, 180, 195,
  202, 203, 206, 260; South-West Face, 134

Frost, Tom (mtr.), 58

Ganges (r.), 84
Garhwal, 99
Gasherbrum III (m.), 225
Gasherbrum IV (m.), 142
Gaurisankar (m.), 216
Gertsch, Frau, 20, 28, 40
Ghirardini, Ivan (mtr.), 226, 227, 230, 231; Jeanne
  Marie G. (wife), 226, 230, 231
Ghunza (v.), 171, 172, 173
Gilgit (v.), 257
Gilkey, Art (mtr.), 235, 236, 248
Glenmore Lodge, 92, 95
Gohar (p.), 221, 224, 227, 228, 229, 230, 231, 247,
  250, 251, 252, 255
Greater Manchester Council, 94
Greene, Graham, 101
Grindelwald (v.), 18

Gspaltenhorn (m.), 15
Guillarmod (mtr.), 162
Gurdjieff, 149

Habeler (mtr.), 46, 146
Hans (tr.), 100
Hanuman (m.), 53, 55; the monkey god, 55, 123
Hardie, Norman (mtr.), 19
Harlin, John (mtr.), 19
Harrer, Heinrich, 19
Herat, 88
Hidden Peak, Karakoram (m.), 46
Himalayas, 19, 40, 41, 42, 44, 45, 46, 52, 55, 78,
  99, 112, 128, 161, 165, 174, 192, 214, 226, 259
Hindu Kush, 92
Huche (v.), 221
Hunza, 221

I Ching, 181
Indian Mountaineering Foundation, 49
Interlaken, 15
Islamabad, 135, 136, 137, 157, 158, 161, 215, 219,
  223, 226, 257, 262, 263, 264
Istanbul, 47, 88, 89

Jannu (m.), 179, 205, 206
Jeff (mtr.), 246, 249, 252
Jewhurst, Allen, 135, 138, 139, 140, 218, 222,
  257–8, 263
Joshimath (v.), 50, 52, 83, 98, 107, 119, 124
Junfrau (m.), 15
Jungfraujoch, the (vantage point), 22

K2 (Karakoram 2) (m.): 1st expedition, 127–58,
  159, 160, 161, 164, 180, 262; 2nd expedition,
  214–55, 259, 260, 263–4; Abruzzi Ridge
  (South-East Spur), 131, 228, 229, 231, 232,
  247, 264; Angel Peak, 143, 144; Black Pyramid,
  234; Godwin Austen glacier, 231, 235; maps of
  (1st expedition), 137, 147, 151 (2nd expe-
  dition), 232; Savoia glacier, 143, 227, 262, 263;
  South Face, 235, 239; South-West Ridge, 143;
  West Ridge, 131, 143, 215, 227, 228, 232, 262
Kabul, 85, 86, 88, 89
Kalanka (m.), 44, 62, 118, 119
Kami (cook), 168, 179, 187, 192
Kangbachen (v.), 173
Kangchenjunga (m.), 160–213, 214, 215, 216, 234,
  249, 263; maps of, 174, 175; North Col, 177,
  179, 180, 188, 189, 193, 194, 200, 208, 209, 263;
  North-East Ridge, 162; North Face, North
  Ridge, 176, 187; South-West Face, 162, 197, 204
Kapoor, Inder, 50
Kapoor, J. D., 48, 50, 84, 98
Karachi, 218, 219, 257, 263, 264
Karakoram range, 46, 128, 138, 152, 161, 216,
  257; *see also* K2

Kathmandu, 43, 88, 163, 164, 167, 192, 193, 208, 263
Khan, Shere (cook), 141, 154
Khumjung, 164
Khyber Pass, 84
Kleine Scheidegg (v.), 18, 21, 22, 27, 28, 29, 32
Kumar, Colonel N. (mtr.), 162
Kurz, Toni (mtr.), 18, 32

Lake District, 16, 43
Lata (v.), 50
Lauterbrunnen (va.), 15, 18, 20, 28
Lawrence, T. E., 168
Lhotse (m.), 159
Lister, Chris, 135
Ljubljana, 90
London Rubber Company, 132, 138
Louise (girlfriend), 135, 159, 160
Louise (secretary), 129
Love and War in the Apennines, 188

Magic Mountain (shop), 214, 253
Mahdi (p.), 223
Makalu (m.), 195, 202, 206
Maria (girlfriend), 218, 252
Martin (mtr.), 92
Mashad (t.), 47, 88
Masherbrum (m.), 142, 237
Matterhorn (m.), 14, 97
Maurice (driver), 78
Meetings with Remarkable Men, 149, 150
Mehringer (mtr.), 35
Mekong (r.), 249
Messner (mtr.), 46, 146, 179
Mike (mtr.), 246, 249, 252
Mitre Peak (m.), 226
Mohan Bahadur Thapa (L.O.), 168, 179, 187, 190, 192
Mönch (m.), 15
Montana (resort), 21
Mountain magazine, 46, 132
Mount Everest Foundation (MEF), 43, 75, 94, 163, 217, 218
Mrigthuni (m.), 44
Muriel (girlfriend), 43, 90, 94
Mürren (resort), 15
Muztagh Tower (m.), 142

Naik, N. D. (Sherpa mtr.), 162
Nanda (goddess), 55
Nanda Devi: (m.), 52, 53, 54, 55, 62, 101, 111–12, 115; (mtr.'s daughter), 112
Naturfreundhaus, the (hostel), 21, 22, 40
Neelkanth: (m.), 50; 'Motel', 50, 52, 98
Newby, Eric, 188
Newsnight, 217, 218, 252

Nima Tensing (Sherpa), 164–5, 168, 171, 175, 182, 185, 186, 187, 189, 193, 194, 209, 210, 211
Nuptse (m.), 159, 216, 262

Odell, Noel (mtr.), 53
Ogre (m.), 130, 159
Olsen, Jack, 17

Pache (mtr.), 162
Paiju (m.), 139, 140
Pangboche, 164
Pang Perma, 173
Paphlu (v.), 221
Patta, Flight Lieutenant, 99, 100
Punmah (r.), 225, 256

Quamajan (p.), 141, 144, 153, 154, 221

Ram, Munshi, 49
Ramani glacier, 53, 75
Reni (v.), 50
Renshaw, Dick, 13–17, 20, 21, 22, 23, 24, 25, 26, 27, 28, 29, 30, 32–3, 34, 35, 36, 37, 38, 39, 40, 41, 42, 43, 44, 45, 46, 47, 49–50, 52, 53, 54, 55, 56, 57, 58, 59, 60, 62–81, 83–6, 90, 91, 92, 96, 97, 101, 107, 111, 112, 121, 124, 216, 217, 218, 219, 220, 223, 224, 227, 228, 229, 231, 233, 234, 235, 239, 240, 241, 242, 243, 244, 247, 248, 250, 251, 253, 254, 255, 256, 257, 258, 259, 261, 263, 264; Daniel R. (son), 258
Righi, de (mtr.), 162
Riley, Tony, 128, 130, 134, 135, 146, 150, 156, 262
Rishi Ganga, 50
Rishi gorge, 53
Rishi Kot (m.), 53, 55
Roberts, Peter, 49, 52, 53, 54, 79
Robinson, Tony, 138, 139, 140
Roche, André (mtr.), 44
Royal Geographical Society, 44
Ruth (mtr.), 118–19, 120, 121, 122, 123–4, 125, 157, 262

Sadia Aerofreeze, 217
Sammy (coach operator), 89
Sarwat, Major (L.O.), 220, 222, 224, 225, 227, 228–30, 234, 236, 237, 239, 245, 246, 247, 249, 251, 253, 254, 255, 257
Scheidegg, *see* Kleine Scheidegg
Scoop, 149
Scott, Doug, 93, 130, 132, 133, 134, 138, 140, 141, 142, 143, 145, 146, 148, 149, 152, 153, 154, 155, 156, 157, 160, 161, 163, 164, 165, 166, 167, 169, 171, 172, 175, 176, 177, 180, 181, 182, 183, 184, 185, 189, 190, 193, 194, 195, 196, 197, 198, 199, 200, 201, 202, 203, 204, 205, 206, 207, 208, 209, 210, 211, 213, 214, 215, 216, 217, 218, 219, 220, 223, 224, 227, 228, 262, 263, 264

Sedlmayer (mtr.), 35
Seigneur, Yannick (mtr.), 161
Seven Pillars of Wisdom, The, 168
Shafiq ur Rahman, Captain (L.O.), 136, 140, 157, 220
Sherlock, Peter, 218
Sherpa Cooperative, 163
Shipton, Eric (mtr.), 44
Shivling (m.), 40, 42
Shōgun, 253
Sikkim, 161, 162, 163, 184, 190, 195, 206
Sillitoe, Alan, 199
Sind desert, 219
Singh, Bhupal, 50, 98, 125
Singh, Bijay (p.), 52
Singh, Hart (p.), 53
Sinkiang province, 234
Skardu (t.), 136, 137, 157, 158, 220, 221, 222, 224, 256, 257, 262, 264
Skyang Kangri (m.), 230
Sony, Mr, 98
Stefan (first climbing partner), 36
Streather, Tony (mtr.), 162
Sue (Jim Duff's girlfriend), 124
Sven (tr.), 87–9
Swain, Mr (of Sadia Aerofreeze), 217

Tamur (va.), 167
Tehran, 47, 88

Terai region, 165
Tibetan Book of the Dead, The, 181
Tilman, Bill (mtr.), 53
Tim (L.O.), 230
Today, 217
Trango Towers (m.), 142, 225
Tut, *see* Braithwaite, Paul
Twins Peak (m.), 175, 176, 177

Urdukass (camping spot), 141, 142, 224, 225, 226, 256

Varanesi, 48
Vera (tr.), 89–90

Wanda (mtr.), 225
Waugh, Evelyn, 149
Wengen (v.), 15
Western Cwm (Everest), 158
White Spider, The, 19
Willie (tr.), 48, 78
Wilson, Ken, 46, 90, 132
Wolfe, Dudley (mtr.), 235

Yalung glacier, 161
Yasu, 98, 119–21, 122, 123, 124

Zermatt, 97

JOE TASKER was born in Hull, England, in 1948. From rock-climbing in his teens, he became increasingly drawn to mountaineering and he made many remarkable ascents in the European Alps and in the Himalayas, where he pioneered routes of extreme technical difficulty. As well as the climbs described in this book, he was a member of the team that made the first ascent of Mount Kongur in China. In early summer 1982 he was a member of the British Everest Expedition that set out to climb the mountain on the previously unattempted East-North-East Ridge. Joe and his companion Pete Boardman died as they were making a final assault on the summit.